Iran's Quiet Revolution

Offering a new perspective on Iran's politics and culture in the 1960s and 1970s, Ali Mirsepassi challenges the prevailing view of pre-revolutionary Iran, documenting how the cultural elites of the Pahlavi state promoted a series of striking *gharbzadegi* or "Westoxification" discourses. Intended as ideological alternatives to modern and Western-inspired cultural attitudes, these influenced Persian identity politics and projected Iranian modernity as a "mistaken modernity," despite the regime's own ferocious modernization programme.

Focusing on the cultural transformations that defined the period, Mirsepassi sheds new light on the Pahlavi state as an ideological gambler, inadvertently empowering its fundamentalist enemies and spreading a "Quiet Revolution" through secular and religious civil society. Proposing a new theoretical framework for understanding the anti-modern discourses of Ahmad Fardid, Jalal Al-e Ahmad, and Ali Shari'ati, *Iran's Quiet Revolution* is a radical reinterpretation of twentieth-century Iranian political history that makes sense of these events within the creative, yet tragic, Iranian nation-making experience.

ALI MIRSEPASSI is the Albert Gallatin Research Excellence Professor of Middle Eastern and Islamic Studies at Gallatin and in the Department of Middle Eastern and Islamic Studies in the Faculty of Arts and Science at New York University, where he is also the director of the Iranian Studies Initiative. He is the author of numerous books, including *Islam, Democracy, and Cosmopolitanism* (2014), *Transnationalism in Iranian Political Thought: The Life and Times of Ahmad Fardid* (2017), *Iran's Troubled Modernity: Debating Ahmad Fardid's Legacy* (2018), and co-editor of *The Global Middle East* series, with Arshin Adib-Moghaddam and also published by Cambridge University Press.

The Global Middle East

General Editors

Arshin Adib-Moghaddam, SOAS, University of London
Ali Mirsepassi, New York University

Editorial Advisory Board

Faisal Devji, University of Oxford
John Hobson, University of Sheffield
Firoozeh Kashani-Sabet, University of Pennsylvania
Zachary Lockman, New York University
Madawi Al-Rasheed, London School of Economics and Political Science
David Ryan, University College Cork, Ireland

The Global Middle East series seeks to broaden and deconstruct the geographical boundaries of the "Middle East" as a concept to include North Africa, Central and South Asia, and diaspora communities in Western Europe and North America. The series features fresh scholarship that employs theoretically rigorous and innovative methodological frameworks resonating across relevant disciplines in the humanities and the social sciences. In particular, the general editors welcome approaches that focus on mobility, the erosion of nation-state structures, travelling ideas and theories, transcendental techno-politics, the decentralization of grand narratives, and the dislocation of ideologies inspired by popular movements. The series will also consider translations of works by authors in these regions whose ideas are salient to global scholarly trends but have yet to be introduced to the Anglophone academy.

Other books in the series

Iran's Quiet Revolution

The Downfall of the Pahlavi State

ALI MIRSEPASSI
New York University

CAMBRIDGE
UNIVERSITY PRESS

CAMBRIDGE
UNIVERSITY PRESS

University Printing House, Cambridge CB2 8BS, United Kingdom

One Liberty Plaza, 20th Floor, New York, NY 10006, USA

477 Williamstown Road, Port Melbourne, VIC 3207, Australia

314–321, 3rd Floor, Plot 3, Splendor Forum, Jasola District Centre, New Delhi – 110025, India

79 Anson Road, #06–04/06, Singapore 079906

Cambridge University Press is part of the University of Cambridge.

It furthers the University's mission by disseminating knowledge in the pursuit of education, learning, and research at the highest international levels of excellence.

www.cambridge.org
Information on this title: www.cambridge.org/9781108485890
DOI: 10.1017/9781108641852

© Ali Mirsepassi 2019

First published 2019

Printed and bound in Great Britain by Clays Ltd, Elcograf S.p.A.

A catalogue record for this publication is available from the British Library.

Library of Congress Cataloging-in-Publication Data
Names: Mirsepassi, Ali, author.
Title: Iran's quiet revolution : the downfall of the Pahlavi state / Ali Mirsepassi.
Description: Cambridge, United Kingdom ; New York, NY : Cambridge University Press, 2019. | Series: The global Middle East ; 9 | Includes bibliographical references and index.
Identifiers: LCCN 2019008501| ISBN 9781108485890 (hardback) | ISBN 9781108725323 (paperback)
Subjects: LCSH: Iran – History – Pahlavi dynasty, 1925–1979. | Iran – Social conditions – 20th century. | Reza Shah Pahlavi, Shah of Iran, 1878–1944. | Iran – Civilization – 20th century. | Islam and politics – Iran. | BISAC: HISTORY / Middle East / General.
Classification: LCC DS317 .M57 2019 | DDC 955.05/3–dc23
LC record available at https://lccn.loc.gov/2019008501

ISBN 978-1-108-48589-0 Hardback
ISBN 978-1-108-72532-3 Paperback

Contents

Acknowledgments

This book was planned as a research collaboration with Mehdi Faraji. We researched and wrote two chapters of the book, "De-politicizing Westoxification: The Case of *Bonyad Monthly*" and "Iranian Cinema's 'Quiet Revolution' (1960s–70s),"[1] and did some more research. However, Mehdi's academic life became more demanding, and he decided to stop working on the book, while I continued working on and writing the rest of the book. Mehdi later helped me with transliteration and stylistic editing. I am very grateful to him, and he should be credited for important sections of the book. As always, Tadd Fernée helped me in editing this book, and I would like to express my deep appreciation for his considerable contribution.

I would like to thank the two reviewers of an earlier version of the manuscript of this work whose comments and suggestions for revisions helped improve the quality of the book. I would also like to express my gratitude to Maria Marsh, Middle East Editor at Cambridge University Press, for her enthusiastic interest in this book and for her support in its publication.

---

[1] The two chapters were published as co-authored pieces: "Iranian Cinema's 'Quiet Revolution': 1960s–70s," with Mehdi Faraji, *Middle East Critique*, September 2017; and "De-politicizing Westoxification: The Case of *Bonyad Monthly*," *British Journal of Middle Eastern Studies*, December 2016.

Note on Transliteration

The transliteration of Persian words and names follows the system suggested by the *Iranian Studies Journal* (available from https://associa tionforiranianstudies.org/journal/transliteration), with the following exceptions:

- Consonants with the same sound are not differentiated. So *ghayn* and *ghaf* are both represented by gh, and *hamza* and *ayn* are represented by '.
- Current Persian pronunciation has been followed, except for Arabic words in an Arabic context (for instance, in reciting the Qur'an). In such cases the *International Journal of Middle Eastern Studies* transliteration rules were followed.
- For individuals' names, their own preferred transliteration was used if it was accessible. If not, the most common transliteration was used. In cases where the same name is transliterated in different forms, one form was chosen for the text of the book (but not the Bibliography and citations) for consistency. In general, omission of *ayn* and *hamza* was preferred when a name is commonly transliterated without those signs.

Dates

In some cases, two dates are used to cite Persian materials (e.g. 1395/ 2016). In such cases, the first date is based on the solar hijri calendar, which is currently used in Iran, and the second one is its equivalent Common Era date.

Introduction
The Quiet Revolution

In remembering the 1978–9 Revolution, there is a scholarly convention of memory capturing our imagination. A consensus seems to be evolving that, at the cultural and intellectual levels, the revolution represented a sharp cultural war opposing the "modernist" Pahlavi state to a fiercely traditional "religious" opposition. Following this un-thought template, the revolution is recalled as a major confrontation between modernity and tradition. This book ventures a different and more nuanced analysis, arguing for a convergence of anti-modern, spiritual, and nativist discourse in both the Pahlavi state and the Islamist revolutionary movement. By focusing on the cultural transformations defining the 1960s and 1970s, the historical logic driving the revolution along anti-secular and anti-Western paths becomes considerably clarified. The complicating factor in this picture is the Pahlavi state's pursuit of a Western and modernist model in economic and social policies, but an ideologically anti-Western attitude in the cultural and even political campaign to win public hegemony.

This book therefore tells the following story: a cultural and intellectual transformation occurred in Iran in the 1960s and 1970s whose quietness was matched only by its penetrating sociological depth. An all but unnoticed Iranian cultural movement pre-shadowed the spectacularly dramatic social drama of the 1978–9 Revolution. The Pahlavi dynasty is routinely recalled wistfully as the great lost project of Iranian modernization, burned in the revolutionary crucible from which the Islamic Republic of Iran arose like a specter to disturbingly haunt the achievements of post-Enlightenment civilization. In the post-1978 decades, a nostalgic image of pre-revisionary Iranian modernization has emerged – often imagined by Iranian exiles and foreign commentators as Iran's modern "paradise lost."

A timely counterintuitive analysis of Iran's pre-revolutionary period can provide an antidote to the intellectual stasis that has beset studies of Iran's 1978–9 Revolution over the last few decades. This stasis derives from an uncritical modernist–traditionalist dualism that supposedly explains the central stakes of the 1978–9 Revolution in an affirmation of orthodox postcolonial themes. This simplistic template cannot withstand close empirical scrutiny, as the contents of these chapters will demonstrate. This book firstly focuses on the anti-modern substance of Iran's Quiet Revolution, an anti-secular cultural project, actively fostered between the state and the opposing forces with which it was locked in deadly combat. Secondly, this analysis of a socially conflicting but imaginatively overlapping ensemble illustrates the larger ideological vista of anti-modern discourse in Iran and transnationally. Through the multiple institutional bases of a developing society, the material and social sources of the variously symmetrical and conflicting forms of the anti-modern imaginary are explained. These explanations crack the orthodox surfaces of postcolonial dogmas on the 1978–9 Revolution and revolutions elsewhere.

The very quietness of the pre-revolutionary Iranian transformation lends itself to a misleading description regarding the glittering social and cultural "conversion experience" that the Iranian state and society underwent in those years. The Quiet Revolution went unnoticed because the cultural and intellectual mutation was a sensorium, encompassing cinematic, journalistic, and other cultural dimensions. Intellectually, it had its roots in the most obscure visions of such troubled figures as Ahmad Fardid. Its very pervasiveness, by contrast, was in transforming Iran's public sphere and state institutions through emotionally accessible images and narratives. Most interestingly, this many-sided Quiet Revolution captivated the Pahlavi elite class's imagination in an irresistible and fatal spell. And the Pahlavi elites, at the pinnacle of state power, were only one site in the widespread distribution of an anti-modern ideology that served the conflicting social interests of varying elites, subordinates, and other protagonists in a general struggle over the crystallization of modern power in the Iranian nation.

This book explores the possible connections, and discursive continuity, in the two decades preceding the 1978–9 Revolution, to the revolutionary movement driven by a violent anti-modern ideology. We see that the anti-modern ideology of the Quiet Revolution constituted a veritable web, ensnaring a surprisingly varied and conflicting cast of social protagonists. This ideology successfully mobilized the Iranian masses, particularly the urban middle class. The chapters in this book each focus on a defining cultural and intellectual space shaping the Iranian social and cultural life of the 1960s and 1970s. It studies the amazing convergence of anti-modern ideas, values, and ideologies as produced, embraced, and publicized by the opposition, religious as well as secular, and the secular, modern Pahlavi state. The militant hostility to modernity and the West shared by state-sponsored institutions and intellectual figures on the one hand and by those opposing the Shah's regime on the other has different origins. It was used for different means, with spectacularly contrasting ends. In both cases, however, a nation-making imaginary was constructed upon a common conceptual binary: the soulless modern West is pitted against spiritual Iran, or the East. And yet the very conflicting nature of its deployment illustrates the superficiality and emptiness of this imagined binary.

In the two decades preceding the 1978–9 Revolution, the Pahlavi state and the myriad civil society institutions were both captivated at the discursive level by the "anti-modern" imagination. This idea had a lengthy history in modern Iranian intellectual life, to say nothing of the West and its colonial victims, but had only a marginal role in Iranian cultural and intellectual sensibilities until about the early 1960s. This certainly flies in the face of assumptions that Iran and "those Muslims" have always been anti-modern. Iran's anti-modernism is of quite recent vintage. For the Pahlavi regime's opposition, as for many public intellectuals, the anti-modern discourse performed two critical functions. Politically, it undermined the Shah's autocratic modernization project and fostered resistance to Western cultural influence. It provided a powerful sense of national solidarity, invoking Iranian and Islamic past traditions and identity as an alternative to Western values. Its deployment is even more interesting, and is scarcely explored by scholars who accept the conventional modernist–traditionalist narrative. For the Pahlavi state, anti-modern ideology served to foster a "cultural" – that is, ideological – source of national legitimacy. By offering a "local" and cultural identity, the "anti-modern" ideology justified the Shah's autocracy and undermined the powerful Iranian left, with its claim to universalist and cosmopolitan ideas. In the same way, it undermined the claims of liberals who promoted a democratic sensibility that could be brushed off as "culturally inauthentic." Ultimately, it endeavored to subvert the heritage of Iran's Constitutional Revolution, which had envisioned a ground-up, popular, and secular mode of national modernization. By defining both the radical Iranian left and liberals as

Western-inspired, and alien to Iranian and Islamic tradition, the Pahlavi state endeavored to establish itself as the authentic governing force of Iran, against the historical tide of political and cultural imperialism. This "cultural war," clearly, centered on the marshalling of discourses for the strategic purpose of undermining political opponents. The sincerity of the respective actors is a matter of secondary consideration. The aim of the Quiet information war was to foster national hegemony for one's own cause and destroy opposing nation-making ventures. There was therefore little in these imaginaries that was natural. Yet – and here is where many scholars have fallen into a trap – the very success of these movements depended upon their appearing to be the unreflecting, unselfconscious, "natural" embodiment of the "real" Iran.

The scholarly quest to understand the root causes of the 1978–9 Revolution – employing myriad templates, from mode of production to postmodernism – has neglected the pervasive cultural and discursive shift in Iranian political culture in the pre-revolutionary decades. Scholars perceive the revolution as the confrontation between a modern state and the traditional or religious masses. This includes those of the "older" Orientalist tradition and advocates of the modernization paradigm. It also includes more critical scholars on the left, who see the traditional masses as heroes (postmodernism), or a potentially anti-capitalist force for the more conventional left. For these left-leaning scholars, the Iranian case is a counter-Orientalist event that resists "rational" explanation or understanding. It is either the overcoming of oppressive hegemonic reason (postmodernism) or an irrational upsurge of protest by the traditional masses (the conventional left). Across the spectrum, from old-fashioned Orientalists, to optimistic but disappointed modernizers, to leftist postmodernists and old-school Marxists, there is a fixation upon this conventional abstraction that has obstructed sight of a concrete and well-documented cultural and social turning in pre-revolutionary Iran. When this turning is rendered visible, all the categories based on such received abstractions are reduced to chaos.

This book challenges this entire constellation of scholarly perspectives. It argues that what seemed to be a modern and modernizing state strategically embraced an anti-modern and anti-Western cultural attitude in a specific political gamble that went horribly wrong. The Pahlavi elites took a serious and well-conceived political gamble, which ended in their violent annihilation. This gamble has been routinely overlooked because of the persistent dogma that the Pahlavi were committed cultural modernizers. In fact, the Pahlavi operated upon several contradictory tracks: political, economic, and cultural. This deadly cocktail eventually undermined the Pahlavi state's raison d'être, making it vulnerable to the challenge of political Islam as a mass uprising from the streets.

The above "blind spot" in recent Iranian history explains why the 1978–9 Revolution continues to pose an "unthinkable" paradigmatic challenge to the social sciences "canon." It is repeatedly invoked as an enigma, a unique historical moment falling outside the net of all established historical explanations. It is thereby passed off as a miracle, the proof of Foucault's irreducible integrity of the local event. Revolutions, the long-accepted theory holds, transpired only under conditions of impoverishment and extreme economic hardship. A nation was consumed in a foreign war or civil strife, or the state was severely mired in internal factional conflict. Yet all the empirical evidence reveals Iran's revolution as transpiring amidst the highest achievements in economic development, and the Pahlavi state as boasting the securest power and firmest stability within the Middle East region. The Shah was enjoying the pinnacle of his rule. Was this a revolt against the conventionally accepted idea of "revolution"? Or have we failed to fully grasp the social situation that produced the revolution? If so, how can this situation be explained? It seems that basic sociological and historical categories may require reexamination if we are not to slide into the widely trumpeted but fanciful thesis of "Islamic difference." Yet the misplaced concreteness of the all-purpose word "Islam" does not explain the 1978–9 Revolution as the magical occasion that Westerners and Easterners alike fondly dreamed of. On the contrary, there was a clear sociological dynamic. The illumination of this dynamic adds potentially important new perspectives to our received sociological optic. It also proves more interesting than the quasi-religious myth of "exceptionalism" that has clustered around scholarly memory of the event, providing a fanciful resource for literary-critical-style interpretations of this formative twentieth-century moment. It is not too late to understand lucidly and rationally what transpired in Iran during those decades: on the contrary, we emphatically must, in order to chart a better future for a nation that demonstrated an amazing political and cultural creativity throughout the twentieth century before being ensnared in the Islamist error.

Beginning in the 1960s, Iranian public life underwent a "quiet," yet existentially transformative, sociocultural reformation. This undocumented reformation prepared the ground for the highly cataclysmic subsequent years. The so-called "Silent (or Quiet) Revolution" was the backstage rehearsal, without which the 1978–9 Revolution remains – through the prevailing optic of the social sciences – an unintelligible, freak episode. A transfixing and determinate event may have unfolded before the eyes of the world in 1978–9, but it requires contextualization against the silent revolutionary background. The 1960s and 1970s provided the social settings, the institutional resources, a new vision of the world, and what we might call a "national spirit." This rendered possible the revolutionary mobilization and launching of a very public revolt. As a result, the self-proclaimed "ancien régime" crumbled in a short span of time.

Most of the existing scholarly and popular literature on the 1978–9 Revolution focuses on either postrevolutionary Iran or the earlier history of Islam and Persia's past traditions. Actual events, symbolic meanings, and iconic images encircling the 1978–9 Revolution have overshadowed the critical role of the so-called "Quiet Revolution" that unfolded over the two prior decades. The contemporary story of the 1978–9 Revolution, therefore, remains incomplete. It is available in fragments, without having been fully told. The time is ripe – given the unrelenting scholarly and public fascination with "Islamism" – to tell the history of the "quiet transformation" in a systematic way. This story concerns a "lifeworld." It transpired during one of the most important periods in Iran's history, as well as having undisputed global significance. A systematic analysis of the period throws a serious spanner in the works of scholars who enthusiastically envision the 1978–9 Revolution as a "great religious event" based on "scriptural" criteria (e.g. Bruce Lawrence). Such quiet enthusiasts of 1978 argue that, although horrible in its way, the event portended a necessary spiritual corrective to the oppressive evils of secular modern materialism.[1]

The Iranian cultural elite (artists, filmmakers, writers, scholars, and other urban elites), at precisely the moment of modernizing the nation and systematically destroying the traditional Iranian countryside, developed a nostalgic desire for the simple, innocent, and pure village

---

[1] Bruce B. Lawrence, *Defenders of God: The Fundamentalist Revolt against the Modern Age* (Columbia: University of South Carolina Press, 1989).

life. Why did cosmopolitan and privileged elites (mostly based in Tehran), at the crest of Iran's drive for modernization, suddenly become profoundly emotional concerning the virtues and lost innocence of a peasant world they had never known – and were actively demolishing? By identifying this broad and strange cultural tendency among Iranian elites, we can better understand the place of Ahmad Fardid in Iran's modern history. Fardid was precisely such an intellectual: a privileged, if marginalized, Western-educated intellectual with a religious background. He was part of Tehran's urban elite during the violent state drive for modernization in the 1930s. We can hence better understand how Fardid, tortured by guilt and confusion, created a complex ideology of a return to the pure roots. He evoked an ahistorical "East" that has never existed in the real world. This Heideggerian fixation, in time, came to nurture not only Fardid's own hunger for power and influence, but also the rising Islamist politics that promised utopia in a return to the pure source of Shi'ism.

In Chapter 1 I argue that if we observe the history of twentieth-century Iranian scholarship on Sufism, we note an intriguing transnational and circulatory transition. From the balanced accounts of Sufism, considering its complex strengths and weaknesses, we see a shift into a post–World War II new wave of uncritical adulation of the Sufi tradition. Interestingly, this stream was particularly shaped by the intervention of French scholars who were inclined toward religious mysticism and who hated the secular liberalism of their home country (at the time of ongoing French political polarization between the Catholic revival and secular republicanism). A reconstructed Iranian Sufism became the refuge for notable scholars from Henry Corbin to – surprisingly – Michel Foucault. Meanwhile, a second, domestic stream inspired this new wave in Iranian scholars of the new middle classes, often Western-educated, who felt disgust with both the West and Pahlavi tyranny, and sought "authenticity" – often in Western philosophical sources (e.g. Heidegger). A third stream emerged from the Iranian left that was more critical of Sufi anti-rationalism. These discourses helped to inflame the emergent Quiet Revolution, which inspired Iranian intellectuals with a new faith in an Iranian utopia beyond the promises of Pahlavi development, the liberal achievements of the Constitutional and National Front eras, and the bitter disillusionments of Western neo-imperialism. By helping to foster a mood of anti-Western nativism, it produced the ideological conditions for the

Islamic Revolution as a new political experiment in twentieth-century nation-making.

Chapter 1 examines the postmodern turn inspired by the intensified Sufi discourses. A set of binaries defines the genre: a fairytale celebration of violence and cruelty, an attraction to scaling new human heights that erase the subjective agency of modernism, and a collapsing of past and future in a utopian imaginary wedded to transcendental forces. The chapter explores the attraction of this new movement for intellectuals – a poetic attraction, based on mystery, the world as a blank canvas, which permits everything. It analyzes the dangerous significance of these discourses for power – a dismissal of the relevance of evidence, where lies and truth coalesce. Based on the work of Mark Lilla, Richard Wolin, and Jeffrey Herf, it contributes a new chapter to the twentieth-century history of intellectual flirtation with political authoritarianism.

Chapter 2, "De-politicizing Westoxification: The Case of *Bonyad Monthly*," analyzes Iranian modernity in the final years of the Pahlavi state, and the non-political roots of the emergent anti-modern ideology. It begins with a focus on the Pahlavi state, showing how – contrary to the prevalent portrayal – the regime embraced an anti-modern ideology at the very height of its ambitious national development project. Faced with pressures to liberalize, the regime preferred to secure hegemony through fostering an ideology of Iranian and Islamic authenticity that harshly criticized the West and democracy. It sought to appropriate aspects of the left and religious discourses that were then challenging its authority. This is shown through an analysis of *Bonyad Monthly*, a journal sponsored by the Princess Ashraf Pahlavi foundation. It helped to shift political debates toward cultural terms, evoking Iran's ancient past, and voicing spiritual prescriptions concerning the fallen human condition.

It thereby doubled ideologically with a growing anti-Pahlavi mass movement. Upon examination, both the discourse of the regime and the mass opposition derived from the *gharbzadegi* concept popularized by Jalal Al-e Ahmad, although formerly invented as an arcane discourse by the Heideggerian Ahmad Fardid. By taking this gamble, the Pahlavi regime helped to secure its own downfall.

Chapter 3 focuses on the life and thought of the prominent personality Ehsan Naraghi. Here, we see how Islamist ideology had a social genesis in the often secular and irreligious sensibility of an erratic and eccentric intelligentsia. They eclectically embraced multiple, conflicting ideologies, including *gharbzadegi*, in ignorance of the fact that it would destroy the basis of their very way of life. The ideological flirtations of these individuals, possessed of important social power, had a ricocheting effect upon Iran's public ideological fabric in these crucial decades. Between the 1930s and 1970s, a generation of Iranian intellectuals embraced the culture of the high life, an intelligentsia indifferent to the stark realities of the world. They remained immune to serious commitment, imagining themselves as visionaries and guardians of Iran's eternal culture. These included Fardid, Bagha'i, and Naraghi, who negotiated opposing elements in a parallel fantasy universe. Naraghi was Swiss-educated, and close to the Pahlavi monarchy and the secret police, or SAVAK. Yet he embraced the anti-modern *gharbzadegi* discourse, attending the Fardidyyeh meetings organized around Ahmad Fardid. He also flirted with involvement in the Tudeh Party (the pro-Soviet Communist Party in Iran). He worked for the Iranian government following the 1953 coup, promoting ethnographic fieldwork and a "spiritual" return to Iran's villages. Naraghi was hailed as a great Iranian sociologist, working through the royal court, SAVAK, the universities, media, and conferences to produce a nativist sociology that was highly critical of the West. In so doing, he rejected the relevance of the modern legal process for Iran and the gains of the Constitutional Revolution, urging a return to the inherent tolerance and goodness of traditional Iranian culture. He went so far as to prescribe Sharia as a solution to the world's problems. All the while, he entirely passed over the social realities of contemporary Iran. While fearing revolution, and possessed of an aristocratic temperament, he helped to beget the 1978–9 Revolution.

Chapter 4 analyzes the importance of Iranian cinema in the Quiet Revolution. The New Wave shaped public perceptions of the Pahlavi modernization process. It was key in making a new Iranian national "imaginary" and the accompanying cultural institutions. This was one extremely potent expression of *gharbzadegi*, produced by talented cinematic artists who were mostly urban, upper-class, and cosmopolitan (i.e. Western-educated). The chapter is a further testament to the transnational genesis of the Quiet Revolution. Yet these artists produced a narrative celebrating a rural village reality that they had never seen and that was being destroyed by the regime that sustained their cultural achievements.

The chapter analyzes these fascinating figures in terms of Raymond Williams' theory of the pastoral, as a split notion of modernity idealizing a lost rural past. The wide spectrum of New Wave cinematic motifs is analyzed, including celebrations of Iranian Sufism, the pastoral hero, the virtuous poor, and the beauties of myth. The New Wave's cinematic narratives helped to construct binaries of purity–impurity, spirituality–materialism, rural community and the selfish urban individual.

Chapter 5 tells the story of an important modernist architect and his world of art. It focuses on the *Garden between Two Streets*, a book that features dialogue between Iranian intellectuals involved with the Tehran Museum of Contemporary Art (TMOCA) from before and after the 1978–9 Revolution. Their voices represent three visions of Iranian modernity: the secular-autocratic, the cosmopolitan left, and the Islamist-pastoral. Reza Daneshvar is a left-leaning Iranian novelist, speaking with the architect–designer and founder of the TMOCA, Kamran Diba. The author of the preface, Alireza Sami-Azar, was the TMOCA director under the Islamic Republic. Most strikingly, we discover that these three ideologies are neither pure nor watertight, but blurred and overlapping, concerning the central categories of Islam, modernity, and the nation. This unlikely conjuncture strikingly confirms the thesis of an underlying convergence between multiple sociological carriers for the *gharbzadegi* imaginary, among opposing social interests. There is an interlocking of secularism and nativism, and despite serious tensions over "memory" between the leftist Daneshvar and Diba, the encounter complicates the conventional accounts of modern Iran's past–present disjuncture. In Diba, we see a striking embodiment of the Quiet Revolution: his class-based estrangement from Iran's masses, his imaginary projection of this as a "foreign worldview," his yearning for a spiritual politics, and, despite his atheism, his flirtation with building mosques in public spaces to generate a "new modernist spirituality." He goes so far as to describe the fad for Islamic artistic flirtation among the elite as an Iranian equivalent to American Pop Art, suggesting how blindly he stumbled into the political populism that fed the popular wave of the 1978–9 Revolution. Such compelling evidence mandates a serious sociological rethinking of what, superficially, appeared as a "great religious event" to both casual observers and the ideologically predisposed. An almost farcical cultural episode, it is far from the regular optic of scriptural revival as an explanation for the spread of the *gharbzadegi* ideology in the pre-revolutionary years.

Chapter 6 is a critical examination of the Shah's self-description as a modern "spiritual" man. This chapter focuses on a particular text in ironically shaping the Islamist revolutionary climate, *Toward the Great Civilization*, the central ideological self-proclamation of the Shah in the late 1970s, on the eve of the revolution. It traces a transitional conjuncture, little noted by scholars, between the 1921 coup and the Pahlavi regime of the 1960s and 1970s. From a perverse affinity with the Constitutional Revolution's modernism (because this had concerned popular empowerment and freedom, but was turned to authoritarianism), the second Pahlavi dictator drew conceptual resources from the *gharbzadegi* discourse and spiritual Islam. In an ultimate irony, the regime embraced the *gharbzadegi* discourse of its opponents – rather than opting for more political openness under growing middle- and working-class pressures – and thereby hastened its own doom. This chapter places the White Revolution in an entirely new light, subverting the prevailing image of a modernizing, Western-friendly regime. In fact, the Shah embraced a version of Islamic mysticism that put him in the company of such figures as Henry Corbin and Ahmad Fardid, not least in terms of a cosmic narcissism that placed him at the center of world events. Like the other protagonists in this history, the Shah lived in a fantasy reality – based on disturbingly postmodern tenets – and ultimately paid the price of a descent into irreversible disaster.

Chapter 7 analyzes two historically seminal intellectual debates in defining the Iranian nation that illustrate how the Quiet Revolution involved socially dispersed interests combined in the strategic embrace of anti-modern ideology to realize conflicting goals. I argue that nation-making is a complex and multilayered process, material, institutional, and creative. There is, firstly, a 1930s debate on the legacy of the French philosopher Henri Bergson as a pretext for a radicalized and innovative discussion of Persian *erfan* and Islamic mysticism. Secondly, there are the televised postrevolutionary "ideological debates" on how to either "reconcile" or reject Marxism with respect to Islamic and Iranian traditions, shortly following the 1978–9 Revolution. I argue that the juxtaposition of these two public debates highlights an important rupture in Iran's public intellectual history. We see an integrally defining moment in the Quiet Revolution. There has been scholarly confusion over whether the nation is a "natural" entity, permanently existing, or a historically produced creation of collective imaginings. The dominant social imaginary unconsciously shapes the competing discourses to which individuals and communities subscribe consciously. The losers endure great suffering in seeking to recover existential security. There is a risk of the social imaginary becoming normalized, as if nature and culture were one, in the historical course of societal development. In the struggle over the modern Iranian social imaginary, this chapter analyzes two focal periods. It depicts two key intellectual debates, each embodying the broader ruptures in the social imaginary of modern Iran. These "debates" both concern the relationship between the religious and secular understanding of the world. In endeavoring to grasp how Iran has been "imagined" in modern times, we happen upon a broader perspective on the Iranian production of a distinctive "social imaginary." The history of modern Iran is, simultaneously, a historic battle of competing social and cultural visions for imagining Iran's past and for determining the nation's future.

Chapter 8 demonstrates how the present book builds upon my earlier study of Ahmad Fardid's thought.[2] The *gharbzadegi* philosophy is the complex site of a transnational circulation of ideas, producing the Iranian political imagination in its mutually antagonistic variants. As Fardid was influenced by the *fin-de-siècle* French critique of modern Western rationality pioneered by Bergson, Spiritual Islam, in Corbin's vision, drew inspiration from Fardid. Fardid spent eight years in post–World War II France and Germany, deriving inspiration from Heidegger's critique of Western modernity, and coined the Persian term *gharbzadegi* (Westoxification). Using Weber's theory of "elective affinities," the chapter highlights the theoretical implications for key beliefs underpinning postcolonial theory. Certain demonstrably unfounded assumptions include: 1) Orientalist knowledge is more nuanced than usually assumed, based on a formulaic reading of Edward Said; 2) the authenticity of the local is often more influenced by Western ideas than is supposed; 3) modernist and liberal hegemony in the West is marginalized in the non-West; and 4) the positionality of the postcolonial itself, as a voice claiming to be local, is often a voice or voices coming from the West.

---

[2] Ali Mirsepassi, *Transnationalism in Iranian Political Thought: The Life and Times of Ahmad Fardid* (Cambridge University Press, 2017).

These chapters explore two important theoretical points. They analyze the political and discursive function of anti-modern ideology. They also point to the presence of a "strong," clear, and mutual affinity between the state's new ideology of "spiritual Islam," nativist identity politics, and the opposition of the masses to the idea of *gharbzadegi*. They did not share the same political position, as the opposition targeted the Pahlavi state as being responsible for the national sickness of *gharbzadegi*. However, there were considerable intellectual and cultural – as well as moral – overlaps. If we compare the artistic career of Diba – his elite background and passion for the imagined lives of the common people – with that of the New Wave revolution in Iranian cinema (notably *The Cow*), we find a paradigm of the pastoral wedded to mystical politics of spirituality emerging in the popular Iranian consciousness as a new nation-making imaginary. It had its intellectual counterpart in the works of Fardid, Al-e Ahmad, and Shari'ati, but it reached a mass public through the architectural and cinematic creations of intellectuals who had a strikingly similar profile. Culturally Westernized, they were raised in elite urban families, studied in the West, encountered the counter-modernist ideologies of the West, confused the left and religious revolt, and created striking nativist ideologies – all of which had little to do with traditional religion and the popular lifeworld that, for them, was more alien than the *brasseries* of Paris. And, in an ultimate irony, the Pahlavi royal family seized upon this ideology for the purposes of their own survival – believing, falsely, that it would bolster their hegemony for a coming "new age."

The Naraghi and *Bonyad Monthly* chapters, by means of a colorful political biography and the analysis of a monthly intellectual journal, present a more representative portrait of the new Pahlavi ideology. These two chapters show how militantly anti-modern and anti-democratic the intellectual elite of the Pahlavi state in fact were, despite a frequent, but false, depiction of them as forward-looking and enlightened modernizers who were subverted by a murky obscurantism emerging from a mysterious religious past. In fact, they were destroyed by a movement with which they shared an overlapping ideology and with whom they generated a new national imaginary that served their adversaries and destroyed themselves. It is like the classic chariot-race scene in the 1959 film *Ben-Hur*, when the hero seizes his rival's whip and pulls him from the horse to his death under trampling hooves, two rival soul-brothers making use of the same deadly weapon to achieve supremacy. The slave pulls down the master with his own weapon. As in the film, in the aftermath they became all but indistinguishable from their victims and even their followers.

In conclusion, reflecting on the experience of the Shah and the centrality of the imagination in nation-making, we see the great risk and danger in the ideological game of embracing the politics of "spirituality." This gamble brought about the ruin of the Shah and his system, as his own writings amply and tragically testify.

1 | *The Allure of the "Anti-modern"*

The worth of the legacy of Sufism. It is a fact that Sufism is a deep-rooted and precious tradition. But it is also mystifying and sinisterly ominous [*shum*]. It is a prized treasure, of new and original ideas and literature. Assortment of mysteries of human wonders. However, this cherished tradition also has a troubling legacy. It is for those who produced this cultural capital and for those who have received this tradition. The destiny of Sufism, that is, the story of those who created this tradition, has both dazzling moments, but also some dark corners.[1]

Abdolhossein Zarrinkub, *The Worth and Legacy of Sufism*, 1983

These words hail from Abdolhossein Zarrinkub (1923–99), a distinguished Iranian scholar of Islam and Sufism. The above quotation is from his book *The Worth and Legacy of Sufism*. Zarrinkub, in two volumes (volume II is called *Trail of the Search for Sufism*),[2] celebrates the Iranian Sufi and *erfan* (Persian mysticism) traditions, evincing sympathy for Sufism. However, being also a fair-minded scholar, he routinely maintained a healthy distance from his study topics. Zarrinkub knew that he could neither uncritically worship the Persian *erfan* nor permit himself to become the unconditional adulator of the Sufi tradition. In both his volumes, Zarrinkub makes sure to discuss the troubling history and flaws of major Sufi figures, and the ideas they spread, by analyzing their thought in critical detail.

Despite his personal interest in and admiration of this cultural tradition, Zarrinkub attempts to remain impartial and avoids making one-sided judgments about Sufism. He writes:

---

[1] Abdolhossein Zarrinkub, *The Worth and Legacy of Sufism*, 5th edition (Tehran: Amir Kabir, 1983), p. 151. All translations of quotations are the author's own, unless otherwise stated.

[2] Abdolhossein Zarrinkub, *Trail of the Search for Sufism* (Tehran: Amir Kabir, 1978).

In fact, throughout the history of Sufism, there were many naïve people, as well as charlatans. Hence, an arena of claims has unfolded among them [Sufis], with many making claims, and others denying them.[3]

In a second book on Iranian Sufism, *Trail of a Search*, Zarrinkub points to the critiques that Iranian and Islamic scholars have made of Sufism. He clearly shows that important critiques of mystical thought and Sufism exist in the literary and intellectual history of Iran and Islam.[4] Zarrinkub especially emphasizes social critiques of Sufism, noting that "some have looked at Sufism from social, ethical, or literary and historical perspectives."[5] He even refers to several contemporary scholars, such as Mohammad Ghazvini and Ahmad Kasravi, and their critiques.

Iran's complex historical and literary context – a strong mystical and spiritual understanding of Islam (in Henry Corbin's idiom, Persian or Spiritual Islam), combined with the cultural prominence of Persian poetry in its manifold sophistication – provided the ideal seedbed for a flowering of wild images and flirtations with the irrational in a modern world darkened by war, poverty, and disorder. Yet the twentieth-century appropriation by Westerners and Iranians alike of Iran's heritage as the citadel of modern irrationalism occludes and whitewashes multiple critical and rationalist streams in Iran's national traditions. This chapter highlights how the irrationalist construction took place, in a transnational dynamic based on an anti-modern ideological core that was both barren and capable of responding to human emotional needs.

The role of Sufi cheerleader was reserved for, and most eagerly embraced by, certain Western scholars, who celebrated Persian and Islamic spirituality as a refuge from the secular liberalism they despised within European society. This Eastern temptation constituted an inception in Iranian society that paradoxically fostered a proudly nativist revolt of indigenous authenticity. These Europeans included the celebrated scholars Henry Corbin and, to a lesser degree, Michel Foucault, among others. It also included those Iranians who, while studying in the West, happened to discover "mysticism" during disorienting

---

[3] Ibid., p. 152.
[4] Abdolhossein Zarrinkub, *Continuation of a Search for Sufism in Iran* (Tehran: Amir Kabir, 1983), pp. 9–47.
[5] Ibid., p. 36.

periods in Europe or the United States. With a renewed sense of purpose, they imagined mysticism as integral to their own yearning for Iranian authenticity. Upon returning to Iran, they bore the European counter-modernist ideologies that would buttress the Islamist revival in its mission to suppress local inauthenticity in left-wing and liberal Iranians. They were either Heidegger's children, including Ahmad Fardid, Daryush Shaygan, et al., or ideological anti-modernists, seeking to re-create "traditionalism" as an alternative to modernity for the Iranian situation in contemporary times. Seyed Hossein Nasr and Ehsan Naraghi are two important examples. Other Iranian intellectuals, more radically inclined, such as Ahmad Kasravi or Taghi Arani, were critical of the political or social use of *erfan*. These individuals were equally critical of the anti-rationalist tendencies, and disturbing practical implications, of embracing a politicized *erfan*. These latter figures, however, have become marginalized.

The blandly uncritical celebration of *erfan* by Iranian scholars is a more recent intellectual fashion. This new wave of scholars is above all "anti-modern" and hostile primarily to modern secularism. They hail the Islam of pre-modern Persian Spirituality, a convenient means of vocalizing their hatred of the modern world.[6] Ahmad Fardid's lifelong embrace of *erfan* provides a good example. Fardid preached and cele-brated *erfan* as a moral and conceptual weapon, suitable for under-mining so-called *elm-e hosuli*, i.e. rational and analytical thinking. Despite this, he scarcely followed the "softer and kinder" side of the Sufi tradition, in lifestyle, politics, or the treatment of others. As a man, he was dogmatic, harsh, self-centered, and politically reckless. Following the revolution of 1978–9, Fardid attacked Mehdi Bazargan and developed a political alliance with Ayatollah Khalkhali.[7]

Fardid's intellectual profile exemplifies a certain template. His embrace of "mysticism" derived less from a spiritual sensibility than from a strong desire to reject modernism in all its aspects. He found his model in the Heideggerian confrontation with modernity, whose strange intellectual innovation recast traditional conservatism as the

---

[6] Steven Wasserstrom, *Religion after Religion: Gershom Scholem, Mircea Eliade, and Henry Corbin at Eranos* (Princeton University Press, 1999); Mark Sedgwick, *Against the Modern World: Traditionalism and the Secret Intellectual History of the Twentieth Century* (Oxford University Press, 2004).

[7] For more details on Ahmad Fardid's political views and activities, see Mirsepassi, *Transnationalism in Iranian Political Thought*, Chapter 8.

new radicalism for a troubled twentieth century. It follows that traditional "mysticism" and contemporary "anti-modernism" have been invested with common core assumptions and sentiments, in a growing transnational movement united by a postmodern revivalist attitude. Mysticism's core elements are well-known: anti-rationalism, and a creative primacy of intuition over empirical science, of spirituality over the material, of community over the individual, and of the local over the cosmopolitan. The idea of mysticism, both historically and in its recent "spiritual" incarnation, overlaps with various anti-modern discourses, and this has been especially so in modern Iranian political experience. Indeed, the 1978–9 Revolution seems to have produced a new paradigm of popular revolution, attracting a wide section of the traditional radical left under the rubric of postmodernism. In this study, I want to point to two less-acknowledged similarities:

1) Their ambiguous and almost "fairytale"-like language embodies certain binary opposites: the appeal to beauty and love doubles with a celebration of harsh violence, moral cruelty, and intellectual rigidity. The promise of achieving a heightened level of human reality doubles with the denial of "man" as a subject or agent, and an insistence on "his" being a vehicle for a more transcendental force. A radical general vision for the present time combines with conservative sentiments, with a correspondingly confusing vision for the future. The "fairytale" future is often difficult to distinguish from the past, making the "postmodern condition" a dead ringer for the historical pre-modern.

This intellectual ambiguity invests the mystic and anti-modern sensibilities with an almost poetic quality, one that is potentially very attractive. It presents a kind of mystery to be solved, a blank canvas upon which to paint. Simultaneously, it proposes a set of ideas that potentially permits everything. In this space, the creative mind can enjoyably thrive in the absence of clear boundaries (social or political). What is less often noted is the potentially tragic political possibilities of this field, for it provides a realm for deception and ungoverned power. Michel Foucault's fantastical writings about the 1978–9 Revolution, and the possibilities of the Islamic state, are only one sorrowful example.

2) As attractive as the mystic, anti-modern discourses may appear on an abstract and rhetorical level, they can produce tragic practical results and massive violence. It is axiomatic that many totalitarian

political movements, leaders, and intellectuals, by invoking the authentic, the spiritual, and the aesthetic, create the political conditions for hell on earth. There is an almost total break between ideas and practice. And, strangely, this is consistent with the type of thinking they advocate. If one is to believe that "myth" represents the truth, or, as Henry Corbin argued, that the "imaginal" is the only truly objective reality, while the material is disparaged, then everything is permitted. No compelling reason exists for providing hard evidence or social facts. More importantly, no difference exists between lies and empirical truth. In this context, neither truth nor reality derives from reason or logic, facts, or evidence, but are instead intuitively grasped – very likely, by the chosen few (as Corbin would have it).

As Mark Lilla has argued, these transnational intellectuals viewed "modernity" as a catastrophe, experiencing nostalgia for earlier periods, infused with mystic fervor, when societies were coherent wholes invested with rich symbolic orders. The thirst for redemption has repeatedly pushed public intellectuals to embrace authoritarian regimes, secular or religious, because they promise to resolve the grand themes of creation, mortality, the soul, the sacred, and the End of Time. Ernst Bloch embraced the German Democratic Republic as the real New World, and, accepting an East German teaching post, declared the country the fulfillment of the messianic promise of Moses and Marx.[8] This political recklessness culminated, in 1957, in his being banned from teaching in East Germany, despite publicly abasing himself before the regime. In 1961, he was forced to seek asylum in West Germany. There, denouncing Western capitalism and the Eastern bloc, he became a university-based guru for radical students, urging packed lecture halls to reject the existing world and focus upon the horizon of the "not-yet-conscious" world, which was to emerge from the jungles of the developing world. Bloch's intellectual and political profile is strikingly comparable to his Iranian anti-modern and millennial contemporaries, who similarly blundered into naïvely utopian complicity with a regime prepared to destroy them.

---

[8] Mark Lilla, *The Stillborn God: Religion, Politics, and the Modern West* (New York: Vintage Books, 2008), p. 291.

The Reckless Seduction of the "Anti-modern"

Even a cursory scan of twentieth-century history provides a disturbing historical landscape, replete with examples of precisely such ideologically conditioned political tragedies. Anti-modern ideas and movements in Germany, Japan, Afghanistan, and elsewhere grew from the sublime ideological ideal of restoring the idealized indigenous community as a spiritual project. Although these historical experiences have left us with the starkest of memories, and never a shred of success, we see the politics of the mystic anti-modern continuing to attract populations and intellectuals. What makes the "anti-modern" worldview so powerful and produce such an appealing and exciting set of ideas?

What makes these ideas appealing, firstly, is they represent the antithesis of everything as it now exists. As such, they are utopian and express a widespread attitude of revulsion against an unjustly set-up world, a visceral rejection of deep inequities in the present world political order, and anger over its coercive but whitewashed history. The modern hegemony of the West, exemplified by colonialism, is based on capitalism and the plutocratic power of the rich. Mass society is coldly selfish and individualistic, and nobody cares as millions perish in misery. The smug superiority of the Western ruling classes, upholding a superficial, money-driven Western culture, claiming superiority in metaphysically empty science while taking the moral high ground in the name of liberal democracy and justice, has sickened people the world over with its anonymous violence and hypocrisy. Look how the poor go to work in deadly factories and construction sites like slaves, like Indians in Qatar, dying anonymously and buried in shallow graves, without even a letter to their families fading away in ghettoes at home, while the elite get wealthier.

The anger over such perceptions occludes the subtler reality of a world of interweaving circuits of power, ideas, and images, a world that undermines the underlying imagining of a monolithic West and a supinely vulnerable East more representative of the colonial era. We must vocally recognize these crimes while yet formulating a more updated and realistic theoretical template. For populations have been attracted precisely to the prosperity and freedom seen in Western societies, while states have been forced to modernize to survive. The anti-modern mystic ideology teaches that this modernist attraction is based on an illusion. It appeals to our desire for purity. Modernity is the root of all the worst evils in the world: environmental destruction, poverty, prejudice, and the crisis of cultural meaning. It also includes an aesthetic attraction: the beauty of being among the gods, of seeing our innermost feelings united with stars and sunrises, is a consolation for suffering. This aesthetic has a political corollary in fostering collective power and belonging among countless estranged people. For millions at the losing end of ruthless mass job markets, it replaces existential confusion with order. In its name, people create networks that provide help and support. There is a forgotten spiritual power that promises all that capitalism denies most of us: solidarity, equality, meaning, identity, status, self-worth, and mobility. Here is where the radical utopianism enters. This wonderful life awaits us in the revival of our indigenous cultures, the network of the honest and humble masses who are the wretched of the earth. We have but to wipe out capitalism, the urban middle classes who prey upon the misery of others, and live together in a restored community of spiritual meaning – because these cultures are ontologically sanctioned, and not merely the cold product of epistemology and instrumental rationality. Just as the utopianism of these fashionable theoretical postures illustrates their irrelevance to change in the practical world, we can analyze their sociological coherence in appealing to intellectuals on a transnational level.

The "anti-modern" ideologies are not necessarily a coherent collection of ideas. It is more of a shared attitude and cultural sensibility that has emerged the world over, with its roots in religious thought and traditions. It has been labelled "reactionary modernism" by Jeffrey Herf,[9] while Raymond Williams regarded it as "pastoral modernity."[10] It is the idea of "Religion after Religion."[11] It is a militant desire to "invent" the tradition after it no longer exists in historical form.

In French post-structuralism, these ideas received a more sophisticated expression. The post–World War II generation, coming of age in the 1960s, were sickened by their national Enlightenment and secular republican traditions, which they equated with the hypocrisies of colonialism, class rule, Americanization, and the empty universalism of reason. They plunged into the Heideggerian reservoir of "politics as

[9] Jeffrey Herf, *Reactionary Modernism* (Cambridge University Press, 1984).

[10] Raymond Williams, *The Country and the City* (New York: Oxford University Press, 1973).

[11] For an excellent discussion of this subject, please see Wasserstrom, *Religion after Religion*; Sedgwick, *Against the Modern World*.

being" to create a radical alternative to Marxism, which they identified with the unfashionable Sartre and the shocking excesses of Stalinism and Maoism (although some of them also had their brief romance with both). Communism and capitalism were two expressions of a single Western metaphysic. A nebulous spirituality arose in "discourse analysis" committed to the "rebirth of language" and the "death of man." Because of this fanfare, when Foucault saw the 1978–9 Revolution he interpreted it as the first great postmodern revolution. The Iranian masses had broken through the colonially inspired "limits" of "modernity," creating a new society based on Sufi-like traditions of belonging and spirituality.

In more recent times, we see the emergence of more nuanced and sophisticated varieties within "postmodernism," notably in "postcolonialism," touted excitedly by left-wing American university professors in the 1990s as "this new radical theory coming out of India." Under the leadership of the mysterious Ranajit Guha, it was a "critique of the entire Western tradition of thought and politics." Subaltern studies were celebrated by these professors as the "first authentic voice of South Asian historiography about itself," as if the entire history of modern Indian historiography (nationalism, Marxism, etc.) were nothing but "West-struck" colonial lackeys. They were no different from their pro-Empire adversaries in the Cambridge School, for they too unconsciously embraced the "Western paradigm." They thought themselves autonomous, but were mentally colonized. Identity was the key word. The irony was that these "new theories" had drunk deeply from Heideggerian waters. Emerging in the 1980s, they drew inspiration from Foucauldian post-structuralism. Their debt to Heidegger and Foucault was vocal (they administered fierce tongue-lashings to any who dared criticize Heidegger for his "Nazi past"). Their unspoken inspiration was undoubtedly the 1978–9 Revolution, for their works centered on the "new" revolutionary power of traditional religious mobilization in hastening the doom of the hated Third World national bourgeoisie and global capitalism. In some nebulous way, this "new theory" was linked to the radical legacy of Marx (supposed discoveries in Marx's final writings revealed a conviction that a "new beginning" was fated to emerge from the non-Western world of the colonies).

Meanwhile, beyond the luxurious theoretical ruminations of the academy, similar religious-identity-based mass movements emerged (Muslim, Hindu, etc.) to be embraced, be seduced by, and even to die for, among countless youths seeking a utopian alternative to the dead-end world of late capitalism, and the increasingly nauseating recurrence of futile hypocrisy in cynical liberal political machines. The genuinely radical potential of these movements revealed itself with the 9–11 attacks, embraced by excited left-wing academics as the "first genuine and last remaining real challenge to the survival of global capitalism," as Osama bin Laden sat, like the cat that ate the cream, upon a colorful carpet in Afghanistan, on video, inviting US forces to come and confront us – "if you are real men." What guts and authenticity! This guy abandoned a life of US-backed wealth and privilege to live in exile in a cave! Meanwhile, conversion to the new Islamist networks raged apace in the jails and ghettoes of the wastelands of late capitalism. This reveals an astonishing elective affinity between the lost but vaguely left-wing elites of the ivory tower and the equally lost but infinitely more wretched Global South, exiled underclass languishing in cells and ruined streets.

Theoretically, as this panoramic sketch suggests, the anti-modern mystic exists on the borderline dividing, on the one hand, the quest for good and justice and, on the other, the nihilistic violence of self-destruction. Our reflections on "anti-modern" ideas, movements, and sentiments therefore should not take them too lightly, as a fad or a simple sojourn in evil, for they derive from innermost human psychological dynamics. Yes, they are dogmatic and ideologically narrow, and ugly to confront, yet they also have the simple persuasive power of TV to souls adrift in the wasteland, where lifetimes slip humiliatingly by in impotence and emptiness. They have the magic quality of music or the cinema, shocking and electrifying, yet seductive in their multiple forms and shades of promises of belonging, status, social mobility, cosmic connection, family, revenge, truth, moral rightness, and love. In this way, they reflect other cults, including the appeal of "white nationalism," with its shocking Nazi ideological basis for extended networks of family belonging (a force in economically and culturally devastated Eastern Europe), and above all the sociological logic of street gangs. They provide the opportunity to be someone, to be loved and prosper, and to be right, from having been a marginalized dog, and there is no more powerful drug than this chance to "come out of the dark" and "enter the light."

If everything about the anti-modern seems counter-contemporary and deeply impractical in its totalizing rejection of everything, it also

reflects the basic desires and cherished ideals of human communities.[12]
It calls for the fulfillment of cultural and moral authenticity, offers
communities the familiarity of shared values and moral sentiments,
and calls for a more "real" and "meaningful" way of living and, more
importantly, of dying in the world. This is the core message of the
widely popular *Tibetan Book of Living and Dying*, with its constant
digs against the shallow Western and modern culture of denying death,
written by a popular and successful Tibetan exile in France. The appeal
of this book (recounting how poor and traditional Tibetans face pain
and death with a cheerful smile) among the literate middle classes of
Europe and America, being told they are shallow, inauthentic, and
empty, remarkably demonstrates the pervasive depth of the anti-
modern sensibility – and not just amongst political radicals. The elective affinity extends beyond university left-wing radicals and recruits to
twisted hypermodern versions of Islamist jihad – it encompasses the
average Westerner in their everyday quest for meaning in modern life.
All three categories are consumers of the anti-modern utopia which,
while undoubtedly a dream, yet temporarily fills some hole. The anti-
modern privileges what is fantastic and mystical over the dullness of the
measurable and calculable. The north Indian Tibetan exile city of
Dharamshala is filled with young Americans who, having "fled" pros-
perous homes in a vocally impassioned anti-materialist revolt, seek
spiritual enlightenment in the expanding "spiritual market" of the
city's labyrinthine backstreets. Most importantly, the anti-modern
always tells captivating narratives about humanity, its desires, and,
still more vividly, all that we most deeply fear. It is about political
spirituality – the archetypal fascination of ascent beyond what is
bureaucratically routine, moderate, boring, and uninspiring. The anti-
modern is more attractive by far to the elite, political or cultural, and
helps them to mobilize the poor, or the unhappy middle classes. That is,
beyond being another drug on the global capitalist market, it is also
a government strategy for managing and diverting populations in a bid
to avoid substantial political change with real consequences for the
future.

The anti-modern seems hostile to the materialism of the modern
world, and looks down on wealth and power, seeing these as petty or

---

[12] Alexander S. Duff, "Heidegger's Ghosts," *The American Interest*, Vol. 11, No. 5
      (February 25, 2016).

inhuman, embodying the modern quest for material gains and the "will to power." Instead, the ideology of the anti-modern offers a boutique of moral ideas, justice, authenticity, meaning, and higher forms of existence in the universe of "spirituality." The "spirituality" discourse is offered as the fantastic prescription for all that is wrong and evil in the modern world. The traditionalists understand it as the revival of the glorious past tradition, the modern middle classes find it a refuge from the dullness of ordinary life, the "Western elite" is attracted to it because of its exotic quality, and the Eastern elite see it as a tool for its own survival and a return to the golden days when everyone knew what they wanted.

But there is also a sociological reality to the anti-modern desire. That is, the anti-modern discourse is aristocratic, projecting the upper-class desire for authenticity and high tradition, but it is also populist and even anti-intellectual. It is the royal road to authoritarianism, unconditional loyalty, and the narrative that empowers the racketeers of the earth. This is its "spiritual" quality.[13]

Post-mythical humanity is not, and will never be, perfect. It cannot even promise to be so. Because of the "fall of God," it is also the end of the mythical. If only man knows what is possible, as Kant argues, then there is no way for ideas outside of the modern tradition to come and claim absolute meaning and be received enthusiastically. Kant suggests that only "reason" can know what is rationally possible, while also acknowledging that there are other areas of knowing outside of the rational. Therefore religion, or other forms of thinking, can help us to understand. What is important, for Kant, is that these remain two separate realms of knowing.

Here, anti-modern "anti-rationalism" can potentially fulfill essential values, namely, the acknowledgment that the human condition is in part inherently "mysterious" or inaccessible to rationality and scientific method. This "vacuum" is more imagined than real. In modern democratic societies, there are spaces for the arts, creativity, and the "non-rational," and the possibility of going beyond cognitive experiences. It is in music, cinema, art, fashion, literature, the private sphere, and even the visual media in general (e.g. the entire world of graphic design,

---

[13] Richard Wolin, *Heidegger's Children: Hannah Arendt, Karl Löwith, Hans Jonas, and Herbert Marcuse* (Princeton University Press, 2001); Mark Lilla, *The Reckless Mind: Intellectuals in Politics* (The New York Review of Books, 2001).

video games, IT). Upon reflection, it is the very diversity of centers of meaning that causes moderns – the rich and the poor – to feel lost in a polarizing and unsettling world. To live in peace with difference in the clustered hyper-sensorium of modern societies is a difficult challenge. However, the anti-modern imagines the non-rational (aesthetic and intuitive) as the central and principle organizing spiritual force of our lives. This is personal escapism and political disaster. All that modern democratic societies offer can be dismissed as distraction and entertainment, occluding the all-important encounter with "being" or God. In the political sphere, this leads to the collapse of the public sphere and some form or other of authoritarian rule. Life is to be lived by eternal rules, with consequences in worlds beyond, and this life is merely a bridge and a trial. Secular expressions of creativity are seductions, destroying our true purpose as the created beings in a cosmic design. Certainly, respected American academics vocalize this view, such as Bruce Lawrence, who expressed euphoria over the 1978–9 Revolution. Lawrence's rhetoric, in a more educated idiom, echoes the ranting of the adolescent Dharamshala hippies against the empty trap of materialism, the urgency of escaping the "US drag" to obtain higher enlightenment, and the invariably hostile jostling among multiple would-be gurus who all dream of outdoing their rivals and enthroning themselves at the summit of a marginal cult. In all seriousness, our contemporary universities are in danger of becoming such cults, and the students minds thereby poisoned for a new generation.

The adoption of Sufism essentially requires authoritarianism

2 | *De-politicizing Westoxification:*
The Case of Bonyad Monthly[*]

This chapter presents the Iranian state's anti-modern ideology in its "non-political" aspect, articulated intellectually in the discourse of "Westoxification" (*gharbzadegi*). The story highlights a strange irony: intellectuals, loyal to the Iranian state, precisely as it violently imposed "material" modernization upon society, collaborated with the state in providing a hospitable cultural space for a radical, anti-modern ideology. This chapter demonstrates how the Pahlavi state elite undermined themselves. Their fall resulted from an almost blind hostility to modern Western ideas and the embrace of an imagined Iranian spiritual superiority, posited politically as an alternative to the modern nation-building project.

The Pahlavi state, a formidable agent of secular modernization, encountered a legitimacy crisis, under pressure from an expanding middle class and widening public aspirations to political participation. In refusing to "liberalize" and open democratic space, the Pahlavi state instead embraced what, with hindsight, proved a highly dangerous, and indeed fatal, gamble. It appropriated the anti-Western, and deeply anti-secular, Westoxification discourse that had been voiced by religious and leftist regime opponents. The regime sought thereby to de-politicize the growing public movement, employing the Westoxification ideology to delegitimize democracy as inauthentic and focus popular animosity abroad. The result was precisely the opposite of their intention, and a mass political movement erupted that destroyed the regime.

The Westoxification project was propagated most powerfully by intellectual and cultural figures close to the royal court. These powerful ruling-class elites were mostly educated in the West (Seyed Hossein

[*] This chapter is a revised version of an article, "De-politicizing Westoxification: The Case of *Bonyad Monthly*," by Ali Mirsepassi and Mehdi Faraji, in *The British Journal of Middle Eastern Studies* (December 2016): 2–21.

27

Nasr, Ehsan Naraghi, Daryush Shaygan, Ahmad Fardid, et al.), or, in one case, was actually from the West (Henry Corbin). This chapter will focus only on the materials published in one journal, *Bonyad Monthly*, sponsored by the Princess Ashraf Pahlavi Foundation.

In February 1977, less than two short years before the 1978–9 Revolution, the Princess Ashraf Pahlavi Foundation launched a new journal called *Bonyad Monthly*. It announced its mission to address the most critical cultural and moral issues in Iran at a very crucial time in the nation's history.[1] The inaugural issue of *Bonyad Monthly* featured an editorial by Ashraf Pahlavi, the Shah's twin sister. Explaining the mission of the journal, she offered her own analysis of the "civilizational predicaments in the contemporary world."[2] The editorial continued: "We are in a period of transition to a new modernity, the achievement of which is impossible without culture and thought."[3] This "new modernity" is described in purely "cultural" terms. It is contextualized within Iran's past traditions, and with almost no mention of modern culture: "For nations with a historically lengthy culture and civilization, the future is a *tabula rasa*. It can be changed to fit the proper and desirable form as required by the civilization."[4] A rather vague and fleeting explanation is given of "the new modernity."

Ashraf Pahlavi subsequently proceeds to offer "spiritual" prescriptions for what may be wrong with the contemporary "human condition." She issues a call for the "recovery" of meaningful cultural roots for Iranian national identity:

The more that cultural, educational and research institutes are productive and widespread, and people possess knowledge and spiritual insight, the better equipped we will be to deal with future challenges. With this in mind, the most pressing issue facing humanity in today's world is to achieve "meaning" and "virtue." This must be spread throughout human relationships.[5]

It is highly ironic that, at the same time, Iranian opposition groups – particularly those with Islamic leanings – were mobilizing the Iranian masses by way of a very similar "spiritual" rhetoric. This oppositional discourse targeted the Pahlavi monarchy, and particularly its "Westoxificated" cultural policies. In a movement paradoxically

---

[1] Ashraf Pahlavi, "A Space to Think," *Bonyad Monthly*, No. 1 (March 1977): 3.
[2] Ibid.   [3] Ibid.   [4] Ibid.   [5] Ibid.

echoing the Pahlavi regime's own discursive posture, the regime was harshly condemned for its moral and political corruption.

Ashraf Pahlavi's editorial specifies the mission of both her foundation and *Bonyad Monthly*:

It has always been my dream to allocate all of my wealth, as well as my life energies, to providing a scientific, cultural and artistic space, even a small place, for dialogue and intellectual creativity. It is intended for those who endeavor to excel within the domain of culture and knowledge. Now that this foundation has been established, we hope to be able to take the significant steps to introduce Iranian culture and civilization to the world. We aim to support and encourage those scholars who are interested in clarifying the important role of Iranian culture in shaping world civilization, and in achieving the ideal of peace and human rights. We shall make this foundation a "school" for research work, new thinking [*no-andishi*], and global connections among scholars.[6]

Ashraf Pahlavi, to all appearances, felt an inner conflict concerning her views on human rights. She advocated both a more Iranian-based cultural identity and a project of "new thinking," involving the embrace of "human rights." This, however, was routine rhetoric in the second Pahlavi-era discourses about Iran's role in the world. Greater scrutiny reveals the shallow way in which such ideas as human rights and modernity were used. Reference to them was always tangled up in qualifications betraying a lack of serious commitment. The Pahlavi discourses expressed an anti-modern modern outlook. As we will see, the essential idea was to call for the subjugation of the Universal Declaration of Human Rights, under the demands of national sovereignty.

The first page of the special issue features Ashraf Pahlavi's address to the 34th International Summit for Human Rights of the United Nations. In the middle of the address, she criticizes the Universal Declaration of Human Rights: "In fact, the Universal Declaration of Human Rights, which embodies the legacy of Western thought, has certain deficiencies. These deficiencies are not related to the tenets of the declaration, but are due to its ignoring the realities."[7]

---

[6] Ibid.
[7] Ashraf Pahlavi, "Human, the Third World, Rights, and Justice," *Bonyad Monthly*, Special Issue (April 1978): 3.

Ashraf Pahlavi, or her ghostwriter, echoed the regular autocratic secular state argument. This proclaims that, despite being for modernity and democracy in general, i.e. willing to embrace "the tenets'" of democratic politics, they nevertheless ask the world for a special understanding of their unique situation. The world, the argument goes, must simply trust them, and understand that "the realities" of their societies require a very different way of practicing and conceptualizing human rights and democracy. Ashraf Pahlavi argues that state sovereignty and autonomy must have priority over the human rights of citizens: "Here, it should be noted that, once the declaration was passed, nobody thought of the right of independence of nations. By doing so, in fact, they deprived the nations of the whole ensemble of civil and political rights mentioned in the declaration."[8]

She goes so far as to criticize the discourse of human rights by bringing in the issue of economic justice and equality: "It should be noted that the economic exploitation of the Third World is an obstacle to the realization of human rights – this problem has not been ended, and we have to put more effort into it."[9]

In another part of the address, Ashraf Pahlavi says:

We should consider that human rights in different societies have different faces. It depends on issues such as age, culture, and the level of political and civil evolution within those societies … So, applying common criteria in every society is not possible, and international cooperation without respect to the specific realities is impossible … This means that nobody can impose their lifestyles or beliefs upon others. The age of exploitation, war, and bullying is over. It is time for cooperation and understanding.[10]

Ashraf Pahlavi's view is highly puzzling. Initially, she wants to affirm Pahlavi Iran's belonging to nations of the world committed to democracy and human rights. However, she borrows the colonial discourse of civilizational stages to imply that Iranians are currently too backward culturally to be ready for full human rights and democracy. This was also Atatürk's argument in Turkey in the 1920s. Ashraf Pahlavi takes this argument a step further, to make the case that the Universal Declaration of Human Rights is culturally imperialistic, because it fails to acknowledge local difference and specificity. As a Western-originated idea, it seeks to impose a mindless legal uniformity upon

[8] Ibid.   [9] Ibid.   [10] Ibid., 163.

all world civilizations, regardless of their local history and cultural specificities. This refers, she makes clear, to the implementation of human rights and democratic politics, which is clearly unsuited to Iran at its current civilizational stage. This peculiar ideological concoction combines anti-Western Third Worldism, leftist critiques of imperialism, and a strong cultural conservatism. Ashraf Pahlavi's contradictory view is, indeed, also represented in most of the materials published in the journal.

State-Sponsored Westoxification

The monthly journal *Bonyad* contains materials reflecting a perspective distinctively similar to the Westoxification discourses of Ahmad Fardid and Jalal Al-e Ahmad. The popularization of these lofty intellectual discourses in a widely distributed public journal reflects the de-politicization of the *gharbzadegi* ideology in a publication sponsored by the Princess Ashraf Pahlavi Foundation. *Bonyad Monthly* used the de-politicized ideology to construct a "culturally authentic" narrative for the rule of the Pahlavi monarchy – while simultaneously, and inadvertently, undermining their own regime of modernization from above. In an ultimate irony, the Pahlavi state came to fatally confront the forces of mass-mobilized political Islam – their destroyer, with whom they nevertheless shared a basic discursive foundation, in variations on the *gharbzadegi* discourse.

For Al-e Ahmad, *gharbzadegi* was intended primarily as a political concept. He had also meant it as a sociological description of how modern Iran had come into historical existence. Politically, he had described *gharbzadegi* as top–down autocratic modernization, in a tyrannical (and colonial) and destructive plan for social change. Al-e Ahmad, of course, was referring mostly to the autocratic Pahlavi state. In this respect, he certainly had a point. However, as with some contemporary postmodernist academics, Al-e Ahmad could not imagine any other way for Iran to embrace modernity. His vision projected the Pahlavi development mode as the only possible modernity. This view was ironically influenced by the modern German and French Romantic existentialists who shaped his ideas. Following their totalizing anti-modern visions, Al-e Ahmad suggested Iran's past tradition – Islamic traditions and agency of the Ulama – as viable political alternatives to the current plan for modernization.

This political reconstruction of *gharbzadegi* seems a betrayal of its original philosophical genesis in the radically anti-modern critique of the Heideggerian Fardid. The original philosophical "master," Fardid strongly disapproved of Al-e Ahmad's political appropriation of *gharbzadegi*. He regularly criticized Al-e Ahmad's failure to understand the true philosophical meaning of this "spiritual" term as a critique of Western metaphysics and the "humanist" desacralization of the human imagination.

The writings of the *Bonyad Monthly* journal and the Pahlavi state's ideology in general are, paradoxically, close to Fardid's articulation of *gharbzadegi*.[11] One could argue that certain critics utilized Al-e Ahmad's term to condemn the Shah's dictatorial polices. Meanwhile, however, Fardid's understanding of the *gharbzadegi* concept was utilized to legitimize autocratic political rule among Pahlavi intellectuals and others close to the regime.

Iran at a Cultural and Moral Crossroads?

Bonyad Monthly was published from March 1977 to November 1978. As the title suggests, the journal was published monthly, and a total of twenty issues came out. The following chart represents the most frequent subjects of the articles published in the two-year history of this journal.

The distribution is interesting

Bonyad Monthly, *Issues 1–20: (March 1977–November 1978)*

Subjects	Number
Critique of Western civilization	29
(Thought/lifestyle/technology/violence/injustice)	
The greatness of Iranian civilization	24
Islam, *erfan*, and spirituality	19
The East/the West	16

Our aim, in this chapter, is to demonstrate the de-politicized, antimodern ideology of *Bonyad Monthly*. In line with this rationale, we

[11] Of course, Fardid's use of *gharbzadegi* after the revolution was very political and at times close to Al-e Ahmad's meaning of the term.

have carefully reviewed all the issues of the journal and done our best to represent all relevant materials published in those issues:

1. We have included materials from all twenty issues of *Bonyad Monthly*.
2. Based on our reading of the twenty issues of the journal, we have categorized all the references and quotations thus: The West/the East, modernity/modernization, progress/technology, consumerism/capitalism, Islam/spirituality, and Ancient Iran/the modern world.
3. We have included and analyzed editorials, essays, short pieces, scholarly articles, poems, book reviews, interviews, advertisements, letters, reports, and translated articles.

A review of the twenty issues of the journal clearly shows the editor and writing staff had very systematically established a clear mission for it. This was a direct response to what they perceived as a cultural and moral "crisis" in Iran, and perhaps worldwide. Their vision concerned a choice: should Iran's future be defined in terms of the Western, or Eastern, civilizational space?[12] In a recent interview, Alireza Meybodi, the journal's editor, described his own thinking at the time in the following way:

I believed that we were facing a crossroads. We had to make an existential choice: West or East? Al-e Ahmad had put forward the concept of Westoxification. Ehsan Naraghi's books were published. And the clash of the East and the West was a heated topic among academics, students, and intellectuals.[13]

It seems that *Bonyad Monthly*'s editor and contributors imagined the East and West as an oppositional binary universe. This totalizing world vision itemized the cultural, moral, historical, civilizational, and even psychological components of Iranian/Eastern identity. These were specific qualities opposed to Western forms of being and thinking. This wave of Iranian thinkers attempted to demonstrate that the East in general and Iran in particular possessed unique and essential

---

[12] During the 1970s, many Iranian intellectuals and philosophers associated with the Pahlavi state wrote extensively about Iran's Eastern, or Asian, moral and civilizational mission. This perhaps culminated in the International Conference on the Dialogue of Civilizations, held in Tehran in 1977. Shaygan and Naraghi, in particular, participated in fomenting this civilizational ideology. But it is also present in the Shah's various speeches and addresses.

[13] Interview with Alireza Meybodi, Los Angeles, CA, April 26, 2015.

characteristics. It was an attempt to articulate an identity politics. Firstly, they argued, Aryan civilization was the bedrock of all other civilizations. Secondly, according to them, the soul or spirituality, and the morality, of the East/Iran was unique in the world. Thirdly, they identified certain golden ages in the history of Iran, in both Ancient and Islamic Iran. Fourthly, these thinkers evoked Iranian civilization's enormous potential to rise like a phoenix from the ashes. Fifthly and lastly, in identifying these unique Iranian characteristics they prophesied the regenerated nation's ability to successfully adopt modern technology. Yet, they insisted, Iran would maintain its Eastern identity and forge a new pathway for the world. These ideological notions, articulating the terms of a struggle against the West, existed in three categories: the cultural potential of Iran, Iranian/Eastern *erfan* or spirituality, and the uniqueness of Aryan civilization.

One section in the *Nowruz* (Iranian New Year) Special Issue was entitled "persons of the year 1977."[14] The nominations included the following categories, selected by *Bonyad Monthly*: journalism, essay, research, book, satire, philosophy, music, and others. Ahmad Fardid was selected for philosophy. The reason for his nomination was explained in the following terms: "due to the discussions provoked by Fardid on *gharbzadegi*, and due to his breaking of philosophical silence in the press and on TV, and his participation in public debates."[15] Ehsan Naraghi was selected in the Compilation Section upon the following basis: "due to the compilation of treasuring one's Own Identity (*Ancheh Khod Dasht*), which instigated an important debate in Iranian intellectual circles."[16]

In the second year of its publication, most of the issues contained a section titled "Farhang-e Velayat" (native or home culture). This section introduced certain folk cultures and literatures, including fairytales, *ta'ziye* (Shi'a plays), and other traditional forms of narrative and performance.[17]

---

[14]   Editor, "Persons of the Year 1977," *Bonyad Monthly*, Special Issue (April 1978): 12–17.
[15]   Ibid., 13.   [16]   Ibid., 16.
[17]   For example, see: Abolghasem Faghiri, "Village Culture: Kaka Siyah," *Bonyad Monthly*, Special Issue (April 1978): 166–167; Abolghasem Faghiri, "Village Culture: New Year's Game in Shiraz," *Bonyad Monthly*, No. 14 (May 1978): 92–93; Mohammad Hassan Raja'i Zafrei, "Village Culture: Ta'ziyeh in Rural Areas," *Bonyad Monthly*, No. 16 (September 1978): 84–85;
Abolghasem Faghiri, "Village Culture: Kharkan Daughter," *Bonyad Monthly*, No. 20 (November 1978): 53.

1 The Supremacy of Ancient Iranian Culture

Many articles in *Bonyad Monthly* feature a sharp contrast between Iranian and Western "cultures." Within this context, Iran is imagined in two basic ways. It is either the ancient imperial Iran of the pre-Islamic period, or it belongs within a broader historical epoch that is Islamic and spiritual but still pre-modern. The West, or Western culture, is defined in terms of the dominance of science and technology. It is presented as if nothing remains in modern Western life and culture except for technology. What is conspicuously missing from this picture is, firstly, the contemporary and really existing Iran of the ruling Pahlavi monarchy and, secondly, the Western literary and artistic world. There are only some periodical hints concerning the "materialist" nature of modern Western science.

Ezzatollah Homayunfar, in an article, clearly represents this line of thought:

We [Iranians] have fallen behind the West in science and technology ... but in culture, not only we do not lag, but we could be a role model for humanity. As in the past, we created the basic rules of peace and comfort for being human. We produced art (not the erotic and lunatic arts of this time) for humanity ... Our technical world, poisoned by science, needs a brilliant culture. The guidance for this culture can't be Bertrand Russell, Albert Camus, André Malraux, Ernest Hemingway, Agatha Christie, and so on.[18]

In the third issue, there is a letter from Switzerland. E. Jazayeri, the writer of the letter, asks *Bonyad Monthly*'s editor to "make a connection with the Swiss people, and let them know how amazing Iranian culture and civilization are."[19] The author expresses disappointment that Swiss people know so little about the glory of Iranian history and culture. He proclaims: "Iran is the birthplace of Persian culture and language, and human civilizations have enjoyed this infinite resource. It is the right of all human beings to be aware of such an inspiring and innovative source of thought."[20]

[18] Ezzatollah Homayunfar, "Messenger of Peace," *Bonyad Monthly*, No. 1 (March 1977): 4.
[19] Ezzatollah Jazayeri, "A Letter from Sweden: Let Nobel Heroes Know That We Are Heroes As Well," *Bonyad Monthly*, No. 3 (June 1977): 21.
[20] Ibid.

Said Fatemi, a journalist and politician, who was formerly the personal assistant of Prime Minister Mohammad Mossadegh, discusses in another piece the role of symbols in Ancient Iran and warns us that:

Gharbzadegi leads us to overlook Iranian civilization. Abandoning who we are, and the luminous culture of our history, is an unforgivable betrayal. We must recognize our fatherland and explore its culture. We must make our youth aware that they are the heirs of such an eternal spiritual power. This is our duty. If we don't do this, we will deeply regret it in the future.[21]

Here, it seems the *gharbzadegi* discourse is used to totally overlook and dismiss the realities of modern Iran, and indeed the modern world. Said Fatemi was seemingly urging a return to pre-modern and pre-Islamic Iran, while using the civilizational discourse to avoid discussion of contemporary Iranian practical challenges. What does "eternal spiritual power" mean? When did real, living Iranians ever possess such a power in their actual lives? There is an amazing absence of either historical detail or sociological analysis.

The modernist poet and literary translator Farrokh Tamimi contributes an essay titled "The East or the West" in the special issue of *Bonyad Monthly* on "The Third World: Struggle for Identity." He writes:

Today, I, as an easterner from Iran, want to save myself from the invasion of adverse Western effects. The only refuge is my national identity. I would like to adopt the best features of Western civilization, while preserving my national identity in pure and uninfected form. This is the real problem, and we expect to hear an important idea from these debates [on Iranian TV's Channel 2].[22]

Tamimi's desire to be a "modern" man and his yearning for "belonging" to the authentic Iranian identity were perhaps the prevalent discursive narrative of much Iranian intellectual thought in the 1970s. This is abundantly represented in the many issues of *Bonyad Monthly*. We see it expressed in intellectual debates, history, and even state-sponsored cultural institutions. However, while the "desirable" aspects of Iranian and Islamic culture and civilization are explained (albeit in

---

[21] Said Fatemi, "Social Symbols of Ancient Gods of Iran," *Bonyad Monthly*, No. 7 (October 1977): 14.

[22] Farrokh Tamimi, "The East or the West," *Bonyad Monthly*, No. 10 (January 1978): 30.

generalities and sloganeering), there is rarely any serious attempt to explain what is "good" about modern or Western culture. Such explanations become almost impossible because the East, Iran, and Islam are systematically defined as the opposite of the West. These dichotomies are evoked in terms of Eastern spirituality vs. Western materialism, rational thinking, and the domination of technical knowledge.

These tendencies are exemplified in another article, titled "The West and the East from the Eastern Point of View," by Naser Ranjbin. He argues that the "East" can utilize modern Western technology, in conjunction with its own traditions, to reject modern Western culture. The "East" can, at the same time, also create a unified and dignified human community:

Despite Western misgivings, the Eastern man will forge his own thought, by way of his resilient and innate civilization. The Eastern man will embrace Western technology, but will respond with a big "No" to Western culture and thought, which will soon decline ... The Eastern man must master the new technology to be upon an equal footing with the West. The East may thereby bestow and extend its traditional and cultural values, and lead the world with its ancient civilization. In this way, we will have a unified humanity, where human beings are not separated into Eastern and Western.[23]

Mohammad Reza Tajoddini makes a similar argument, in a poetic style, in a piece entitled "The East and The West":

Once the Eastern sun
Was infected by the Western plague
Night expanded its new domain ...
Now, my dear East!
Oh, the leader of the past glorious days
Will you return the crown of the sun to my tribe, again? ...
Who knows?
Maybe
There is still fire under the ashes
To heal my Eastern tribe's plague
Maybe
Who knows?[24]

[23] Naser Ranjbin, "The West and the East from the Eastern Man's Point of View," *Bonyad Monthly*, No. 10 (January 1978): 32–33.

[24] Mohammad Reza Tajoddini, "The East and the West," *Bonyad Monthly*, No. 10 (January 1978): 37.

There is hardly any attempt to offer serious analysis or arguments, or present even the slightest evidence for these grandiose claims.

In one of the last issues (No. 18) of the journal, merely a few months before the fall of the Pahlavi state, an editorial opinion piece by the journal's editor criticizes the industrial West while encouraging the Third World to rise and achieve independence:

If the Western industrial countries control the twentieth century, the next century, without any doubt, will belong to the Third World. The experience of the last century shows that industrial and technical power makes humans materially strong, but spiritually feeble. This makes the Third World awaken ... If the twentieth century is the century of industrial and technological power, the next century will be the century of freedom and independent powers.[25]

There is not a hint of clear thinking or any attempt to reason in this line of argument. Upon what basis may we argue that Western countries are only strong materially? What is the basis for arguing that the Third World is the center of spirituality? And even supposing that these two propositions might be valid, why is it that the Pahlavi state was doing everything to invest Iran with material strength?

Iraj Vahidi, in *Bonyad Monthly* No. 7, writes an essay on the "Revival of Iran's Global Stake."[26] He argues for the revival of the ancient Iranian sciences as an alternative to modern Western scientific domination:

The world-historical role of Iran in the dissemination and development of science and culture is undeniable. Far back in history, our scientific schools were always more important than other scientific, cultural, and artistic centers throughout the world ... What is important, now, is the revival of the global share of Iran in science and culture. This is the only means by which we can ensure our scientific clout. The world may thereby accept Iran as a center for scientific exchanges, and not as an importer.[27]

The militant hostility toward modern and Western cultural domination is also evident in issue No. 14 of the journal. An interview is published with the new director of the state-run news agency, Pars. The title of the report and the issue's cover feature, "The News Imperialism," introduce the news agency as a mode of resistance against

---

[25] Editor, "Freedom Means Having No Wish," *Bonyad Monthly*, No. 18 (September 1978): 3–4.

[26] Iraj Vahidi, "Revival of Iran's Global Stake," *Bonyad Monthly*, No. 7 (October 1977): 3.

[27] Ibid.

so-called "news imperialism." After a report on the well-equipped agency, with its new technologies and new offices, the director writes:

The empowerment and expansion of Third World news agencies permit Third World countries to have their own voices, and to cover their different events without any intermediary. In fact, the mainstream news agencies only cover the bad and negative news in the Third World. These include natural disasters, terrorism, coups d'état, etc. They do not pay attention to their [Third World] economic, political, and social achievements. The only way to resist this unpleasant situation is through the emergence of powerful news agencies in Third World countries.[28]

Another interesting example of the unreality of identity rhetoric in the journal is an advertisement for the "Mahestan housing project." The title reads: "A City with Identity: A Combination of Tradition and Technology."[29] However, as far as one can tell from the pictures, these buildings merely resemble other "modern" buildings in Tehran.

2 Iranian Spirituality Encounters the Soulless West

In the journal's inaugural issue, the lead piece presents an interview with the French Orientalist scholar of Shi'a Islam Henry Corbin. The interview is titled "An Interview with Henry Corbin: The Inner East." The interviewer, and journal editor, summarizes Corbin's responses in a very poetic and mystical prose:

Henry Corbin is skeptical about the West. He finds the spiritual civilization of humanity in Sohrewardi and Molla Sadra. In our conversations, Corbin consistently contrasts Eastern illumination [*eshragh*] with Western philosophy. He believes that the realization of the true history of humanity is only possible through an alliance with Oriental culture.[30]

[28] A report on the Pars news agency and an interview with Mahmood Jafarian, Editor, "The Pars News Agency: A Way against the News Imperialism," *Bonyad Monthly*, No. 14 (May 1978): 47 and 174.

[29] "Mahestan Housing Project Advertisement," *Bonyad Monthly*, No. 2 (April 1977): 58.

[30] "An Interview with Henry Corbin: The Inner East," *Bonyad Monthly*, No. 1 (March 1977): 6. The interview has been reported in an extremely Romantic writing style about the so-called spiritual East and Corbin's approach to spiritualism in the East, especially Iran. It seems that the interviewer has not translated Corbin's sentences into Farsi exactly, but produced a combination of his feelings toward Corbin and Corbin's ideas.

It is rather hard to distinguish whether the ideas expressed in the interview are Corbin's or the editor's own. However, the entire conversation is overflowing with Romantic and Orientalist images of the "East," combined with a dark illustration of the modern West. In response to a question about spiritualism, Corbin points out that:

The West is descending into a scientific and sensory world, while the illumination philosophy is inhabited with human spiritualism … You live in a space filled with spiritual and mystic traditions. You live in a world in which Avicenna, Molla Sadra, and Sohrewardi have existed. In fact, you live in a world that has all the necessary essentials for the spiritual transformation of the human condition. In the poor and miserable West, there is no spirituality, which is humanity's most important need. The West knows nothing about *eshragh*, by which the world can be emancipated. Sohrewardi, in his philosophy, always pays attention to a system of spiritual teaching. His approach is thorough. He doesn't think of human mortality. Rather, his aim is to achieve human eternality, which is an Avicennian concept.[31]

Of course, these fantastic ideas about Iran, expressed in 1977, had little to do with the reality of Iranian life as experienced by contemporary Iranian people. These writers, however, formed an important part of the contemporary elite intellectual world, which included Corbin and his Iranian associates. One wonders if those involved in state-sponsored journals and similar institutions were genuinely blind to the realities of Iranian life and culture. Alternatively, they may have found spiritualism a fanciful escape from the harsher realities taking place around them.

In response to the question, "How did you discover Oriental philosophy and become interested in it?" Corbin replies: "I started my philosophical education after World War I, with Etienne Gilso. We were looking for a new meaning in philosophy. He led us toward the path with his institute (Medieval Studies). Therefore, through studying medieval philosophy, we tracked Avicenna's ideas."[32]

The interviewer asks, "What do you mean when you say that Easterners have to be unified? Do you mean it as a 'political act'?" Corbin replies: "I prefer to say a 'spiritual act'." The interviewer further enquires: "You mean a spiritual act against the non-spiritual West?" Corbin explains: "You can live in the West, but think in an

---

[31] Ibid., 8.   [32] Ibid.

Eastern way ... or, you can live in the East, and think in a Western way. Thus, if I say 'the East,' I mean: 'the inward East' [*shargh-e darun*]."[33]

The journal's editor, Alireza Meybodi, in an essay titled "The Crisis of Self" makes an argument resembling the anti-Western argument in Jalal Al-e Ahmad's Westoxification:

In the West, "the Self" is separated from the world ... The relationship between humans has reached its lowest point ... The West has chosen a reversal of history: "I" is closer and closer to tools and instruments, and is far away from nature and human truth. The achievement, however, of historical value requires an opposite direction. That's why everything in the West is inverted: ethics, justice, freedom, and democracy are all displaced.[34]

Meybodi's logic seems influenced by assorted ideological lines. A quasi-Marxist analysis of modern human alienation is combined with a "mystical" and almost exotic representation of the "East." This is very similar to the notions articulated by Fardid and Corbin concerning "Eastern Spirituality":

When we contrast the East with the West, we see that the East has kept its *haya* [shame, modesty]. The crisis of "self" has not reached it, to turn the humanity of man [*ensan-e ba ensan*] into man deprived of humanity [*ensan-e bi ensan*]. The factor that maintains this *haya* is the culture of the Eastern "I" [*farhang-e man-e shargh*]. The Eastern "I" is still consciously or unconsciously resisting the temptations of Western humanism ... In the West, this is a tool. Things are moving forward, rather than human beings. That is right! It is the machine that is becoming the giant, not the human being.[35]

There is also an essay by Pajuhesh on the domination of the West over the East, titled "The Horrendous Domination: How the West Made Eastern 'Brains' Homeless." The argument is based on the East–West binary, in terms of the spiritual East and the technological and amoral West. The author states that:

before colonialism, all invasions were military. Nowadays, however, this domination has taken on new dimensions: political, economic, and intellectual ... The West wishes to impose its supremacy upon the East because of its technological civilization. It has forgotten, however, that its

---

[33] Ibid.
[34] Alireza Meybodi, "The Crisis of Self," *Bonyad Monthly*, No. 3 (June 1977): 4–5.
[35] Ibid.

religion comes from the East ... The West is ruthless, heartless, selfish, and arrogant ... The West has given nothing to the East but misery, corruption, and decay. However, the awakened East will break the chains of political, economic, and intellectual captivity. The East will destroy *gharbzadegi* and remain standing through its ancient traditions. This is so because the criterion of Eastern *erfani* thoughts suggests the fact that philosophy is not a Western phenomenon. Rather, it is rooted in the East. In fact, matters that pertain to humanity come from the East. Whatever is material and commercial, by contrast, comes from the West. The West is a merchant, and its commodity is human blood. Its capital is plundering other countries.[36]

In the same issue, there is a review of a book by Nasrollah Seifpur-Fatemi on Sufism. At the beginning, the reviewer writes:

Iranian Sufism has carried the rich treasury of the Eastern mastermind to the superpower world: the world in which hundreds of crimes are committed every day; to the world deprived of lyricism [*taghazzol*]; to the world devoid of meaning; to the world without poetry. This is the world in which the Western man enthusiastically hovers over the East ... Sufism made a great intellectual transformation in Iran, and its light has arrived in the West now.[37]

Ironically, this style of writing for the sake of writing (*ensha'nevisi*) contains very little meaningful argument or any hint of logic, or historical or factual evidence. The mode of argumentation, rather, is to repeat the idea of the East–West binary opposition in a Romantic way.

Another article, by Said Fatemi in the fourteenth issue, titled "I was Crude, Attained Experience, and Burned" (*Kham Bodam, Pokhteh Shodam, Sukhtam*) makes reference to Molavi's spiritual self-realization.[38] The author writes: "Molavi's thought represents one of the most brilliant embodiments of the Iranian soul, which exemplifies Eastern spirituality. Molavi's thought is the epitome of *erfani*, and the deep soul and unique politeness of the East, particularly Iran as the cradle of Eastern civilization."[39] An article by Zia' Nur on pantheism

---

[36] Pajuhesh, "The Horrendous Domination: How the West Made Eastern 'Brains' Homeless," *Bonyad Monthly*, Special Issue (April 1978): 47 and 174.

[37] Nasrollah Seifpur-Fatemi, "Review of *Sufism*," *Bonyad Monthly*, No. 6 (September 1977): 74.

[38] Said Fatemi, "I was Crude, Attained Experience, and Burned," *Bonyad Monthly*, No. 14 (May 1978): 8–11.

[39] Ibid., 10.

explains Molavi's spiritual thought and *vahdat-e vojud* in his Masnavi.[40] The author further articulates his idea in four additional articles in different issues.

In the twentieth issue there is an article by Ebrahim Safa'i titled "Khayyam and Meterling."[41] Safa'i argues that similar ideas are shared between Morris Meterling and the Iranian poet Khayyam: "When you read Meterling's writing" it is "as if he has been Khayyam's student, and was inspired by Khayyam."[42] The idea is that there are almost no new or original ideas in the modern West. All that is worthy of attention has already been said by Iranian literary and cultural figures.

3 The Uniqueness of Aryan Civilization

In an interview about mythology, Said Fatemi attempts to show that ancient Greece had very little to offer. It was Aryan civilization – Aryan is defined as Eastern – that was the foundation of all other civilizations. He claims that:

Myths travel from the East to the West. Contrary to popular belief, Greece had a weak culture, civilization, and mythology. It has borrowed its entire apparent cultural cohesion from the East, especially from Aryan civilization ... In fact, the entirety of the glorious and great civilization of Greece is nothing but an appropriated civilization from the East and Iran ... Egyptian civilization had more direct effect on Greek civilization. The point is, however, that Egyptian civilization borrowed most of its elements from Aryan civilization.[43]

Fatemi was a regular contributor to the journal. He wrote at least one article on Ancient Iran in every issue of the first year. The general approach in all his writings, as well as his interviews, was to display the greatness of Aryan civilization. His essential message was that Aryan civilization was the foundation of all other important civilizations. Astonishingly, these assertions are made without a hint of

---

[40] Zia' Nur, "*Vahdat-e Vojud* and Its Display in Masnavi," *Bonyad Monthly*, No. 2 (May 1977): 20–25.

[41] Ebrahim Safa'i, "Khayyam and Meterling," *Bonyad Monthly*, No. 20 (November 1978): 37–40.

[42] Ibid., 38.

[43] Said Fatemi, "An Interview with Said Fatemi: Myths," *Bonyad Monthly*, No. 2 (May 1977): 63–64.

evidence, analysis, or historical fact. His writings are written in a poor literary style and are strongly redolent of propaganda.

For example, in the article "Thirty Centuries of Human Anthem," Fatemi writes about the "barbarism of the West against the spirituality of the East." He claims that the East is "the symbol of the great human consciousness ... When the Greeks' acquaintance with the great Iranian civilization started, thanks to Zoroastrianism, they learned many things about human dignity."[44] At the end of the article, Fatemi concludes: "whether in subjects of spirituality and the intellect, or in mythology, Indo-Iranian traditions have always had supremacy over Greek thought. The Aryan race has always been the standard-bearer of the greatest human civilization, upon numerous grounds."[45] It seems that, for him, Aryan is a code-word for Iran and his praise of ancient Iranian culture.

Fatemi further argues that "for ten centuries, Greek civilization had contact and conflict with Iranian civilization. It was always, however, under the control of the spiritual power of Iran. The spread of Mithraism [*Mehrparasti*] in Greece and ancient Rome was the first sign of this spiritual inspiration."[46] He explains, in much detail, that myths, religions, and rituals in Greece and Rome were rooted in the Persian idea of Mithraism. In another article, Fatemi continues this line of argument: "Mithraism spread from Iran to other countries. It appeared in different forms of god, like Apollo ... In many Roman temples, there are different statues, paintings, and even coins which show the influence of Mithra [*Mehr*] in the West."[47] Said Fatemi also wrote an article titled "The Presence of Old Myths in Modern Thought."[48] Here he explains the necessity of myths in ancient life, and their legacies in modern life.

There is also an academic article titled "An Introduction to the History of the Culture and Civilization of Ancient Iran" by Ardeshir

[44] Said Fatemi, "Thirty Centuries of Human Anthem," *Bonyad Monthly*, No. 4 (July 1977): 17 and 66.

[45] Ibid., 67.

[46] Said Fatemi, "Historical Cryptology of a Religion," *Bonyad Monthly*, No. 8 (November 1977): 43.

[47] Said Fatemi, "The Universalism of a School," *Bonyad Monthly*, No. 9 (December 1977): 24–25.

[48] Said Fatemi, "The Presence of Old Myths in Modern Thoughts," *Bonyad Monthly*, No. 5 (August 1977): 18–23.

Khodadadian, Professor of the National University in Tehran.[49] This is a historical article covering the ancient to the medieval periods. The article makes a case for how Aryan heritage survived, despite multiple invasions, throughout the history of Iran. There is also a second part of Ardeshir Khodadadian's article on pre-Islamic literature and languages, "Avesta Literature." It reviews Avesta throughout history.[50] It reviews Zoroaster's *Gathas* as a treasure of Iranian civilization.[51] While all these pieces are written with the aim of glorifying Iran's past, there is hardly any serious attempt at historiography or critical analysis.

Iranian Identity and Modern Anxieties

Issue No. 10 has a special feature on "The Third World: Struggle for Identity." Almost all the materials published are related to ongoing contemporary debates concerning the East and the West, as presented on the weekly Television 2 show. *Bonyad Monthly*'s editor, Alireza Meybodi, hosted this show.

1 The "Good," "Bad," and "Dreadful" West

The Pahlavi state was proud of its socioeconomic achievements and modernization programs in Iran. The state media and various state-run institutions were involved in a vast propaganda campaign. This was dedicated to showcasing the pervasiveness of the Pahlavi-era modernization experience. At least superficially, the state represented itself as a modern and modernizing monarchy. Ironically, the political opposition also believed that the Pahlavi state was arrogantly modern and involved in transforming Iran according to the modern Western model. A more careful examination of Pahlavi ideology, however, reveals a rather different story. The Pahlavi state, particularly under Mohammad Raze Shah's latter rule (1960s–70s), adopted a very hostile and anti-modern/Western attitude. This was evident in the pages of the intellectual journal *Bonyad Monthly*. Almost all the contributors to

---

[49] Ardeshir Khodadadian, "An Introduction to the History of Culture and the Civilization of Ancient Iran," *Bonyad Monthly*, No. 14 (May 1978): 19–32.

[50] Ardeshir Khodadadian, "Avesta Literature," *Bonyad Monthly*, No. 18 (September 1978): 32–33.

[51] Ardeshir Khodadadian, "A Review of Pre-Islamic Literature and Languages," *Bonyad Monthly*, No. 17 (August 1978): 18–19.

Bonyad Monthly made a sharp and almost existential line between what they considered "good" about the modern West, namely, science and technology, and its corrupting culture and politics. Some had a more radical attitude. They blamed secularism and technological dominance in the West for its alleged moral and spiritual crisis. Others, however, were more at peace with the adoption of Western technology.

In the special issue of *Bonyad Monthly* published for *Nowruz* (Iranian New Year) in 1978, Alireza Meybodi has a long essay titled "New Years and Yesterdays" (*Nowruz-ha va Diruzha*). This is a rather nostalgic piece on the loss of the good old days. The essay contrasted all that is new with a bygone but golden age in the past. Apparently, as the author clearly remembers those days, this bygone era was only a few years before our time. Meybodi compares all kinds of material or cultural phenomena: new things, such as radio programs, food items, Pepsi Cola and other soft drinks, the traffic situation, Iranian intellectuals, soccer games, fishbowls, supermarkets, modern medicine, diligent boys and cheated girls, new-year (*Nowruz*) trips, taxis, and much more, with all kinds of old and traditional things, including symbols, behaviors, and beliefs, as well as greetings, parties, gharries (horse-drawn carriages), tradesmen, lemon juice, old radios, bathhouses, zurkhaneh (traditional Iranian gymnasiums), and much more.[52]

In another essay in the same issue, "A Western Tribe among the Ethnic Iranians," we hear a similar line of argument on the decline of the true Iranian identity. The author argues that "The new rich [Iranians] teach their kids that Massachusetts, London, and Nice are better places than Yazd and Shiraz ... They are the reason why the West is considered a symbol of greatness and beauty, while our homeland is perceived as the symbol of despair."[53]

The author also criticizes those parents who send their kids to boarding schools in Europe or the United States, and also those parents who prefer their kids to learn a foreign language from an early age.[54]

In the same special issue, Mohammad Hossein Adeli has an essay on "Consumerism and Narcissism." The author argues that consumerism

---

[52] Alireza Meybodi, "New Years and Yesterdays," *Bonyad Monthly*, Special Issue (April 1978): 8–11.

[53] Bonyad Monthly, "A Western Tribe among the Ethnic Iranians," *Bonyad Monthly*, Special Issue (April 1978): 34–35.

[54] Ibid.

is one of the consequences of industrialization and modernization, and that it "makes people in the developing countries into consumers . . . the consequence of which is loneliness."[55] He further argues that "[t]his equation shows our description of contemporary humanity: hungry, human-consumer, and human-dependent human, which means catastrophe. How can we expect to live our lives when we have lost them?"[56]

There is an interview with Mehrdad Avesta (1930–91), a poet and literary critic, on the relationship between literature and *erfan*. After explaining the uniqueness of *erfani* (mystical) literature, Avesta argues that:

Because of technical and industrial progress, both in Iran and the whole world, civilization has reached the point where one doesn't have time to think. The more there is progress in our civilization, the less we have time to spend for spirituality and thought. The media captures people. When, as a result, the ideal life for a young man is a singer or actor's rich life, they can't follow a gnostic like Molana.[57]

In the fourth issue of *Bonyad Monthly* there is a section on the Persian language. There is a very short piece by Ahmad Fardid, "Routinization of the Persian Academy" (*Aknunzadegi-ye Farhangestan-e Zaban-e Farsi*). There are also other articles and essays on the same subject. They all follow Fardid's main argument on the Persian language. Fardid argued that:

With Martin Heidegger, I believe that "language, which is the house of being, is in ruins in the world." That's right, today's language is the language of modernization; it is the language of industry; it is the language of the status quo; but it is not the language of thought. Today's language is a tool for power, dominance, and hegemony over others, and any kind of being. The language the Persian Academy has constructed suffers from presentism [*aknunzadeh*], and this language will not create culture, literature, and art in the future. We have to think of tomorrow's language; a language in accord with thinking and meaning; a language beyond egoism [*ananiyat*] and presentism [*aknunzadegi*]. To find this language, we, first, must make people,

---

55 Mohammad Hossein Adeli, "Consumerism and Narcissism," *Bonyad Monthly*, Special Issue (April 1978): 42–46.
56 Ibid., 46.
57 Mehrdad Avesta, "An Interview with Avesta about Literature and Erfan," *Bonyad Monthly*, No. 17 (August 1978): 82–87.

especially young people, familiar with thinking, and let them gradually make their thinking language. What we have today is the language of the mass media: the language of the radio, television, and the newspapers, which people inevitably follow.[58]

In the same issue, there is an essay and an editorial calling for radio and TV programs on the Persian language. Also, there is an essay by Reza Davari (a former student and close follower of Ahmad Fardid's) on the standard language. From another angle, Meybodi, in one essay, discusses the purification of the language after colonial and political influence. He writes that "The presence of a foreign language and culture among a population could be dangerous when it results in a political and economic presence, and lays the foundations for colonialism ... Arabophilia [*Tazizadegi*] is not our problem. It happened in the past. Now we should be aware of, and deal with, the penetration of Western culture and language."[59]

Issue No. 9 features a review of Reza Davari's book *The Status of Philosophy in Iran's Islamic Era*. One of Fardid's students, Mohammad Reza Jozi, wrote the review.[60] The reviewer emphasizes that Davari lacks any "original idea," insisting that the book is "repeating Heidegger's and Fardid's ideas, both in form and content, without referring to them." Another problem, according to Jozi, is that there are "many paradoxical and selective ideas" in the book. For example, Jozi states that "Davari believes that philosophy is necessary for the essence of the history of Islam. According to Fardid, by contrast, philosophy is not necessary for the essence of the history of Islam, and he criticizes Western metaphysics."[61]

In the article's conclusion, Jozi argues that Davari's "book tries to cover spirituality and the significance of the history of Islam by means of Western metaphysical paganism [*zandagheh*]. Although prophecy and Shari'a with Prophet Mohammad are finished, Mohammad's

---

[58] Ahmad Fardid, "Presentism of the Persian Academy," *Bonyad Monthly*, No. 4 (July 1977): 5.

[59] Alireza Meybodi, "Linguistic Doctrine for Language," *Bonyad Monthly*, No. 4 (July 1977): 5.

[60] Mohammad Reza Jozi was a student of Ahmad Fardid's before the revolution. He became one of the prominent advocates of Fardid's ideas after the revolution, and a well-known figure in the postrevolutionary period.

[61] Mohammad Reza Jozi, "Review of *Position of Philosophy in the History of the Islamic Iran*," *Bonyad Monthly*, No. 9 (December 1977): 56–57.

guardianship [*velayat*], which is based on the truth of his religion, is not interrupted."[62]

2 The Moral and Cultural Decline of the West

In *Bonyad Monthly* No. 5 there is an interview with the Heideggerian philosopher and former student of Ahmad Fardid, Reza Davari. In this interview, Davari is asked about the effects of technology on the future course of the Third World. In his response, Davari offers a very dark and Heideggerian view of Western culture:

We can no longer expect philosophy to save Western culture. If the history of the West has a future, it will be determined by the future thought which is not philosophy. Since we [the Third World] are implicated in the history of the West, we must beware of – or at least, not pose the idea of – saving the West.[63]

Unsurprisingly, he then makes the point that, perhaps, the final hope for the West lies in embracing the East:

Philosophy cannot save the Third World countries either. But if they are deprived of philosophy, they will face even more confusion. They need philosophy, so that they can order their own sense of rationality and common sense ... Today, more than ever, human beings know that technology is unleashed. Even humanity itself is captured by, and subordinated to, technology. Human beings wish that they could take control of technology. If you see how, these days, some Orientalists recommend that people adopt the ancient Eastern customs and manners, it's because they are looking for a heaven on earth to save Western civilization. But if they think they can change the path of history with their plans, it's a delusion of the West.[64]

In a similar line of argument, the journal's editor, Alireza Meybodi, rebukes Western metaphysics and advances the routine but crude "Heideggerian" argument that:

Physics remains the same in Havana or in Manchester ... But what is different in the world is human faith ... We live in a pluralistic period ... Although God, truth, and salvation are not exportable, the policy of the

[62] Ibid., 62.
[63] Reza Davari, "An Interview with Reza Davari," *Bonyad Monthly*, No. 5 (August 1977): 32.
[64] Ibid.

dominant human-type, system, and ideology of the West is to impart a certain God, truth, and freedom to the global subalterns ... The presence of Western patterns and logics in the West is normal [*badihi*] and hegemonic, but their presence in the East is perceived as unnatural [*zed-e badihi*].[65]

Meybodi then proceeds to argue that the "concealed" ideas of the East are steadily becoming disclosed and more visible:

The problem of the global subaltern man, who lacks political and economic organization, yet who lives in the so-called Third World, is that what seems unknown [*zed-e badihiat*] is gradually becoming known [*badihi*] ... The human is a physical being that lives between life and death ... what makes the human eternal is history. That is, history gives the human a permanent identity and meaning. If the contemporary Iranian is still alive, it is because of the prior establishment of a permanent identity through his enriching culture, poetry, and morality. This included a respect for their own truth and virtues. While many nations may have even appeared before Iran, no trace remains of them upon the earth. Thus, I declare that humans have two choices: they can either consent to the physical [material] life, or, while living life, they can engage in the eternal meaning-bestowing power of history.[66]

Meybodi subsequently advances a "spiritual" critique of the concept of "progress":

Here is the problem: human beings think that they are involved in progress, because of material and technological advancements ... The fact is that the momentary flash of human life in the West has surpassed all, but we can't call it the progress of history ... Apparently, the West feels guilty about its eroticized and materialistic life, so, to find solace, it has decided to take revenge upon the truth.[67]

Bonyad Monthly No. 9 is a special issue devoted to *gharbzadegi* (Westoxification). The back-cover photo features pictures of Jalal Al-e Ahmad, Seyed Hossein Nasr, Ahmad Fardid, and some other Iranian intellectuals. The issue is titled "The East or the West: The Intellectual Debate." In fact, the only relevant essay on *gharbzadegi* in this issue is the editorial. This title seems to have been used because of the debates

---

[65] Alireza Meybodi, "Consummation of History," *Bonyad Monthly*, No. 1 (March 1977): 32.
[66] Ibid., 33. [67] Ibid., 34.

taking place, at the time, on the TV 2 program hosted by *Bonyad Monthly*'s editor.

In the editorial piece, Meybodi states that the "elite TV 2" television channel has drawn vast public attention. According to a survey, 59 percent of the programs on this channel are cultural, 32 percent are political, and 18 percent are entertainment. Citing the survey, the editor concludes that the popularity of TV signifies a new era in Iranian television history in producing high-culture products.[68]

The lead piece in this issue, by Shahkar Shams, is titled "*Gharbzadegi* in the Production System." The author explains:

In the East, human beings have kept their human qualities. In the West, meanwhile, human beings are about to change into something inhuman. Contrary to popular belief, the cause for this is neither technology nor industry, per se. The root cause is the presence of a specific production system, which can be traced back to the European Industrial Revolution, and bourgeois historical consciousness ... In this system, the human being is in the service of production, and production is in the service of profit ... which is in the service of a certain group.[69]

The author then proceeds to offer a critical view of both capitalism and socialism. He argues that both economic systems are part of the same modern, secular, and Western universe. If the above line of reasoning is hard to understand, and the author's confusing arguments seem self-contradictory, the following turn in the argument seems comical and mind-numbingly silly:

When we mention the West, we intend both capitalist and socialist production systems. The European and American proletariat faces its counter-self, in the same way as the socialist proletariat. The difference is that in the socialist system, the government, which possesses the means of production, replaces the counter-self. Meanwhile, the duty [*resalat*] of the Eastern human being is not to fight against the West, and especially not against industry and technology. Rather, they should battle the bourgeois consciousness that has turned the human into an industrial tool and consumer anthropoid. Therefore, the duty of the Eastern man is to find an Eastern

---

[68] Editor, "The End of the Age of Sandwich Images," *Bonyad Monthly*, No. 10 (January 1978): 13.

[69] Shahkar Shams, "*Gharbzadegi* in the Production System," *Bonyad Monthly*, No. 9 (December 1977): 3.

production system which is rooted in economic honor [*sherafat-e eghtesadi*].[70]

In issue No. 17 of the journal there is a piece by a professor of law at Tehran University, Reza Mazluman, titled "Imitation and Social Frustration." The author, who was also a well-known royalist political figure, attempts to offer a sociological analysis of violence and its root causes. In a seemingly scholarly fashion, he explains various theories of "imitation." He then provides examples from around the world, including Iran and the United States, depicting the underlying relation between media violence and its subsequent social replications. This is clearly the author's attempt at explaining what was going on in Iran at the time; however, the journal almost exclusively uses cases of violence in the United States to criticize the West for events in Iran.[71]

In issue No. 8, the journal has a translated article by the French-American environmentalist René Jules Dubos (1901–82) titled "Against Technology."[72] The original English title of the article is "In Defense of the Environment." The author, a well-known micro-biologist, proposes a social-evolutionary approach that he believes capable of overcoming environmental problems, in favor of an ecologically balanced environment. He argues that humanity has the capacity and resilience to solve contemporary environmental problems. He is optimistic about the future. *Bonyad Monthly*'s choice of title, however, is misleading, and seems intentionally chosen to imply a totalizing vision that the author did not in fact have in mind.

There is another essay in the same issue, by S. Sahand, titled "The Age of Technology [*Felezsalari*]."[73] The author argues that we live in an age surrounded by technology and the machine: "Contemporary man imagines himself as being free ... but how can we escape from the increasing waves of radio and television? The mass media which stimulates people, like any other kind of drug, necessarily has side-effects."[74]

---

[70] Ibid.

[71] Reza Mazluman, "Imitation and Social Frustration," *Bonyad Monthly*, No. 17 (August 1978): 4–7 and 86–97.

[72] René Dubos, "Against Technology," trans. A. Azarang, *Bonyad Monthly*, No. 10 (January 1978): 14–17.

[73] S. Sahand, "The Age of Technology," *Bonyad Monthly*, No. 18 (September 1978): 85–86.

[74] Ibid., 86.

In the same issue an article by Arthur Miller is published in Persian. This piece discusses literature and consumerism, and is titled "Literature and the Consumer Society."[75] The article analyzes authors and their readers in the modern era, and suggests that mass media and mass production make every work and every author public. The journal, however, uses certain sentences as pull-quotes to imply that Miller is against the modern world and technology. As in previous articles, the editors routinely extract passages out of context to present a distorted representation in conformity with the anti-modern ideology of *Bonyad Monthly*.

Issue No. 15 features an article on "Racism and Apartheid" by the Bonyad Monthly Research Group.[76] It discusses discrimination and apartheid against black people in South Africa. Issue No. 16 subsequently features an essay by Farrokh Tamimi titled "A Letter to His Excellency."[77] In the form of a letter to the South African authorities, it criticizes racism and apartheid. It incorporates quotations from Islamic texts and the Qu'ran, as well as the Bible and prominent scholars, and condemns the racial situation in South Africa.

In the same issue, there is a translated article on racism, "The Dreams of Black America." It features interviews with ten black professionals and experts on racism in the United States.[78] There is also another essay on racism and apartheid in South Africa, based on the memoires of a traveler named Dan Jacobson.[79]

Bonyad Monthly's nineteenth issue also focuses on race and racial politics. It features an essay by the Caribbean-American novelist Frank Hercules titled "To Live in Harlem."[80] There is also the second part of Dan Jacobson's article on apartheid in South Africa,[81] and another

---

[75] Arthur Miller, "Literature and the Consumer Society," trans. Mehdi Khamush, *Bonyad Monthly*, No. 16 (July 1978): 14–17.

[76] Bonyad Monthly Research Group, "Racism and Apartheid," *Bonyad Monthly*, No. 15 (June 1978): 3–13.

[77] Farrokh Tamimi, "A Letter to His Excellency," *Bonyad Monthly*, No. 16 (July 1978): 12–13.

[78] Paul Sh. Pierce, "The Dreams of Black America," trans. Hadi Dastbaz, *Bonyad Monthly*, No. 18 (September 1978): 20–22.

[79] Dan Jacobson, "Memories and Dangers of Travel to South Africa," trans. Farah Barari, *Bonyad Monthly*, No. 18 (September 1978): 23–28.

[80] Frank Hercules, "To Live in Harlem," trans. Hadi Dastbaz, *Bonyad Monthly*, No. 19 (October 1978): 14–15 and 27.

[81] Dan Jacobson, "Memories and Dangers of Travel to South Africa, Part 2," trans. Farah Barari, *Bonyad Monthly*, No. 19 (October 1978): 16–19.

piece, by Milton Ellerin, on the re-awakening of Nazism in Europe.[82] This issue also features a translated interview, "The Ugly Reflection of Colonialism," with the Senegalese filmmaker Mahama Jansoon Traore. The director discusses his experiences and problems as a black filmmaker.[83] This issue, published in October 1978, contains nothing at all about the events then taking place in Iran.

In most of the issues of *Bonyad Monthly* there is either a report or a translated article about increasing violence and crime in the United States, especially about racism there and in South Africa as representative of white supremacism. Even in the scholarly articles, the headlines and subheads are selectively constructed to present highly critical perspectives on the United States and the West.[84]

Intellectual Schizophrenia: Fear of Facing Reality

In this study, we have carefully selected representative materials published in *Bonyad Monthly* to highlight the prevalence of anti-modern ideology in a state-sponsored journal. *Bonyad Monthly* appears apolitical on the critical issues of the time in Iran, but it clearly and systematically engages in a perilous and self-indulgent intellectual exercise. The journal is clearly influenced by the existing currents in the Iranian intellectual life of the 1970s. It should also be noted that *Bonyad Monthly* is only one case among many state-sponsored cultural institutions engaged in similar "nativist," anti-modernity propaganda.

A good example is how one regularly finds the presence of Ahmad Fardid on state-run national television in the 1970s. Ahmad Fardid had derived an anti-Western affirmation of religious traditionalism from his studies of Heidegger. Al-e Ahmad, who condemned the Pahlavi regime's authoritarian modernization program while celebrating Iranian tradition as an authentic alternative had subsequently politicized this "return to the roots" philosophy. The Pahlavi regime, paradoxically, appropriated this discourse of

---

82 Milton Ellerin, "A Report on the Revival of Nazism in Europe," trans. Farah Barari, *Bonyad Monthly*, No. 19 (October 1978): 20–22.
83 Mahama Jansoon Traore, "The Ugly Reflection of Colonialism," trans. Parviz Shafa, *Bonyad Monthly*, No. 19 (October 1978): 23–37.
84 For example, see: Pajuhesh, "Racism," *Bonyad Monthly*, Special Issue (April 1978): 68–72; Bonyad Monthly Research Group, "Racism and apartheid"; Pierce, "The Dreams of Black America"; Jacobson, "Memories and Dangers of Travel to South Africa"; Hercules, "To Live in Harlem." There are three more articles on racism in this issue.

civilizational authenticity, with its anti-Western and anti-modern rhetoric, in the very moment of implementing a violent and rapid state-led modernization program. Within this confusing orbit, *Bonyad Monthly*, under the auspices of the Shah's twin sister, opened a public platform for reflection upon the problem of *gharb-zadegi*. The journal contributed to undermining the legitimacy of the very regime it was seeking to bolster through its intellectual posturing. The journal celebrated a highly romantic notion of pure Iranian identity, while consistently denigrating the West as a slave to material gain, technology, and humanist rationalism. These stereotyped discursive figures became a substitute for even a superficial analysis of existing Iranian political and social realities, and a platform for self-righteous make-believe. Ultimately, *Bonyad Monthly* came to pay the price by facing its own annihilation, as the reality it had systematically ignored fatally exploded in its face.

The *Bonyad Monthly* editors and writers were entirely seduced by their own self-absorption in the mission of recovering the "spiritual" and "mythological" truth about Iran. This was to such an extent that they remained entirely blind to contemporary events in the country. It was not until the November 1978 issue – the final one – that they informed readers, in an editorial, that *Bonyad Monthly* was facing major challenges to continued publication:

While you may or may not like *Bonyad*, it is a legitimate journal. All issues, covered over the last two years, are a testament to our independence of mind. *Bonyad* is a space for thinking … We uphold independence and freedom of thought. We will not exchange these ideals for any material gains. We have pledged our allegiance to our homeland, and our pen is not lent to anything or anyone else … Therefore, we write for love of our country, and you [readers] who cherish thought. If someone wants to censor this right, we will immediately leave it [the journal] and go home. Therefore, we need your intellectual support, so that we can keep this journal independent.[85]

The challenges were far too big for *Bonyad Monthly* to overcome, and this was to be the last issue of the journal ever to be published. Ironically, the forces that led to *Bonyad Monthly*'s downfall were also, just like the journal itself, seeking the "spiritual" recovery of Iran.

---

[85] Alireza Meybodi, "The Beggar of Freedom," *Bonyad Monthly*, No. 20 (November 1978): 4.

However, the intellectual schizophrenia plaguing *Bonyad Monthly* was far from exclusive to this journal. The specific anti-modern discourse, represented in so many writings on *Bonyad Monthly*'s pages, reflected a socially wider discursive turn in the Pahlavi state ideology of the late 1960s and 1970s. There is clear and ample evidence to show that many other cultural and academic institutions, sponsored and funded by the Pahlavi royal family, were similarly engaged in an equally strange and potentially self-defeating "cultural war" against modern ideas. *Bonyad Monthly* was part of this larger discursive shift in the Iranian state's ideological formation. For a seemingly "secular" and conspicuously "pro-Western" state, the appropriation of the *gharbzadegi* oppositional discourse was both existentially unliveable and politically unwise.

An interesting example of the ideological turn is the case of "The Imperial Iranian Academy of Philosophy." The Academy was established in 1974, and was sponsored by the Shah and his wife, Farah Pahlavi. The man responsible for this new Institution, Seyed Hossein Nasr, has an interesting biographical history. Nasr, a member of Iran's ruling elite, spent most of his early life in the United States:

Much of the young Nasr's intellectual universe was Western. His father's library contained Montesquieu and Voltaire, as well as Persian classics, and he was sent to high school in New Jersey [*Peddle School, an elite boarding school in Hightstown, NJ*] at the age of 12, for reasons that are not entirely clear. From New Jersey he proceeded to the Massachusetts Institute of Technology, majoring in geology and geophysics.[86]

Seyed Hossein Nasr, in an experience resembling that of Ahmad Fardid, underwent an intellectual "crisis" in the United States. He consequently abandoned "science," and embraced religion and tradition:

In his second year at MIT, Nasr experienced what he later described as "a full-blown spiritual and intellectual crisis," as he began to feel the limitations of natural science as an explanation of reality. With his faith in physics eroded by lectures on the Manhattan Project by Robert Oppenheimer (who quoted from Hindu texts), and a discussion with Bertrand Russell, Nasr turned to philosophy, though he completed his degree in science.[87]

---

[86] Sedgwick, *Against the Modern World*, p. 153.   [87] Ibid., p. 154.

After he finished his graduate work at MIT in 1956, Nasr pursued a PhD degree in the history of science at Harvard University. After Harvard, Nasr returned to Iran as a professor at Tehran University, where he was the dean of the Faculty of Letters, and later was appointed president of Arya Mehr University (Sharif University), in 1972. After he left his position as president of Arya Mehr University, Nasr was appointed chief of staff to Farah Pahlavi. He was very close to her, and she appointed him head of the Imperial Academy of Philosophy in 1970.

Seyed Hossein Nasr was also close to some well-known figures in the Shi'a establishment. These included, notably, Ayatollah Motahhari, perhaps the favorite disciple of Ayatollah Khomeini. Nasr invited Motahhari to join the Academy:

Nasr introduced the teaching of Islamic philosophy, and successfully worked with his friend Ayatollah Motahhari (who introduced Islamic philosophy into the Department of Theology at about the same time) to spread understanding of, and interest in, Islamic philosophers, both within and outside of Tehran University. Both Nasr and Motahhari also lectured on these subjects to more general audiences at the Hosseiniyeh-e Irshad, a celebrated institution of the time.[88]

Ayatollah Motahhari was to become a leading political figure in the 1978–9 Revolution and was appointed by Ayatollah Khomeini head of the Revolutionary Council. The fact that he also was admired by Seyed Hossein Nasr shows the common ideological belief that the "old" and the "new" regimes shared.

[88] Ibid., p. 158.

3 | Ehsan Naraghi:

Chronicle of a Man for All Seasons*

In many ways, the story of Ehsan Naraghi is the story of Iran, a country that has demonstrated an extraordinary capacity for survival. Throughout history, Iran has overcome numerous challenges that have left the country shaken but triumphant, battered but never beaten.[1]

James A. Bill

The generation of Iranian intellectuals who were active in shaping Iranian modernization in the 1930–70s presents fascinating biographical chronicles. These display multiple layers, including paradox, vacillation, and duplicity in their lives and mental habits. Men of culture and politics, they were "adept" at living a "high life" of almost total indifference. They were immune to a commitment to serious ideas, political visions, or ethical positions.[2] Yet they imagined themselves all the while as "visionaries," and all-knowing guardians of the Iranian nation and its culture.

One cannot but wonder, as James Bill intimates, whether their lives and ways of thinking helped to shape the ultimately baffling character of modern Iranian life; or whether they were the mere victims of a very troubling history of modern Iranian experience. We, of course, know

---

* In this chapter we cover Ehsan Naraghi's life and thought only up to the revolution of 1978. He led a life of great influence after the revolution and until his death in 2012.

[1] James A. Bill, "Review: *From Palace to Prison: Inside the Iranian Revolution* by Ehsan Naraghi, trans. Nilu Mobasser (Chicago: Ivan R. Dee, 1994)," *The Middle East Journal* 49, No. 1 (winter 1995): 144.

[2] There are, of course, exceptions: Mohammad Mosaddegh, Gholamhossein Sadighi, Ahmad Shamlu, and others, who lived lives deeply dedicated to their own political or cultural commitments. There were also other political and cultural figures (Ali Akbar Siyasi [1895–1990] is a good example) who decided to turn a blind eye to the overall corruption and dictatorial nature of the political system, but kept some level of integrity and courage in areas of their own responsibilities. This is what Siyasi did as the head of Tehran University. He was rather uncompromising in maintaining the university's independence.

better than to dismiss in a cavalier manner this entire generation of political and intellectual figures. However, such figures of indifference were so influential in Iranian national life that we cannot reasonably categorize them as the exceptions. They were indeed the norm, to the point where we might plausibly label them the indifferent generation of "high living."

The lives and thought of such individuals as Ahmad Fardid or Ehsan Naraghi, wrapped in layers of complex paradox and mystery, often require a veritable archeology in order to uncover and recover the truth about them. These individuals, members of Iran's cultural and political elite, seemed to embody the majority of the binary categories most opposed to the experiences of modern life. They seem, to all appearances, to have lived within a parallel universe that combined the modern and the pre-modern, the West and the East, radical and conservative, and dogmatism and nihilism. They were constantly negotiating these opposed elements, with seemingly no desire at all for choosing one over the other or living at peace with both.

Ehsan Naraghi was certainly a member of this particular elite society of Iranian political figures and intellectuals. He grew up in a family with a long religious lineage. His parents, however, established the first secular school for girls in his hometown of Kashani. His father, a nationalist reformer and scholar, was definitely open to new ideas. Naraghi moved to Tehran and finished high school in the capital city. At college, he became involved with the Tudeh Party. Dropping out of college, he left Iran to study in Switzerland. Now a Western-educated young man, Naraghi became close to Ayatollah Kashan. Later, in the 1960s and 1970s, he rose as a political figure, enjoying close connections to Queen Farah, Amir-Abbas Hoveyda (the prime minister), and Hussein Pakravan, the head of SAVAK. At the same time, he was also involved in an intellectual and cultural project of nativism and anti-Westoxification.

Naraghi was close to Ahmad Fardid, too, and he regularly attended the Fardidyyeh meetings. He also wrote a series of books of anti-Western and anti-modern content. Most of his writings were influenced by Fardid's anti-modern philosophy. However, Naraghi, in contrast to Fardid, was a temperate and moderate person. He may, though, have shared certain personality traits with Fardid. Both of them had large egos and were careless with the truth. Despite this, Naraghi also enjoyed helping others. Although he lived his adult life between Iran and Europe, his vision and intellectual commitment were those of an anti-modern pastoral man. His emotional attachment was to the country, rather than the city.

Naraghi's Life and Times

Ehsan Naraghi was born on September 14, 1926 in Kashan, a city in central Iran. He came from a prominent religious family with a long history of a high scholarly status. Two of his paternal grandfathers were noted Shi'a scholars. Mulla Mohammad Mahdi Naraghi (1716–94) was a leading mujtahid (a senior Shi'a scholar) in his time, and Mulla Ahmad Naraghi (1771–1829), a prominent faqih (the most senior Shi'a scholar), was the first Shi'a theologian to propose the idea of the Guidance of Jurist (*velayat-e faqih*).[3] Ayatollah Khomeini later drew upon the idea to write his own theology of the Islamic State.[4]

His father, Hasan Naraghi (1896–1989), was also interested in religious matters, spending many years as a seminary student. However, he lived through the Constitutional period, during which his writings developed a more reformist and modern outlook. Ehsan Naraghi acknowledges that his father was inspired by such political figures as Seyed Jamal al-Din Asadabadi (Afghani) and Seyed Hasan Taghizadeh.[5] The latter was a modernist politician who advocated a "total capitulation" of Iran to Western modernity.[6] Hasan Naraghi also studied modern and secular sciences, and learned the French language. He graduated from the Etihad School (previously known as the Tehran Alliance School) in 1935.[7] Ehsan Naraghi's mother, Rakhshandeh Gohar (1899–1987), also received a Western-oriented education. She graduated from the American School for Girls in Tehran.[8]

---

[3] Mohsen Kadivar, *Government of the Guardian* (Tehran: Nashr-e Nei, 1998), p. 105.
[4] Ibid., p. 107.
[5] Ali Mirsepassi, *Intellectual Discourse and the Politics of Modernization: Negotiating Modernity in Iran* (Cambridge University Press, 2001), p. 63.
[6] Safa al-Din Tabarra'ian, *Soft Like a Sponge: Evaluating Ehsan Naraghi's Role in the Second Pahlavi*, Vol. I (Tehran: Moasseseh-ye Motale'at-e Tarikh-e Mo'aser-e Iran, 2013), p. 34.
[7] The school was at first a branch of the Alliance Israélite Universelle, an international Jewish organization founded in 1860 in Paris. The Alliance inaugurated its first school in Tehran in 1898.
[8] The American Schools for Girls were established first in Orumieh in 1848 and then in other cities like Tabriz, Isfahan, and Tehran. The American School for Girls in Tehran was established in 1875. At the beginning, just Christians,

After Ehsan's parents married in 1917, they moved to Kashan. At this time, there were no "secular" schools there – the city only had Islamic schools (*maktabkhaneh*). His mother, according to Ehsan Naraghi, did not intend to send her daughters to religious school. Ehsan's parents decided to establish a modern school in Kashan. They established the Elementary School for the Education of Girls (*Dabestan-e Danesh-e Dushizegan*) in 1929.[9] The school was later expanded to include a high school.

Ehsan Naraghi's father was a prolific writer and scholar, and a cultural activist. His contemporaries viewed him as a respected public figure. He edited and published a series of religious texts written by the earlier generation of religious scholars in the Naraghi family. He also published books of his own on the history and geography of Kashan, ancient Persian civilization, and the Constitutional Movement.[10] In addition, he wrote articles and essays for various Iranian journals on the history of art and architecture, Iranian history, cultural artifacts, and religion.[11] Hasan Naraghi was also involved in philanthropy and institution-building. He, among other public figures, founded the Association of Kashan's National Heritage and the National Museum of Kashan.[12] It appears that such scholarly and intellectual qualities, together with his father's public standing,

---

Armenians, and Assyrians attended the schools. The American School for Girls in Tehran was opened to Muslim girls in 1895.

[9] However, Tabarra'ian has found some documents to show that there were some girls' schools in Kashan similar to the Alliance before Naraghi's parents founded their elementary school. Tabarra'ian, *Soft Like a Sponge*, Vol. I, p. 36.

[10] For instance, see Hasan Naraghi, *Social History of Kashan* (Tehran: Moasese-ye Motaleat va Tahghighat-e Ejtema'i, 1966), *Kashan in Mashruteh* (Tehran: Mash'al-e Azadi, 1976), and *A Brief History of Iran: From the Aryans to the End of the Pahlavi Dynasty* (Tehran: Atiyah, 1999).

[11] For instance, see Hasan Naraghi, "Shah 'Abbas's Tomb in Kashan and Its Historical Documents," *Honar va Mardom*, No. 24 (October 1964): 46–49, "Historical Building of Kashan's Telegraph Center," *Tasvir*, No. 29 (March 1964): 21–25, and "Tayer-e Qodsi or Mohaghegh and Fazel Naraghi's Poetry," *Tasvir*, No. 187 (May 1978): 47–50.

[12] The Society for the Preservation of the Historical Monuments of Kashan was established by a number of public figures, including Hasan Naraghi, in Kashan in 1959 to preserve historical artifacts, sites, and buildings in Kashan. The Society founded the Association of Kashan's National Heritage and the National Museum of Kashan as part of its historical preservation project.

marked the young Ehsan Naraghi's life and the formation of his character. We know that he named his father as an important source of his inspiration.[13]

Ehsan Naraghi, following his two elder sisters, attended the secular school that his mother had founded earlier in Kashan. He later attended the Pahlavi Elementary School and then the Pahlavi High School in Kashan. When his family moved to Tehran in 1944, Ehsan enrolled in the prestigious Dar al-Funun High School as a senior student, graduating in 1945.[14] Naraghi entered the University of Tehran's Faculty of Law and Political Science in 1946 as an undergraduate student. This was during the oil nationalization movement. It was a very politically charged time, and university students were deeply involved in political activism. Ehsan Naraghi, like many other students, was drawn to the Tudeh Party of Iran.

Naraghi's involvement with the Tudeh Party is the subject of debate and controversy.[15] Naraghi himself, on many occasions, has emphasized the fact that he never joined the Tudeh Party and that his association with the party was short-lived:

I was a Tudeh Party sympathizer but not a member ... When I was a student [at the University of Tehran] I participated in some leftist activities ... For instance, when there was a strike, we participated. When there was a national interest issue, we defended it. In general, the left-wing party was strong at that time, and we were part of it ... There were the Patriotic Party and the Party of Iran. All of them were interesting to me, and I attended their meetings.[16]

However, there are indications that Naraghi was, indeed, more involved in the Tudeh Party than he later suggested. The idea that the Tudeh Party students' group was the only organized group at Tehran University was not true. We know that Islamic and nationalist student

---

[13] Tabarra'ian, *Soft Like a Sponge*, Vol. I, pp. 51–54.

[14] Dar al-Funun High School was established by Amir Kabir (1807–52), chief minister of Naser al-Din Shah (1831–96), in 1851 as the first state-sponsored, European-style school in Iran.

[15] Naraghi, later in his life, developed a very critical attitude toward the Tudeh Party and Marxism. He blamed the Tudeh Party and Iranian Marxists for what he considered the poisonous intellectual and political environment in Iran.

[16] Ebrahim Nabavi, *Through an Unbaked Brick: Interview with Ehsan Naraghi* (Tehran: Jame'eh Iranian, 1999), pp. 46–47.

associations existed at the time, but Naraghi was not interested in working with them.[17]

We also know that after Naraghi had spent only one year at the University of Tehran, his father arranged for him to leave Iran. He seems to have wanted to keep him at some distance from the very charged political environment at the university. Naraghi left for Switzerland in May 1947 to continue his academic education in Europe. However, in Europe he continued his association with the Tudeh Party. Iraj Eskandari, one of the Tudeh Party leaders, who was based in Paris at the time, confirms that Ehsan Naraghi worked under him.[18] Naraghi attended the Communist Youth Festivals in Budapest in 1949 and Berlin in 1951. He represented the "Iranian Youth," a Tudeh Party front organization, in both of these events.[19] Naraghi claims that he was only involved with the Tudeh Party for two years. Yet, as we see regarding his involvement with the Tudeh Party, it lasted at least from 1946, at the University of Tehran, to the Berlin Festival of 1951, if not even longer.

Iranian intelligence agency (SAVAK) documents show that Naraghi had a rather close association with the Tudeh Party while he was in Europe. One report describes him as "an active member of a Communist group in Geneva and that he was a member of its central committee which has been established by Iraj Eskandari."[20] It is hard to tell if this report is based on hard evidence or not. Naraghi dismisses this and describes his relationship with the Tudeh Party as informal and casual.

After obtaining a BA in the social sciences, Naraghi returned to Iran in August 1952, a few days after the uprising of July 21, 1952 (30 Tir 1331). He was hired by Iran's Statistical Center on September 7, 1953, some three weeks after the coup d'état of August 19. One year later, however, in October 1954, he lost his government job "due to having leftist thoughts and involvement in anti-government activities."[21] It appears that he had maintained a continuing affiliation with the Tudeh Party, and the government consequently grew suspicious of him.

In December 1954, Naraghi was granted a scholarship from the Cultural Association of Iran and France, and left Tehran for Paris to

---

[17] Tabarra'ian, *Soft Like a Sponge,* Vol. I, p. 76.   [18] Ibid., p. 79.   [19] Ibid.
[20] Ibid., p. 83.   [21] Ibid., p. 99.

pursue a PhD program at the Sorbonne.[22] At the Sorbonne, he worked
with Alfred Sauvy (1898–1990), a prominent French demographer, in
the National Institute of Demographic Studies as an intern for two
years. Naraghi was inspired by the work of this Institute, and when he
returned to Iran he established the Institute for Social Studies and
Research (Mo'asseseh-e Motale'at va Tahghighat-e Ejtema'i) at the
University of Tehran in 1958.[23] He also worked on his PhD dissertation at the Sorbonne University under Pierre George.[24]

During his time in Paris, Naraghi cultivated connections with several influential scholars, including Jean Piaget, Georges Balandier,
Georges Gurvitch, Louis Massignon, Henri Lefebvre, and Jacques
Augustin Berque.[25] According to Naraghi, it was Jean Piaget who
introduced him to UNESCO and helped him start a lifelong association with this United Nations organization.

Naraghi conducted research for UNESCO on nomads in the Middle
East. A few years later, in 1960, UNESCO's special fund appointed him
to write a book on the social sciences in Persian for use in Iranian
universities. This book was published in 1965 as *The Development of
the Social Sciences* in Tehran.[26] In the preface to this book, Naraghi
acknowledged his sincere thanks to another Iranian scholar who had
also studied at the Sorbonne, and who later served as a mentor to him.
This was "the scholarly and precious friendship with Dr. Ahmad
Fardid," who helped him find proper Persian equivalents for scientific
terms.[27] In 1965, Naraghi was commissioned by UNESCO to conduct
transnational research on the problem of the "brain drain" in the Third
World. Naraghi's work on this topic received wide publicity, and his
research appeared in *The New York Times* and *Le Monde*.[28] Naraghi
was subsequently made the director of the Youth Division of UNESCO
in 1969. He worked for UNESCO until 1975.

[22] Part of French diplomatic actions in Tehran was to promote French culture and
language and contribute to development, including granting fellowships.
[23] Ehsan Naraghi and Ata Ayati, *A Glance at Social Research in Iran* (Tehran:
Sokhan, 2000), p. 202.
[24] Tabarra'ian, *Soft Like a Sponge,* Vol. I, p. 100.   [25] Ibid., pp. 100–104.
[26] Ehsan Naraghi, *The Development of the Social Sciences in Iran* (Tehran: Nikan,
1965).
[27] Ibid., p. iii.
[28] It was also published in the *Milwaukee Journal*, September 12, 1966: https://news
.google.com/newspapers?id=S00aAAAAIBAJ&sjid=2icEAAAAIBAJ&pg=7196%
2C2406510

While conducting research for UNESCO and developing his international network of connections, Naraghi planned and created the Institute for Social Studies and Research at the University of Tehran. In so doing, he was successful in securing the budget for the Institute outside of the regular sources of university funding, obtaining it directly from the government. The creation of this institute is regarded as Naraghi's highest academic achievement. He also obtained permission to publish an academic publication for the Institute, *The Journal of Social Sciences (Nameh-e 'Olume Ejtima'i)*, in 1963. The first issue of the journal was published in 1968, but, after only three issues, its publication ceased in 1969.[29] The Institute continues to exist. It attracted both senior and well-known Iranian, as well as international, scholars, and also younger intellectuals. Naraghi was particularly interested in bringing in public intellectual figures to do work at the Institute.[30] He later proudly boasted: "the best scholars and intellectuals worked at the Institute. We published Jalal Al-e Ahmad and [Gholamhossein] Sa'edi's monographs. Amir Parviz Puyan, [Habibullah] Peyman, [Mostafa] Sho'a'ian ... worked in the Institute. I helped them and took care of all of them. We had different people, ranging from Islamist and leftist to nationalist. Their political affiliations did not matter."[31]

[29] Publication of the journal was resumed in 1974 with a new team.

[30] In addition, some of the junior scholars who collaborated with the Institute later became famous politicians, including Abolhassan Banisadr and Hasan Habibi. Abolhassan Banisadr (1933–) was a political activist before the 1978–9 Revolution and the first president of Iran after the 1978–9 Revolution. He was impeached by parliament in 1981. Banisadr joined the Institute in 1958 and worked there as an intern for four years. Then Ehsan Naraghi helped him to go to France and continue his education in economics at the Sorbonne. A famous book of his is *Eghtesad-e Towhidi (Monotheistic Economics)* (1978). Hasan Habibi (1937–2013) was a political activist before the 1978–9 Revolution, and studied sociology and law in France. He was among the principal architects of the first draft of the prospective constitution of Iran. After the revolution, he held different positions, such as vice president, minister of justice, minister of science, and minister of culture.

[31] Tabarra'ian, *Soft Like a Sponge,* Vol. I, p. 279. Gholamhossein Sa'edi (1936–85) was a prolific writer and a left-wing political activist. He published more than forty books in different genres such as novels, screenplays, short stories, cultural criticism, and ethnography. The screenplay for *Gav (The Cow)*, directed by Daryush Mehrju'i in 1969, is considered Sa'edi's magnum opus, which announced the emergence of New Wave cinema in Iran. Amir Parviz Puyan (1946–71) was a Communist theoretician, organizer, and political activist. He was one of the original founders of Sazman-e Chirikha-ye Fada'i-ye

The faculty and scholars affiliated with the Institute conducted research in many areas of the social sciences, including urban studies, the study of nomads, rural surveys, and demography. However, the Institute's emphasis was on conducting research on rural areas in Iran.

The Institute published more than sixty books in the first decade of its existence.[32] As Naraghi has frequently repeated in his interviews and books, their research policy in the Institute was to support fieldwork. Naraghi preferred to call the Institute's books "the Eastern insight" against positivism.

Naraghi and the Institute encouraged ethnographic fieldwork in rural areas in Iran. This was perhaps the most popular area of research among those who worked for the Institute. Naraghi later explained that he decided to publish a series of "monographs on Iranian villages," and he asked Jalal Al-e Ahmad to supervise this important initiative.

Under Jalal Al-e Ahmad's supervision, the Institute published a number of highly publicized and well-known "rural monographs."[33] These works were largely influenced by the romantic and "pastoral" anti-modern sentiments promoted in certain intellectual circles, as well

---

Khalgh (Organization of the Iranian People's Fada'i Guerrillas). He developed a belief in the armed struggle in his book *Zarurat-e Mobarezeh-e Mosallahaneh and Radd-e Teori-ye Bagha'* (*The Necessity of Armed Struggle and Refutation of the Theory of Survival*) (1971). Puyan was executed by SAVAK in 1972. Habibullah Peyman (1935–) is a writer and a political activist. He has written a couple of books and articles on human freedom, socialism, and Islamic ideology. He was one of the original founders of Jonbesh-e Mosalamanan-e Mobarez. He was also one of the leaders of Shora-ye Fa'alan-e Mell-Mazhabi (Nationalist-Religious Forces) and a member of Nazhat Khoda Parastan-i Socialist (the Movement of God-Worshipping Socialists). Mostafa Sho'a'ian (1936–75) was one of the original founders of Jebheh-e Democratic-e Khalgh (the People's Democratic Front) that later merged into the Organization of the Iranian People's Fada'i Guerrillas. Because of ideological differences, Sho'a'ian later was expelled from the organization. He was killed in a shoot-out with police in 1975.

[32] Tabarra'ian, *Soft Like a Sponge*, Vol. I, p. 273.

[33] Ibid., p. 281. For instance, some of the well-known monographs published by the Institute include Gholamhossein Sa'edi's *Ilkhchi, An Azeri Village with Sufi Dwellers* (Tehran: Mo'asseseh-e Motale'at va Tahghighat-e Ejtema'i, 1963), *Khiyav and Meshkin Shahr* (Tehran: Mo'asseseh-e Motale'at va Tahghighat-e Ejtema'i, 1965), *Ahl-e Hava* (Tehran: Mo'asseseh-e Motale'at va Tahghighat-e Ejtema'i, 1966), and, with Sirus Tahbaz, *Yush* (Tehran: Mo'asseseh-e Motale'at va Tahghighat-e Ejtema'i, 1963); also, Khosro Khosravi's *Khark Island during Oil Domination* (Tehran: Mo'asseseh-e Motale'at va Tahghighat-e Ejtema'i, 1963).

as among many elites within the Pahlavi state. The "return" to the "village" represented a political and cultural theme whereby many intellectuals were working hard to articulate an authentic identity for the Iranian nation, in contrast to modernity; and German intellectuals, in the early twentieth century, had been involved in a similar cultural movement of "returning" to the country.

Naraghi, of course, was one among many Iranian intellectual figures, and part of the contemporary anti-Westoxification campaign. Henry Corbin and Ahmad Fardid were the two principal philosophers of this current, and Naraghi was close to both of them. The anti-Westoxification campaign was taking place in the media, and in national and intellectual newspapers and journals. Opposition intellectuals and activists on the one hand and state-sponsored institutions and individuals on the other both spread it with great energy. A principal example was *Bonyad Monthly*, dealt with in Chapter 2.

For a sociologist, Naraghi's own narrative of his intellectual transformation is rather non-sociological. He almost totally disregards what was happening in Iran, or in the world, and explains his intellectual transformation in a very personal way. Naraghi suggests that his approach has changed, through his personal rethinking and reflection in the West, during the time he worked for UNESCO in Europe:

In the beginning, I was fond of Western scientific progress, too, like all youth at that time. My colleagues and I, at the Institute for Social Studies and Research, attempted to employ "the scientific" methods in our social research. We wished to see sociology expanded in Iran as a science. However, after years of living again in Europe, I realized clearly the inadequacy of these methods.[34]

Ahmad Fardid also makes a very similar claim. He presents himself likewise as a former Westernized intellectual, who, later in Germany, saw the light. He came to realize how horrible modern and Western culture truly were.

Naraghi was inspired to help create a "nativist," or Iranian, approach to the social sciences. For this reason, he was hostile to the very Western-inspired social sciences in Iran that he had studied for almost his entire time in Europe. Shams Al-e Ahmad, many years later,

---

[34] Ehsan Naraghi, *Freedom, Right, and Justice: A Talk between Esma'il Khu'i and Ehsan* (Tehran: Javidan, 1976), p. 49.

recalled that Naraghi was very critical of Westoxificated Iranians. He charged them with believing in the use of scientific methodology and statistics, and condemned their assumption that no tradition of research and thought existed in Iranian culture.[35]

It is, however, not clear whether he did much serious research in Iran. Naraghi was most successful in securing funding and obtaining the government's permission for academic activities. He also used his own personal connections to invite well-known intellectuals and scholars to the Institute. There did not appear to be any high-quality research and scholarly work. A review of the first issue of the journal indicates the poor quality of the scholarship done at the Institute. Ali Banuazizi welcomed the new journal:

Seems like it turned to a propaganda outlet quickly

> The publication of an Iranian journal of social sciences could serve as a vehicle for scientific dialogue among students of Iranian society and culture. It might gradually make available, to the Persian-speaking reader, the vast body of social science theory and research published in other languages. This is a long-awaited event among Iranian scholars. A number of attempts to realize this objective, at home and abroad, have failed to result in any adequate periodical. None has continued publication beyond more than a few issues. The appearance of *'Olum-e Ejtema'i*, a quarterly journal of social sciences, is therefore a timely response to this genuine need. The journal is published by the Institute for Social Studies and Research of the University of Tehran, with Dr. Ehsan Naraghi as Executive Editor and Mr. Daryush Ashuri as Editor-in-Chief.[36]

However, in his analysis of the materials published in the first issue of the journal, Banuazizi expressed his disappointment at the poor quality and the lack of critical perspective:

> To some extent, the contents of this single issue are representative of the current state of social science research in Iran. There is an almost total lack of analytic and critical studies at either theoretical or empirical levels. There is a good deal of confusion regarding the distinction between social science, on the one hand, and social philosophy and social criticism on the other. There is

---

[35] Tabarra'ian, *Soft Like a Sponge*, Vol. I, p. 281.
[36] Ali Banuazizi, "*'Olum-e Ejtema'i*, a Quarterly Journal of Social Sciences, ed. Ehsan Naraghi and Daryush Ashuri, Tehran: Institute for Social Studies and Research, University of Tehran, 1968–," *Iranian Studies* 2, No. 1 (winter 1969): 45.

a narrow definition of social research, to include only problems of immediate, short-range concern to the various governmental agencies. These include the Plan Organization, the Ministry of Education, or the Land Reform Program; these are some of the characteristic features of social science research in Iran today.[37]

Naraghi's success at the Institute was an end in itself. He used his position as the director of the Institute for self-promotion in Iran and at the international level. When he, as an international figure, returned to Iran after six years, in 1975, he received an immediate appointment as head of one of the top institutes in Iran: the Institute for Educational and Scientific Research and Planning.[38] It appears that the prime minister, Amir-Abbas Hoveyda, proposed this new position to him and convinced him to accept it.[39] Apparently, Naraghi was satisfied with his new high-ranking position: "most of the time I had more power than a minister had ... Besides the power and his [Amir-Abbas Hoveyda's] direct support, I had Farah [Pahlavi]'s support. On different occasions, Farah had asked me to leave UNESCO and return to Iran."[40]

In the last three years of the Second Pahlavi reign, 1975–8, Ehsan Naraghi seems to have achieved his lifelong "dream" of a very public presence in state political life and influence over its institutions. He was a member of many state-sponsored institutions and organizations, and advisor to many leading political figures. Naraghi was particularly

---

[37] Ibid., 46.

[38] The Institute for Educational and Scientific Research and Planning was founded by the Ministry of Science and Higher Education in 1969. The director of the Institute served as deputy minister of Science and Higher Education. However, at Naraghi's request, the government transformed it into an institute with its own board of directors. The Institute was comprised of the Center for Educational and Scientific Planning, the Center for Scientific Documents, Library Services, and a Publications Center. Tabarra'ian, *Soft Like a Sponge,* Vol. I, pp. 464–465.

[39] Amir-Abbas Hoveyda was born in 1919 in Tehran. He was prime minister of Iran from January 1965 to August 1977. He spent much of his earlier career in the Foreign Office and served in Paris, Bonn, Ankara, and New York City. After almost thirteen years of service as prime minster, on August 7, 1977 Hoveyda was replaced by Jamshid Amuzegar. In November 1978 he was detained by the Shah's new government. Two months after the 1978–9 Revolution, he was sentenced to death by the Islamic Revolutionary Court. www.iranchamber.com /history/ahoveida/abbas_hoveida.php

[40] Tabarra'ian, *Soft Like a Sponge,* Vol. I, p. 464.

close to Farah Pahlavi and the many cultural and educational organizations she was responsible for overseeing.[41]

He regularly appeared on national media to be interviewed, and
wrote for various newspapers and magazines. He gave a large number
of lectures and routinely advocated for an authentically Iranian and
"traditional" way of life. He decried the Westoxification of Iranian
cultural and political life. Naraghi contributed to holding an international conference in Tehran in October 1977. The conference, "Does
the Impact of Western Thought Render Possible a Dialogue among
Civilizations?," centered on the idea of dialogue between civilizations.
It was organized by the Iranian Center for the Study of Civilizations,
which was under Farah Pahlavi's supervision. Some leading traditionalists and scholars of Islam, like Toshihiko Izutsu, Henry Corbin, and
Roger Garaudy, were among the guest lecturers. The lectures were
published in Paris as a book titled *L'Impact de la pensée occidentale
rend-il possible un dialogue réel entre les civilizations?*[42]

The more Naraghi's associations developed with Pahlavi officials,
the more his relationship with the intelligence agency in Iran, SAVAK,
was the subject of controversies and debates. He was accused of being
a SAVAK agent and working for them. It was the case that he had an
extensive relationship with several high-ranking SAVAK officials.
However, there is no evidence to support the argument that he was
a member of SAVAK. A confidential document, from the US embassy in
Tehran, shows that a US chargé d'affaires in Iran believed that Naraghi
was "a well-known agent of SAVAK."[43] Naraghi himself later declared
that his position vis-à-vis SAVAK was complicated, and that people

---

[41] Queen Farah oversaw tens of institutes, associations, organizations, and centers.
Her office contained forty staff and was divided into four sections: the health
and treatment section, the education section, the social welfare section, and the
art and culture section. For instance, there were more than fifteen centers under
the supervision of the art and culture section. These included the National
Institute of Iranian Folklore (founded in 1961), the Foundation of Iranian
Culture (founded in 1964), the Institute for the Intellectual Development of
Children and Young Adults (founded in 1965), the Institute for the Shiraz–
Persepolis Festival of Arts (founded in 1967), the Institute of Dialogue between
Civilizations (founded in 1976), and the Imperial Academy of Philosophy
(founded in 1975), among others.

[42] Centre Iranien pour L'Etude des Civilisations, *L'Impact de la pensée occidentale
rend-il possible un dialogue réel entre les civilisations?* (Paris: Berg International,
1979).

[43] Tabarra'ian, *Soft Like a Sponge*, Vol. I, p. 302.

had the right to speculate about his association with the agency. He pointed out that "my position was rather peculiar and if not actually inviting suspicion could at the very least give rise to a degree of confusion."[44]

Naraghi had a particularly close friendship with the second director of SAVAK, Hassan Pakravan.[45] It seems that Naraghi served as an unofficial advisor to Pakravan. Naraghi admits that he conducted "a three-session course on social issues for SAVAK staff to improve the cultural knowledge of its staff."[46] For Naraghi, his association with SAVAK formed part of his wider ambitions, involving grand plans to attain proximity to the centers of Iranian power. As he stated, "I am well aware that, if we decide to do anything on the subject of young people, it would be done through SAVAK. Without SAVAK's permission, no organization and institution can accomplish anything concerned with the youth."[47] This was an interesting statement, considering Naraghi had never been close to the Iranian youth. One could even argue that his ideas about and outlook on Iran were outdated and hardly youth-friendly. Naraghi spent most of his life socializing with the Iranian elite, and his ideas were much to the satisfaction of the older generation of the country.

However, Naraghi's self-image, during the last years of the Second Pahlavi regime, was that of the man of "wisdom," good sense, and judgment. Of course, moreover, the image was of a man of the royal court and a social reformer. He later described his meetings with the Shah, at the end of his reign, as part of his larger reform project:

44 Ehsan Naraghi, *From Palace to Prison: Inside the Iranian Revolution*, trans. Nilu Mobasser (Chicago: Ivan R. Dee, 1994), p. 153.
45 Hassan Pakravan was born in 1911 in Tehran to a family of mixed Iranian and European culture. He was one of the three founders of Iran's secret police, SAVAK, and, from 1961 to 1965, was the head of the agency. He had also spent much of his earlier military career in intelligence and the Second Bureau, which was notorious for alleged cruelty against opponents. For the rest of his life, he had different positions. These included the minister of information, ambassador to Pakistan and France, and senior counselor to the Ministry of Court. Following the 1978–9 Revolution, he was executed on April 11, 1979. Abbas Milani, *Eminent Persians: The Men and Women Who Made Modern Iran, 1941–1979* (Syracuse, NY: Syracuse University Press, 2008), Vol. I, pp. 474–482.
46 Tabarra'ian, *Soft Like a Sponge*, Vol. I, p. 340.   47 Ibid., p. 316.

Despite the fact that, when I sat in front of him [the Shah], I saw this man was no longer able to make a 180-degree change. However, I was still hopeful, and I could not resist not doing this … Because I saw blood, cruelty, and destruction in the revolution.[48]

Naraghi may have been a reformer. He was perhaps advising the Shah against harsh suppression of the growing mass movement. However, statements made by Naraghi after the revolution also present a self-congratulatory image. There is very little attempt at self-examination or reflection on his own rather "misguided" ideology. Nor is there any evaluation of Naraghi's own militant anti-modernity, which he so keenly advocated before the revolution. Naraghi was, of course, fearful of radical social change. He states, "I had a strange fear and horror of revolution … [Revolution] comes like a flood. It brings everything together in a great clash, making reform really hard."[49]

At the same time, he was also part of a larger group of intellectuals, scholars, and political figures, including Henry Corbin, Ahmad Fardid, Seyed Hossein Nasr, and Daryush Shaygan, who each in their own way helped to fuel the revolutionary fire that Naraghi so feared. Fardid, of course, welcomed the Islamic Revolution. Others may have felt ambivalent about it. Naraghi does admit that "there is a correspondence between my ideas on Westoxification and the clergy's. The clerics were against Westoxification, and so was I."[50] Apparently, he just needed time to figure out that his ideas were part of the ongoing Quiet Revolution. As we will see later, Naraghi's ideas were a lot more radical and militantly anti-modern than his calm and moderate personal character, or his temperament, might suggest. In this study, we do not deal with Naraghi's life or thinking after the revolution. However, he seems consistently unreflective about his own thoughts and deeds.

After the 1978–9 Revolution, revolutionary officials arrested Naraghi on three occasions. He was arrested in April 1979 but released after four days owing to Ayatollah Morteza Motahhari's mediation. He was again arrested in December 1979, but after four months he was exonerated and released from prison. The third time he was arrested was in June 1980. This time, he remained in jail for almost sixteen

---

[48] Tabarra'ian, *Soft Like a Sponge,* Vol. I, p. 69.
[49] Nabavi, *Through an Unbaked Brick,* pp. 87–88.
[50] Tabarra'ian, *Soft Like a Sponge,* Vol. I, p. 78.

months. After one and a half years in Evin Prison, the Islamic Revolutionary Court investigated his case. The judge, according to Naraghi, who at first believed that Naraghi was a royalist intellectual, after reading Naraghi's files, books, and articles, realized he was wrong about Naraghi:

I have to acknowledge that, for five years, all Islamic activists, including myself, were misled by the reputation fabricated for you by the pro-Soviet communists. I must confess that, as a student, I myself mentioned your name in a political meeting in Mashhad, to exemplify the type of former regime intellectual that we were vilifying. However, after examining your file, and the books and articles you have published, I realized how unfair I was. As a Muslim, I solemnly plead for your forgiveness, and beg that you accept my apology.[51]

As we know, the judge was not the only person who was confused about Naraghi's paradoxical life and thought – many other people were equally confused.

In the end, the court confirmed that Naraghi was not guilty. All allegations about his relationship with SAVAK and Abulhassan Banisadr (as his intern at the Institute for Social Studies and Research in the 1960s, and his friend in Paris) and his financial abuses were deemed to be without merit.

Released from prison in September 1983, Naraghi left Iran for France the following year. He then rejoined UNESCO, as an advisor to the secretary-director general of UNESCO, from 1984 to 1999, when he retired. During this time, he improved his relationship with the Islamic Republic of Iran. As a special advisor to UNESCO, he was able to facilitate a better relationship between it and the Islamic Republic of Iran, and to contribute toward making Iranian artists visible on the world stage.[52]

Naraghi, for the remainder of his life, was involved upon a regular basis in giving interviews and public talks, and publicizing his views. During this time, he was interviewed by large media and press outlets. He repeatedly described, explained, or justified what he had said and

---

[51] Ehsan Naraghi, *From Palace to Prison*, p. 264.
[52] At this time, Mohammad Reza Shajarian (1940–), a leading singer of Persian music, received UNESCO's Picasso Award in 1991, and Abbas Kiarostami (1940–), a prominent Iranian film director, received UNESCO's Federico Fellini Medal in 1997.

done in the past. Most of the interviews were published in the form of books.[53] In 2007, a biographical documentary film about Naraghi's life and thought was publicly screened in Tehran. In the final scene of the movie, Naraghi, satisfied with his lifelong cultural, political, and intellectual activities, says, "I'm ready to die now, and I'm not afraid of death."[54] Naraghi died in Iran at the age of 86 on December 2, 2012.

An Un-thought Utopia

Within the history of ideas, Naraghi's utopian approach to Iranian and Islamic history and culture presents an interesting case study. What is interesting is the construction of "community." There is an assumption that there is an organic link between a "golden age," "popular culture," and a hierarchical order led by religious jurists. This is the ontology: it requires neither law nor democracy, but produces "justice" spontaneously. It is necessary only to remove Western contamination to bring it to life. Naraghi articulates this "utopian" discourse through a moral claim to cultural authenticity based upon anti-Western ideas. A collective notion of community, Romantically utopian and opposed to the individual autonomy of rationality, is the core image advanced by Naraghi. He inverts the French revolutionary triad to privilege a spiritually transcendent and collectively binding public power of belonging:

> Our traditional culture does not speak of "liberty, equality, fraternity." It states "fraternity, equality, liberty." This indicates that, in our traditional culture, "justice" has priority over personal "freedom." One of the aspects of "justice" is "equality." Our traditional culture, merged with Shi'ism, considers "justice" the most important social value.[55]

Complete opposite of Liberalism

This notion of traditional community guarantees egalitarian justice while stifling individuality for the sake of collective order and a consensus on spiritual meaning. Naraghi suggests that the Islamic political system of the past can be revived and used as a model that will work in superior fashion to any other political system today. The basis

---

[53] For instance, see Ehsan Naraghi's *Impossible Fate* (Tehran: Elm, 2003), *Hormoz Ki's Talk with Ehsan Naraghi* (Tehran: Jame'eh-e Iranian, 2002), and *Freedom* (Tehran: Afkar, 2004); see also Nabavi, *Through an Unbaked Brick*.

[54] See www.roozonline.com/persian/news/newsitem/article/-9e497d6f02.html

[55] Ehsan Naraghi, *Freedom, Right, and Justice*, p. 199.

of ethics is posited in a transcendent realm of obedience to the divine. Because of its ontological moorings, and in contrast to rootless and anarchic Western individualism, the Islamic system is immune to any possible cruelty:

The foundation of Western philosophy rests upon "individualism" and ego- ism. Meanwhile, "Eastern freedom" means being free of "ego." If one can be free of ego, one can't be cruel. This is the Eastern point of view on "freedom." Of course, at any time in history when this way of thinking has weakened, cruelty has gained prevalence.[56]

This quotation contains, in kernel, a coherent ontological notion of collective conformity to a revealed "straight path" and its evil double in individual deviation leading to the wickedness of community ruin. Its neat ontological coherence, however, shatters against any comparison with either contemporary or historical reality. Naraghi's arguments, for a sociologist, are glaringly simplistic. Here, the utopian character of political fantasy is in striking contrast to any factual or secular survey of human history. He praises "Iranian thinkers" for their political or social views in a way that is devoid of historical or sociological context. His call for the revival of past political systems ignores the fact that Iran, as a political entity, did not exist in the twelfth or thirteenth centuries. Its "rulers," moreover, were either Turkish or Arab elites. These examples reveal Naraghi's cavalier disdain for any factual basis in conducting sociological research. This sociological deficit shows its moral hazard in Naraghi's whitewashing of the medieval and auto- cratic nature of the traditional Iranian political system: "All leading Iranian philosophers and scholars, such as Khajeh Nasir al-Din Tusi, Imam Mohammad Ghazali, and Mulla Mohsen Feyz, urged the rulers to be just leaders. The concept of 'justice' in the Orient is as important as the concept of 'freedom' in the West."[57]

This passage can easily be interpreted differently. These rulers did not treat their subjects fairly, and were brutal and tyrannical. They were asked to be just and fair. The centrality of the ideal of "justice" or *edalat*, in the Iranian political context, was precisely because rulers and their states were seen as *zalem* (cruel). Naraghi's is a skewed and arbitrary reading which disregards the popular experience of oppres- sion while unjustly idealizing rulers as incarnations of the pure faith.

[56] Ibid., p. 117.   [57] Ibid., p. 136.

A serious and realistic historical analysis reveals that the centrality of "justice" has nothing to do with any Iranian negative attitude toward freedom. In contrast to the fanciful idealization of a Romantic community through ontology, a concrete sociological analysis of the Iranian tradition of justice is critically required for any clear understanding of Iranian political culture.

Where Naraghi attempts a more "specific" argument, his logic only becomes more fantastic. He totally rejects the utility of a legal system or rights in Iranian society. He argues that societies like Iran's, with its rich moral and cultural tradition, do not need legal codes or systems of rights such as Western societies have. It is a double argument from ontology, indicting at once the West and those Iranians whose authenticity has been tainted by its influence:

Westernized Iranians ... sacrificed "chivalry," "justice," "right," "fraternity," "equity," and all values rooted in our people's soul, which motivated all of the turban-wearing men [*kolah namadi ha*] and veiled women, in favor of an image of "government," "freedom," and "law" that was "abstract" and Western. This had no connection with our historical, social, and cultural background.[58]

Naraghi's argument is a double assault, firstly upon the "West" conceived as a monolithic entity, and secondly upon those Iranians who have faltered in their Iranian cultural authenticity to become Westernized. In this account, they have lost their souls. Both the West and the Westernized Iranian are charged with acting and thinking in ignorance of Iran's (and the East's) true nature. Its true nature is equated with the true soul of humanity, and hence it is beyond the possibility of "cruelty" as an existential deviation from the divine. Like the unveiling of a great secret, Naraghi's construction of the authentic human soul is a curious triangle of ontology, epistemology, and politics.

It translates into a political rallying-cry for a return to the ontological sources, based upon a championing of traditional religious knowledge. Knowledge is construed as concrete rather than abstract, existential rather than scientific. It cements an idealized ontological notion of the traditional family and community as an unbroken and tension-free

---

[58] Ibid., p. 208.

whole. The enemy knowledge, Western and abstract, is embodied in the impersonal institutions of the modern state and economy:

We shouldn't let Iranians undergo a metamorphosis. We have to fight against bureaucracy. We have to fight against the destructive elements endangering family relationships. We have to fight against any kind of deviation from true traditional principles. We have to fight against those elements that prevent the natural growth of individual characters. These are just some examples of challenges that our intellectuals can and should get involved in.[59]

Naraghi is calling for the reawakening of a lost communitarian identity and for being grounded in religion, as against the danger posed by Western modernity. He grounds this call to action within a hastily sketched international scenario that reproduces the fundamentally conspiratorial logic animating his ontology of the Romanticized ideal traditional community. It also includes quasi-leftist overtones in a call for a "realistic" appraisal of Western ideals of freedom in the politics of foreign policy. The fundamentalism of identity politics is united with an injunction that Iranian intellectuals awaken from the naïve, old illusions of anti-colonial struggle as the project of building a politically democratic nation. America is cast in the role of the chief villain, globally linking liberalism and freemasonry, a force for contamination among Iranian intellectuals:

"Pro-American" intellectuals ... are those who stem from freemasonry, and believe in a liberalism of which America is the cradle. The notion that one of America's policies is to defend or disseminate freedom is a naïve idea. ... People need to achieve freedom by themselves. Any nation, by struggling for their independence, could move toward freedom. Thus, a return to national identity is really the critical solution. Unfortunately, our intellectuals, whether because of impatience or ignorance regarding the world situation, have been easily deceived by other nations' sayings of freedom. They believe in Western thought and patterns of behavior, and are unashamed of collaborating with foreigners. If Iranian intellectuals cannot adjust to the current situation in Iran and the world, and continue ruminating upon the old concepts and ideas, they will not be able to transform the situation. As long as our intellectuals fail to detoxify their thought from foreign ideologies, they cannot take a step toward providing justice and freedom.[60]

---

[59] Ibid., p. 260.   [60] Ibid., pp. 259–260.

He doesn't
really
back himself
up, only
more so like
saying stuff

Underlying these arguments is a theory of existential knowledge as the basis for an authentically revived Iranian community. Thus, Naraghi argues: "The West, before the twentieth century, didn't have accurate knowledge of the Eastern system of government and way of thinking." Secondly, and relatedly, we come to those inauthentic Iranians: "some of our intellectuals, who graduated from Western universities, also made the same mistake. They brought this humiliating approach back to our country as a souvenir." Naraghi, in opposition to the West and its Iranian imitators, calls for the implementation of a Sharia-based political system in Iran. For Naraghi, however, both Western and Islamic cultures are abstract ontological categories. He never, for example, explains Sharia law in detail. When he does engage in more concrete analysis, he is very reckless. Ultimately, his notion of authentic Iranian or Islamic community rests upon a broader abstraction concerning an inflated notion of the "East." This "East" is defined by a supposed set of normative or spiritual elements, a unifying ontology in which Iran occupies the historical and cosmic center.

If Naraghi's prescriptions smack of religious "fundamentalism," the careful observer is surprised, upon glimpsing below the surface, to find a curious cocktail of essentially modern ideologies of a secularized messianic nature. Naraghi's reflections on technology and the individual as components of "modernity" attest to a general inclination toward ontology (how things are) or normativity (how things should be), with little regard for historical fact, social reality, or empirical evidence. Unsubstantiated and hefty assertions, devoid of detailed or analytical reasoning, are the mainstay. These statements are made with a robust confidence that excludes either doubts or further deliberation. His methodology, based upon ontology and normativity, rejects detailed analysis of social reality (sociology). Upon close examination, it derives from, firstly, Henry Corbin's analysis of Sohrewardi, for whom "East is Home, and the West is exile," secondly, Fardid's diagnosis of Western decline, and, thirdly, Al-e Ahmad's notion of the soulless Western Machine confronting authentic Islamic being. These are all well-known Romantic tropes, but they received imaginative and original articulation by these thinkers for the Iranian context.

Naraghi, in unoriginal manner, simply follows their lead to develop his own arguments in favor of Sharia and against representative democracy. The West, he contends, is under the spell of a spiritual and moral crisis involving rampant individualism and soulless technological domination. Naraghi identifies "scientism," or the worship of science (*elm parasti*) and technological domination, as the root cause of an existential crisis in the West. He suggests: "Given this situation [domination of the machine], we, as Easterners, should beware of losing our civilization and culture under the onslaught of Western industry."[61]

Naraghi, with a moral undertone, makes statements that are heavily normative. The source of his moral high ground derives less from Iran's traditional religion and more from its modern intellectual culture of Counter-Enlightenment. Moral advocacy appears to be central to his intellectual commitment to Iranian (or Eastern) culture and tradition. He equates the dividing cultural line between West and East with "spiritual" concerns. The organizing principle of Eastern tradition, he contends, centers on the ethics of what is good. Western culture, by contrast, is indifferent to the notion of good and evil:

The people of the East have a commitment to "morality." They believe in what is "right" against what is "wrong." Therefore, their faith in good and evil is a self-regulation of their freedom. Nobody in the East believes that their freedom is boundless. In the West, by contrast, "personal freedom" is like a contest. In this competition, they give the honor to the winner – not to the person who is right.[62]

Naraghi's book *The Alienation of the West* depicts a vision of the fallen Western community as the counterpart to Iran's traditional ideal community. Its cruelty is the result of having strayed from the nourishing ontological roots of that collective justice which is the core of the Eastern tradition. He proclaims this book to be the outcome of his many years of research and observation while living in the West. It is supposedly an inquiry into the intellectual character of Western youth and their worldviews. As an "Eastern" sociologist, he declares his curiosity about knowing the West. Yet Naraghi conflates the specific sociological reality of the youth movements of the 1960s with the overall decline of the modern West as a vast metaphysical "event." He eagerly highlights existing social problems in Europe, drawing an absolute conclusion upon the basis of minimal evidence.

[61] Ehsan Naraghi, *What Oneself Had* (Tehran: Amir Kabir, 1976), p. 17.
[62] Ehsan Naraghi, *Freedom, Right, and Justice*, p. 173.

Upon scrutiny, the book shows very little evidence of Naraghi's own research as a basis for critiquing the "West," or even personal observation from his time living there:

We are aware that our people, like other Eastern civilizations who encountered Western civilization, were stunned and bewildered by technical supremacy and economic progress in the West. Our scholars, politicians, and activists were somehow deceived by the West. They admired [these Western achievements] so much that they failed to notice the adverse features of Western life: those aspects that are irreconcilable with their traditions, spiritual sensibilities, and local conditions.[63]

The entire book remains at the level of empirically baseless abstraction. Naraghi neglects to explain his claims, apart from generalities about the East and West. Questions such as: Was the "Western" encounter in Iran, and other parts of the East, as simple as his description suggests? Is it true that no one raised any objections to the adoption of Western ideas and values? How do we explain the Ulama's resistance to European ideas in Iran and other Islamic counties? Moreover, even leaving aside the past, at the time when Naraghi was writing this book there was evidence of a vast and lively critique of the West and modernity in Iran. Naraghi had friendships with the likes of Ahmad Fardid and Seyed Hossein Nasr. Naraghi, very confidently, and with disregard to the existing reality, claimed: "I will, in this book [*The Alienation of the West*], examine new and unknown aspects of Western civilization."[64]

Naraghi explains, in this rather confusing book, the clever ways the people of the East can cherry-pick the good in the modern West and reject what is harmful to their culture:

Obviously, I don't reject every technical and scientific aspect of Western civilization, which are necessary for progress. The important point is to see that the new sciences and techniques, the creatures of men, can deprive us of human freedom and liberty, making humans into docile slaves. In this situation, Eastern nations must be familiar with new methods of Western scientific experience to enable free and considerate adoption of whatever is useful and necessary. Without being either subjugated or oppressed, and without losing

---

[63] Ehsan Naraghi, *The Alienation of the West* (Tehran, Amir Kabir: 1974), pp. 2–3.
[64] Ibid.

their cultural and spiritual foundations, Eastern societies should be able to take possession of sciences and techniques.[65]

The idealized traditional Iranian community, the central claim of Naraghi's writings, is based upon these essentially baseless, but imaginatively potent, abstractions.

The Iranian Counter-Enlightenment

In a construction of the enemy as inauthentic within the Iranian nation, Naraghi applies his abstract and imaginary schema to the concrete, historical experience of Iran's Constitutional Revolution. This is essentially an argument for an authentic cultural identity:

Why should cultures, such as ours, which consider people as a collective being, follow a so-called rationalism that must reject our culture's metaphysical essence? Why should we abandon the source of our "spirit" [*vajd o hal*], which is the art of our poetic and mystic heritage, and a part of our historically symbolic Iranian identity? ... Isn't this heritage of love, brotherhood and friendship, so vivid in our culture, an antidote to the threat of isolation and indifference in Western societies?[66]

From this utopian spiritual premise, several highly dangerous institutional injunctions followed. Naraghi's indictment of the Constitutional Revolution entailed a rejection of the right to "universal suffrage," a legal system based on laws, and other Western institutions. The appeal of these innovations, Naraghi argued, stemmed from a misplaced enthusiasm for all things Western. He wrote that "the West affected the tenets of the Constitutional Movement," as Western thought patterns were implied in the codification of "the Fundamental Law." The new Iranian constitution, he argued, did something "unnatural" by establishing a representative form of government that involved "voting." By contrast, Naraghi idealizes a supposed organic democracy based on peasant forms of life that preceded the constitutional revolutionary era:

The Iranian peasant, at the beginning of the Constitutional Movement, had what we can call "rural democracy." There was a kind of solidarity of social life in the village, and they participated in the natural life of the village as a holistic unit. They knew their social responsibilities well, and, for a long

[65] Ibid. [66] Ehsan Naraghi, *What Oneself Had*, pp. 183–184.

time, they knew how to defend their interests against landlords. But, with the introduction of the Western method of "voting" in Iran, Iranian peasants lost all of their rights and traditional features. Villagers turned into flocks of sheep, and were taken by landlords' trucks to the ballot boxes.[67]

The population "knowing their place" is equated with the universal soul and with true democracy. This is the basis of Naraghi's argument for spiritual "justice" over the anarchic decadence of Western "freedom." He proceeds to argue that the religious jurists are right. The consensus of the Ulama is a more "natural" and authentic form of democracy for Iran than the secret ballot system: "I, along with jurists [*foghaha*], believe in consensus [*ijma'*]. I believe that only the 'natural' representative of every social strata, group, or class has 'authenticity'." Naraghi describes the secret ballot system as "the Western style, that laid the foundations for fraud, deception, and cheating."

According to Naraghi, the Constitutional Movement hurt rural people, as "rural democracy" was demolished in the new situation. "The first result of employing the Western pattern of 'voting' in Iran was that the position of 'the landlords,' compared to 'the peasants,' once more became stable."[68] He concludes: "I basically believe that, anywhere where there is a 'voting' system, the 'natural election' is terminated."[69]

Naraghi's argument against Western inauthenticity and his affirmation of the universal soul as embodied in Iran's traditional social order lead to the promotion of Sharia as the prescriptive solution to Iran's (and the world's) contemporary problems. Sharia law provides the authentic basis for every gain in true liberty promised by secular modernity, whereas secular modernity has (by its own admission) failed to achieve these lofty aims. Naraghi declares that Western societies have come to acknowledge the failure of their own concept of freedom. He writes: "The West has accepted that indulgence in personal freedom will not lead to social happiness." It is unclear, however, what Naraghi means by "social happiness." Why, we might ask, is it unachievable in the modern West, and where can it be achieved?

An idea in many ways similar to Ayatollah Khomeini's theory of Velayat Faghih, Naraghi's Sharia has a curiously hybrid intellectual legacy: "If we thoroughly read the Islamic juridical [*faqih*] laws, we see that these laws have considered all details of personal rights. These

---

[67] Ehsan Naraghi, *Freedom, Right, and Justice*, pp. 206–207.   [68] Ibid.
[69] Ibid., p. 206.

laws, in fact, have been regulated based on all different possible incidents in our lives and our relations. The rational logic of these laws is extraordinary."[70]

Naraghi's Sharia ideal belongs within the "third way" ideological category, within the twentieth-century Cold War impasse of rival bipolar power blocs. He rejects the opposing modern alternatives in "either 'socialism' or 'capitalism'," opting instead for an indigenous national politics grounded in a cosmic sanction. Although Naraghi does not openly state what kind of economic system he prescribes for Iran, he clearly rules out all of the modern economic models. The "modern," at a highly generalized level, is the enemy. His "third way" is based on religious tradition and the rejection of secular science. The resolution, it follows, argues for a clerical executive branch: "I wish that the cabinet were entirely clerical." He goes so far as to suggest that Friday-prayer imams from every province should take responsibility for government [*farmondari-ye ostan*].

The Plight of the Modern West

Naraghi considers the modern emphasis on freedom and democratic rights as foreign and alien to Iranian culture, and as the product of Western modernity. His Romantic ideal of the restored religious community is predicated upon the rejection of these foreign elements. The idea of justice, and not democracy, is ingrained in the Iranian historical tradition. Iranian culture, moreover, is more in tune with the ultimate reality of human nature, and therefore a cosmically determined sense of social justice. The ideal of a collective social and historical destiny is elevated above the morally corrupt modern individual. Because the community is inherently good by transcendent spiritual decree, there is no need for the divisive and corrosive risk to social solidarity that lies in individual freedom.

Naraghi argues that the "notion of the individual" in the West is of an "atomized self, isolated from society." By contrast, "in the East," the "'individual' is not 'separated from society'." From his perspective, "people in the West fought for freedom," while "in the East people always fought in defense of what is 'right'." Freedom is defined by specific cultural and civilizational contexts: "in my opinion, freedom

---

[70] Ibid., p. 139.

does not necessarily have the same meaning for all people, societies, and civilizations." Within the Islamic social context, including Iran, Naraghi argues, "I believe that we have to consider 'freedom' along with 'good,' 'justice,' and other moral virtues in every society." "Freedom" can be reduced to what is moral and ethical, and it does not have any meaning as such.

In the East, freedom is a collective idea: "The West always wants merely freedom for itself, while the East always sees its freedom related to the freedom of other peoples. That is, the East sees freedom as the freedom of the human being generally, which means 'liberty' [*azadegi*]."[71] In the East, the notion of *azadegi* provides a broader social liberty for the whole of society: "'Western freedom' has an integral relation with 'individualism,' while, in the Eastern *azadegi*, the 'individual' is inseparable from the 'collective.' Freedom in the West means freedom of the individual from social constraints, while an Eastern person doesn't consider custom, manners, and social regulations as a limitation."[72]

The crisis of individualism and technology are resolved into a broader narrative on the spiritual dead-end of modernity. Naraghi's ideal traditional community has its primary adversary in modernity. This is a central notion of all Counter-Enlightenment ideology, quite remote from traditional religious imaginings of an ethical cosmos. Modernity, Naraghi argues, is an artificial and soulless "machine" that has shattered every ethical constraint rooted in traditional cultures, and threatens to destroy all that remains of collectively rooted ethical and existential meaning in the world.

Naraghi's critique of the West and modernity, the obstacles to the restoration of an ideal religious community, is presented as a flawless truth made visible to the public. The Iranian public is asked to accept Naraghi's writings as the "unveiling" of a world cultural map:

> My picture of the West is a sort of a "map," in which such countries as England, France, North America, and Russia are located at the center. Other Western countries are on their periphery. Meanwhile, my picture of the East is also a sort of "map." Iran is in the center, and the Islamic East surrounds it. Beyond this, there are the other eastern countries.[73]

---

[71] Ibid., pp. 86–88. [72] Ibid. [73] ibid., pp. 161–162.

From this imaginary premise, Naraghi further elaborates the Eastern and Western mental distinction as two existentially separate "cultures." The East and the West, he maintains, embody two different moral understandings of the world. Materialism, rationalism, and scientific thinking, combined with technological dominance, are described as the primary attributes of Western civilization. The East, by contrast, is home to the genuine spiritual expression of human life.

Naraghi's elementary notion is based upon the concepts of "incommensurability" and "purity," which are the dual components of an "ontology" of "authenticity." The ideal religious community is pure and authentic, and therefore incommensurable with modern Western values. This utopian conceptual schema permits broad explanations of diverse events and actions without requiring detailed investigation of any.

The East and West, in his schema, constitute two existentially distinct cultural and historical realities. The ideal traditional religious community is starkly contrasted with the corrupt and soulless modernity of Western society. Naraghi advances every imaginable argument, and every type of randomly selected evidence, in order to force this formulaic point into a semblance of plausibility. It is essentially a theory of incommensurability. Naraghi's larger goal, ultimately, is to prepare the ground for insisting that authentic Iranian tradition, culture, and sensibilities are irreconcilable with Western values and modern institutions. The theory of incommensurability correlates to a notion of cultural purity. Western culture will corrupt the historical purity of Iranian culture. Naraghi's aim is to safeguard his construction of the true Iranian culture, while cleansing it of inauthentic foreign or domestic forces.

These ontological declarations, given Naraghi's sociological training and credentials, are nevertheless invested with the authority of his own "first-hand" personal experiences. His declarations promise, in prophetic language, the beginning of the end of Western civilization. Yet, strangely, Naraghi says little that is concrete about his own experiences in any Western country. No serious empirical research underpins his grand arguments, and nor does he seem familiar even with secondary sources. Sweeping references to a supposed moral and cultural crisis in the West are the mainstay, combined with generalized statements about modern experience. At best, his writings are a poor imitation of polemical debates in Iranian newspapers and magazines of the time.

Despite his having studied in Europe for many years, and having received a PhD from a leading French university, the Sorbonne, the dearth of analytical substance or empirical evidence in Naraghi's writings is striking.

Upon careful examination, the analytical deficit in Naraghi's writings is actually the consequence of his chosen methodology. Corbin, Fardid, and Al-e Ahmad were each "deeply" Heideggerian thinkers. Heidegger's ontology explicitly rejects the modern scientific notion of "reality" as a superficial and secondary consideration with respect to more elementary structures of meaning. If "reality" is a "representation" based upon detailed observation, it is far removed from the underlying existential structures that govern the authentic patterns of our daily lives in a collective and public world. Heidegger employed this insight for the purpose of purportedly "uncovering" these hidden structures of "authenticity." It was a highly creative and hermeneutical process, where imaginatively conceived "structures" could be applied to the everyday world to explain its genuine depth. It has always been a point of contention as to whether these "ontological structures" were genuine scholarly discoveries or simply elaborate fabrications of the imagination. Naraghi, using the Heideggerian "depth" methodology, however derivatively and unconsciously, attests to the likelihood of these "structures" as the arbitrary and socially interested projections of a given imagination.

In this methodological spirit, Naraghi anchors his argument in a predictably recherché notion of primal or original truth. Original truth is the source of the ideal traditional religious community, the opposite of the divided and corrupted West based on science and materialism. He argues: "Even 'the truth' in the East is different from 'the truth' in the West." Far from an "objective" observation, this declaration asserts the superiority of the Eastern worldview over that of the West.

Very quickly, the ontological vista peels back to reveal interlinked epistemic and political stakes. "Incommensurability" and "purity," the dual elements of Naraghi's "ontology," are articulated through the comparative analysis of "truth" and "freedom" as culturally relative notions. However, "ontologically," Iran and Islam are "natural," while the West is "artificial." The East is moral, collective, and spiritual, while the West is individualistic and chaotic, i.e. immoral, linked to materialism, rationalism, and modern science.

This all seems more like propeganda then anything else. The regime propping up this friend is more like to give them legitimacy

Within this imaginative landscape, the kernel of a reactionary modernist anti-imperialist critique is observable in the following principle. The East–West cultural bifurcation is found in the Eastern appreciation of "justice" and the Western attachment to a cynically coveted and externally coercive "freedom." "Justice" and "freedom," against the grain of modern political thought since the French Revolution, are split into ontologically dichotomous opposites.

The reduction of the ideal of freedom to a totalizing impulse for global domination certainly derives from a Heideggerian imaginative resource. Naraghi writes: "Some believe that the West has 'freedom' and the East has 'liberty' [*azadegi*]. This is definitely true."[74] For Naraghi, the Western idea of freedom is a political tool, deployed uniquely for the purpose of world domination: "The West always only wishes freedom for itself and for enslaving other nations."[75] The argument is pushed to the following extreme judgment: "I believe that the civilization of the West is 'essentially' cruel."[76] This harsh civilizational condemnation, in metaphysical manner, covers the entirety of history, encompassing ancient and the contemporary times:

The West, on the path of freedom, has ignored "right" and "justice" … Athens was comprised of "free people" and "slaves" and "foreigners." In Ancient Greece, Athens was the "center," while other cities were its economic and cultural "satellites." These relations between "metropole" and "periphery" have continued throughout Western history. The West has always attempted to be the economic and cultural center of the world, while making other countries its satellites. Ancient Rome, as well as Paris and London in the nineteenth century, and Washington, New York, and Moscow in the current time, are all "metropoles." They have been built following the pattern of Athens, and the rest of the world is intended to be their satellites.[77]

What seems, on the surface, like a conventional leftist critique of capitalism, is a deeply conservative reactionary modernist appeal for a restored traditional order, for the traditional left, grounded in the sociological interpretations of Karl Marx and the everyday class struggles of the French Revolution, is remote from this vividly imagined cosmic tableau of conservative Romanticism. In the leftist tradition, an ideal traditional religious community was not a realistic option. Naraghi has replaced the leftist utopia of a just future society based

---

[74] Ibid., p. 86.   [75] Ibid., p. 74.   [76] Ibid., p. 91.   [77] Ibid., p. 146.

upon scientific advances with an ontological notion of a cosmically sanctioned community. In Naraghi's conception, the West is the over-arching nemesis in a fixed scenario where the East is the innocent victim. Yet certain left-leaning critiques of imperialism can be glued onto this ontological fantasy in such a way as to provide Naraghi with a perennial moral high ground. We should reflect carefully upon this ideological construction, which elevates colonialism from a specific practice with an intelligible history to a metaphysical feature inherent to a specific cultural civilization.

For Naraghi, the Western legal tradition represents the unnatural effort to force itself upon diverse cultures for the purpose of sheer power. In Iran, Sharia law has the entirely different function of provid-ing the guidance for living a fully spiritual life. This Sharia law, unlike the unnatural and humanly crafted law of the West, is an extension of the moral design of the universe itself. Naraghi's ideal religious com-munity is a world where individuals live spiritually pure lives, as the cosmic mandate for justice has always intended. They are moral rather than free:

In the East, "morality" and "law" are not separated. The goal of every law in the East is to reach a spiritual state. In the West, meanwhile, the separation of "law" and "morality" allows the abuse of "freedom." The West might have the most comprehensive and complete legal system. When, however, the whole relationship of the people is based on legal precepts, moral codes have no credibility. Freedom is therefore abused by the powerful. The most liberal legal systems, the Western governments, have always infringed both their own citizens' rights and the rights of other nations.[78]

Naraghi applies this critique of secular legalism to the United States. This global symbol of mass democracy and the rule of law is, in reality, a conspiracy to violently impose uniformity upon difference. It is a fundamental betrayal of the seamless natural unity of the ideal religious community that Naraghi aspires to resurrect from the Eastern spiritual tradition:

Consider America. People in this country do not have deep cultural traditions or a sense of national solidarity. There are British, French, Irish, Spanish, blacks, as well as Indians, and also other ethnicities who live there for only

[78] Ibid., p. 150.

a few years. In such a society, the only way to regulate and organize social relationships is to make a strict and severe system of "law" and "codes."[79]

Naraghi argues that, by contrast, the system of justice in Iran can be based purely upon tradition and shared cultural values. He writes: "in Iran, we are dealing with people who have had a historical unity in their language, religion, traditions, rites, customs, and dreams for a long time. Why, therefore, should we prefer the Western judicial system and laws to our own 'ethics' and 'custom'?" Naraghi promotes an informal system of justice mediated by the "elders," without any clear or written legal codes. In a modern and complex social system such as Iran's, this can lead only to a troubling outcome. It can only entail arbitrary rule by the traditional elite. For Naraghi, however, the authentic religious community is a simple and harmonious place, unaffected by the organizational hazards of a large modern society. In his imagining, the modern and very complex Iran of the twentieth century has no place.

The supposed East–West ontological disjuncture is the constant theme pervading Naraghi's reflections upon the contemporary world. The idea of freedom in the modern West is a pretext for a malicious battery of coercive actions. "Western freedom," he maintains, involves the Western desire for freedom exclusively for their own nations. This pattern has characterized the entirety of Western history, and has provided liberal interests with the pretext for enslaving and colonizing other nations. The West has, without exception, been a colonialist force, and particularly so in their relations with Asian and African nations.

Naraghi extends his argument to offer a more "utopian" and "Heideggerian" image of Eastern culture: "The East does not believe in the individual, but instead pays attention to the 'human being'."[80] He then defines the Eastern idea of the "human being" to mean "values such as honor, righteousness, truth, and justice." It is out of such ontological values that he derives a solution to the Western sickness, in seeking to embrace the instrumental benefits of technology and science in conformity with the exigencies of the universal soul.

[79] Ibid., p. 223.   [80] Ibid., p. 175.

Anti-modern Arrogance

Naraghi's political worldview is basically aristocratic, displaying enthusiasm for the Persian medieval tradition of the organization of power. The ideal religious community of his imagining centers on the "ideal type" narrative of the "just" king and his benevolence with regard to his subjects. This is Naraghi's desired political model for modern Iran and is similar to the Pahlavi image of the Shah. This may explain Naraghi's hostility to democracy and modern rights, and his overall acceptance of both the pre- and postrevolutionary political systems. The discourse of rights and democracy, he maintains, is a Western construction. In the East and Iran, the notion of "justice" is ingrained in the cultural and popular imagination of the mass of the people. In his ideal religious community, no tension between ruler and ruled is possible so long as the cosmic mandate is faithfully interpreted and practiced.

Naraghi proceeds to emphasize: "We must achieve new sciences and industries, and use them to facilitate our lives. However, in the meantime, we should be careful to make science and industry follow our authentic cultural identity, and not vice versa."[81] This notion is extended: "A conscious society is one that creates a living and vivid link between its national culture, and Western science and civilization."[82]

This argument is a highly familiar construct in the history of national struggles against colonialism. It contends that local tradition, while spiritually superior to Western culture, must integrate Western science and technology to enhance the nation's material power. Many, including Pahlavi state officials, made this argument regularly. The majority, however, were not so naïve as to believe any country can embrace modern science, technology, and industry while preserving its "traditional" cultural values unchanged. Naraghi embraced precisely such an aim:

We have to completely reject the presumption that "if you want the machine and technique, you have to accept all of their adverse aspects." A sign of the freedom, liberty, and power of awakened nations is their valiant effort to adopt the favorable aspects while rejecting the unfavorable parts [of Western

---

[81] Ehsan Naraghi, *What Oneself Had*, p. 17.   [82] Ibid., pp. 23–24.

civilization]. For doing so, the historical situation of these times is better than any other time.[83]

This simplistic argument, from a person with a PhD from the Sorbonne, is mind-boggling. There is a total disregard for any analysis of the realities of modern social structures, and an insistence on the pure determinism of the mind and will. Naraghi is hostile toward modern democracy and repeatedly locates the root causes of the darkest moments in modern Western history in its admiration for democracy. He suggests that Europe's democratic sensibilities have led to totalitarianism: "Both are appalling examples of resentment toward freedom that arose from 'the West,' the place that most Iranian intellectuals imagine as the cradle of freedom." He further argues:

Thorough and serious research clearly shows that, in the womb of Western societies, there are still many Hitlers and Stalins. Western civilization, in my opinion, when you come down to it, breeds the likes of Hitler and Stalin. "Little Hitlers" and "semi-Stalins" can still be found in Western societies. Political affairs in the West are still controlled by these kinds of people: those who want everything for the West, and dream of keeping control over the rest of the world forever.[84]

However, upon scratching the thin surface of Naraghi's idea of Eastern justice, it is rather insubstantial. Naraghi's idea of justice as the cornerstone of the Iranian–Islamic traditional community lacks any serious basis. Advocating "justice," he attacks liberal democracy and Western notions of freedom. He scarcely explains the nature of Iranian or Eastern "justice" (*edalat*), and, as a sociologist, he fails to portray the historical practice of justice in Iran. The following important ideas are ignored: the rights of individuals or classes of people, the limits of state power, gender equality, and the equality of religious or ethnic minorities. Naraghi's enthusiastic embrace of the Iranian idea of justice omits mention of any of them, as the unified ideal community seems to override any such consideration.

In his conversation with the Iranian philosopher Esma'il Khu'i he brushes against them in discussing the issue of justice. Without explaining what the Iranian judicial system was before the *Mashruteh* period, he condemns it as a Western-inspired model that is bad for the country.

[83] Ibid., pp. 27–29.
[84] Ehsan Naraghi, *Freedom, Right, and Justice*, pp. 69–70.

He writes: "One of the initiatives by Westoxificated [Iranians] was the reform of the judicial system. In doing so, [Ali Akbar] Davar was the leader. Davar ... and his colleagues tried to change the whole judicial system in Iran based on a Western understanding of 'freedom' and 'law'."[85]

Naraghi fails to explain what was so good about the previous system of justice, and why changing it was a bad policy. His dislike of the new judicial system simply derives from its genesis in Western ideas of freedom and the rule of law. Naraghi contradicts his own regular claim that he is a modern person and not an anti-Western intellectual, one who is open to accepting Western ideas. He is in fact very hostile to the Western system of justice, asking: "Does the French Department of Justice perform miracles? As one of my friends said, the Westernized people [of Iran] replaced 'reasons' with 'right' in our judicial system."[86]

Naraghi's critique of the post–*Mashruteh* legal system in Iran is characteristically vague and colored by his anti-Western ideology. Lacking criticism grounded upon any factual basis, he casts empty aspersions. The Iranian legal system was indeed corrupt and overly politicized, and it lacked independence from state intervention. Naraghi, however, has little interest in discussing these issues. He instead condemns it simply because its Iranian founders were inspired by the West and transformed the pre-modern Iranian legal system into something less traditional. The implication is that the absence of "artificial" Western influence, as such, is the key to unveiling the ideal traditional community in all of its "natural" glory.

There are several repeated themes in Naraghi's thought, uttered upon a regular basis and used indiscriminately. These constitute the thematic elements of the ideal traditional community as a spiritual alternative to secular modernity:

1. Pre-modern Iranian culture and tradition were natural, and offered social harmony by emphasizing "justice" over freedom, collective over individual rights, and spiritual over material values.
2. Such ideas as the right to free speech, universal suffrage, and dissent are "alien" to Iranian culture and are part of the problem in Iran.
3. Such modern ideas as democracy, human rights, and liberalism are only veils concealing the true essence of the West and modernity.

---

[85] Ibid., p. 221.   [86] Ibid.

> Democracy and freedom are pretexts for Western arrogance, colonialism, and inhumanity.

Naraghi's opposition to cosmopolitan intellectuals and ideas is most visible in his deeply rooted opposition to the Iranian Constitutional Revolution of 1906. His criticism is neither new nor original. In a familiar anti-Western discourse of the time, first articulated by Ahmad Fardid and popularized by Jalal Al-e Ahmad, the primary cause of Westoxification is the Constitutional Revolution of 1906. While acknowledging that the social and political life of Iran before the Constitutional Revolution required change, he says little about these issues. Rather, he blames the Constitutional Movement and its achievements as the onset of the decline of modern Iran.

The coming of modernity in Iran, marked by secular cosmopolitanism, is the root cause of all the problems in the country. The changes resulting from the Constitutional Revolution were alien to the natural order of things in Iran. Naraghi articulates a Romantic view of the social and cultural norms that he believes existed in Iran before the coming of modernity. Traditional Iranian social and cultural life was far more "natural" to Iranian social settings and superior to what happened following the Constitutional Revolution. These declarations are not based upon any research, or even detailed arguments. He just makes half-baked generalizations and expects others to accept them as the truth. The logic of his arguments is neither philosophical nor sociological. As one critic has put it, Naraghi seems more like a "'Compulsive preacher' than a scholar."

Naraghi, like Fardid and Al-e Ahmad, identifies the roots of Westoxification in Iran in the changes that took place after the Constitutional Revolution of 1906. *Mashruteh* ideas and post–*Mashruteh* Iran exhibit the beginning of the decline of Iran's authentic cultural traditions and the institutionalizing of Western social, political, and cultural values and norms. He argues: "The most significant point in this context is the Iranian 'sense of justice' [*hes-e edalatkhahi*], which is religious and mystic. Therefore, constitutionalism in Iran somehow meant justice [*edalatkhahi*]."[87]

In analyzing the social causes of the Constitutional Movement, most scholars made the mistake of considering it a 100 percent internal or

[87] Ibid., p. 196.

external incident. The Constitutional Movement generally had two goals: cutting off foreign interventions and building a government based on rights, justice, and equity. Historical and social documents prove that these two goals were combined.

Naraghi, in appearance, presents a rather reasonable analysis of the Constitutional Movement. In fact, the main goals of the movement were to limit the power of the monarchy and establish the rule of law in Iran. This was the central aim of the Iranian constitutionalists. However, Naraghi believes that the intellectuals and politicians involved in the movement betrayed the original goal and turned it into something less desirable:

The leaders of the Constitutional Movement wanted the cruel internal and external powers "to leave them alone," and let them build a government based on "justice," "right," and "equity." However, when the Constitutional Movement triumphed through patriots and just leaders [*high talab*], the advocates of the West, freemasons and social democrats, joined the movement and gained the upper hand. Subsequently, this national movement, devoid of any ideal but to achieve "justice," deviated from its original ideal into a Western "liberal" [*azadikhahaneh*] fight.[88]

This is the familiar conservative narrative on Iran's Constitutional Movement. Justice is depicted as the natural outcome of the elimination of foreign influence, as spontaneous as the blossoming of a flower. It has little relevance with respect to the historical reality of the movement, or its aftermath, where justice was a humanly constructed problem within complex and unprecedented conditions. The constitutionalists, from the very beginning, described themselves as *azadikhah* or "freedom lovers" and the movement as *azadikhahaneh*. They also considered the movement a political struggle for the establishment of the rule of law, and they saw no essential conflict between *azadi* (freedom) and *ghanunkhahi* (rule of law). The Iranian constitutionalists were also, it is true, cosmopolitans. They were open to new ideas and, particularly, the achievements of secular and democratic countries. They had traveled to England and France, and translated the works of European liberal thinkers. They also traveled to New Delhi and Russia, and were inspired by movements in those places for reform and democracy.

[88] Ibid., pp. 200–201.

This complex constitutionalist ideology and experience met with mixed results, severe setbacks, and in some ways outright defeat. However, constitutional thinkers looked upon Iran as a complex and dynamic reality, a systemic set of social problems, within a wider global power vista. Naraghi, by contrast, based his entire view of Iran upon a highly simplistic notion of a lost ideal community. Because it was a utopian fantasy, there was no real need for either argument or concrete analysis. The solutions to Iran's problems, he suggested, were to be achieved through a magical process of simply reviving the traditional roots in a process unifying the masses and their leaders. Inauthentic Iranians, like the West itself, would simply perish from their lack of ontological sanction within a pre-made cosmic scheme.

For Naraghi, a similarly facile pattern of utopian imagining was applied to Western experiences to explain contemporary events. The revolt of the youth movement in the West, he contended, was an existential challenge to the core fabric of the modern West. The 1960s and 1970s social movements, he believed, were so radical a turning-point in Western history that he anticipated a total transformation in unimaginable ways. Naraghi also hoped that those Iranians enthusiastic about Western modernity would experience a change of heart upon learning of the problems in the West and turn to a renewed appreciation of their own traditional culture:

I hope this book [*The Alienation of the West*] has made it clear that the age of adoption and imitation of the West, as desired by the former Iranian progressivists [*taraghikhahan*], is now definitively over. The time has come for our nation, and other Eastern nations, to return to their own traditional cultures, and to follow an authentic and constructive thought process, founded on their own culture.[89]

The Alienation of the West opens with an image of the West inspired by Shahab al-Din Sohrewardi's discussion of the West–East binary. This was a prevalent ideology amongst Iranian anti-modern thinkers during this period. Above all, Henry Corbin's writings dwell on Sohrewardi's illumination philosophy and the discussion of *Ghorbat-e Gharb* (the Alienation of the West). Naraghi was indeed close to Corbin during these years, but he neither mentions him nor gives him credit for having previously discussed these issues. Naraghi's

---

[89] Ehsan Naraghi, *The Alienation of the West*, p. 8.

perspective on the East–West binary is devoid of sociological insight and shot through with Corbin's extravagant mysticism:

Shahab al-Din Suhrewardi's book is entitled *The Story of Western Exile* [*al-Ghorbat al-Gharbiya*]. On the whole, the book's content, *The Chant of Gabriel's Wing* [*Awaz-e Par-e Jebrail*] and *The Calling of the Simurgh* [*Safir-e Simurgh*], professes that the East and the West are mystical intimations, originating from ancient Iranian thought. The "East" is the world of light, the symbol of light, and the base for God's special angels, whereas the "West" is the world and symbol of darkness. Gabriel has two wings, according to Sohrewardi, and his right wing is located in the Orient, while his left wing is located in the Occident.[90]

He then reproduces Fardid's similar line of argument about the West and its decline, only modifying it to suggest some possible dash of light in the West:

The Story of Western Exile is the story of man's fall into the material world, or the story of an exiled human being in the West, whereas man's home is the East. When I was writing this book, I kept thinking of Sohrewardi's book. I don't mean that the West is entirely captivated by materialism, or is losing its human values, or that the East is the only place of spirituality, flawlessness, and virtuousness. It is obvious that Sohrewardi advanced the subject from a different perspective. However, a kind of alienation is pervasive in the West these days. It involves alienation from the self, alienation from home, and alienation from one's peers. This state is not related to geographical boundaries. It means that the East and the West are equally likely to be alienated.[91]

Naraghi was seemingly also influenced by Jalal Al-e Ahmad's ideas in Westoxification. The "machine" in the modern West, he argued, has replaced what once was our humanity. For Naraghi, the root cause of the ills in the West stem from "the Machine," which has dominated and colonized Western people's lives: "The increasing rate of crime, violence and cruelty in those societies held to be 'utopia' is hard to find among wild animals. This is the gift of the ascendancy of the machine."[92]

The above statement is scarcely based on Naraghi's own research or personal observation as a sociologist. These are "prophetic" proclamations with weak logic and scant empirical evidence. There is no attempt

[90] Ibid., pp. 9–10.   [91] Ibid.   [92] Ibid., p. 6.

to explain these phenomena in Western societies (the anti-war movement, the women's and civil rights movements, etc.). Naraghi is to all appearances blind to the rich context in Europe for any observer with an open or satirical imagination.

Naraghi's only exercise in sociological analysis is the so-called "identity crisis" among European youth:

Drugs ... have faced the West with a serious hurdle. Their pervasive usage indicates an "identity crisis." This shows that [Western] society has failed to meet the inner needs of the young generation. They have turned to using drugs, because they are living in a state of despair, hopelessness, alienation, and isolation.[93]

Naraghi follows this with a simple sociological argument on the weakening of the structure of the family, and takes this as another reason for youth alienation:

The foundation of the family is increasingly weakening and losing its role in the education of the Occident. Because of the emergence of mass media and fast social change, parents are unable to adapt to these changes. A big gap is consequently being forged between parents and children. Therefore, families no longer meet their children's emotional needs. This is another reason for alienation in the West and the frequency of drug abuse.[94]

[margin annotation: This sounds like a modern social conservate in the US]

According to Naraghi, any social problem discussed in sociology is related to technology and the nature of the West. The source of these problems is the ontological condition of a corrupted modern world, the antithesis of his ideal traditional community:

To sum up, the expansion of urban life and the machine, the excessive consignment of personal affairs to (private or governmental) institutions, and the depersonalizing of human relations, without considering human emotional needs, have produced a critical situation in the West. All thinkers and scholars are acutely concerned. All of them seek new solutions by which human beings could avoid the destruction of their souls due to the evils of individual freedom.[95]

Naraghi's arguments are anecdotal or based upon general references to a few Western writers critical of excessive modernization in the West, and, finally, general discussion of social problems in Europe and the United States (the weakening of family structures, addiction,

---

[93] Ibid., p. 12.   [94] Ibid., p. 13.   [95] Ibid., p. 32.

violent crime, and social fragmentation in urban life). He uses these scattered arguments and references to construct his own "culturist" antidote for the Iranian context. The crisis is essentially cultural, without economic or political causes, requiring the restoration of an authentic spirituality:

The ongoing crisis in the Occident resembles the economic crisis in 1929 in the US, or the economic and political crisis before the Second World War. In contrast, nowadays, there are no significant economic problems, and the world is not threated by any serious global war. The major countries have been successful in transferring the challenging issues to Third World countries. The real current crisis of the West is a moral and spiritual crisis. In other words, it is a kind of civilizational crisis.[96]

It is unclear why Naraghi thinks of the crisis in the West as a civilizational crisis. This is a strange conclusion from one professing to work in the sociological tradition: "Considering that over a century has elapsed since Iranians started following Westerners, they should be cautious of the symptoms ... The symptoms of the crisis exist in five categories: the environmental issue, urbanization, family life and human relationships, the crisis of education, and youth revolt."[97]

After referring to these five sociological problems in the West, Naraghi then hastily returns to the familiar old argument opposing science and spirituality. He reminds his Iranian audience that "Although science is rooted in European culture, it has produced a cultural crisis in the West."[98] He then proceeds to argue that, despite some benefits from science, "there are so many problems and adversities that science, made by the West, is incapable of understanding and finding solutions for them." For Naraghi, scientific knowledge functions as a major obstacle to a real understanding of the "ethical and spiritual aspects of human life." Excessive reliance on scientific knowledge has placed the West in a "terrible situation," so that it cannot "overcome its deeply moral and spiritual crisis."[99]

Naraghi presents the cases of China and Japan as successful examples of modernity. He concludes that societies that refrain from imitating Western development patterns can preserve their authentic national culture and become progressive countries. This position is inconsistent, as sometimes he considers the Japanese experience as an alternative

[96] Ibid., pp. 94–95.   [97] Ibid.   [98] Ehsan Naraghi, *What Oneself Had*, p. 18.
[99] Ehsan Naraghi, *The Alienation of the West*, p. 95.

experience of modernity, while at other times he asserts that the West and the East have essential differences that exclude modernity from Eastern societies. In this account, Japanese difference based upon its unique culture produced its success upon a non-modern path.

What one can conclude from such experiences (of Japan and China) is that:

1. Western culture cannot be universal, and the development of technology, science, and public welfare, and other social progress based on other cultures are possible. Therefore, Western technological and economic priority doesn't mean the supremacy of their social system or cultural life.

2. Every different culture has the necessary capacity and potential to adopt technology in accordance with their spiritual and material needs. Therefore, technical and economic growth and development can be in accordance with their national, spiritual, and cultural institutions and social organizations. These countries make a connection with their own past and history. Considering this, one can realize that the Western model and example of growth and development are not the only pattern for other countries.

It is evident that Naraghi has picked up some ideas here and there from those critical of the discourse of development and its totalizing and universalizing assumptions.

Naraghi concludes that since development models in different cultures have different meanings, subjects like women's liberation should consider cultural conditions:

Progress is not an absolute idea, and is related to every society's conditions. One cannot completely consider different rites and ceremonies as factors for or against progress (dogmatism). In a certain society, large economic entities might lead to progress and, by contrast, in another society, small economic entities might be the main factor in progress. The same is true of women's liberation. Women's liberation is a progressive idea, but if it leads to annihilating a society's humane character and national identity, it is against progress. In rural areas, if modernization and development programs do not use internal factors of growth, those programs should not be considered progressive. On the contrary, they destroy the villagers' character and create chaos in the village.[100]

[100] Ehsan Naraghi, *What Oneself Had*, pp. 45–46.

These are broad ideas that appear to reflect common sense. Many intellectuals and scholars, in Iran and elsewhere, discussed them in the 1970s when Naraghi was lecturing and publishing on them. Naraghi added little to the existing critical discourse on development, modernization, or *gharbzadegi*. His arguments were comparatively simplistic with respect to what Al-e Ahmad had written over a decade before. Naraghi's arguments simply reproduced all of the familiar problems of anti-modern Iranian thinkers.

Preaching the Past, Fearing the Present

Despite his identification as a sociologist, Naraghi had little interest in discussing the political environment in Iran under the Shah. He occasionally spoke about censorship, the lack of freedom of expression, and other political restrictions against writers and academics. However, he took recourse to various cultural pretexts to blame "outside forces" for the absence of political freedom in Iran. Again, his vision derived from a world of ontological make-believe and thereby avoided entanglement with the complex details of empirical reality. The notion of an ideal traditional community, simple and cosmically sanctioned, continued to uphold his argument. Its natural antithesis lay in modernity, the perennial root of all evils:

1. He blames Iranian modernity, and he endlessly speaks of some imaginary historical period, in post-Islamic Iran, where Iranians will enjoy all the fruits of freedom. He neglects to document the freedoms that supposedly existed in the Iranian past, except for describing pre-modern Iran as the culturally "natural" state of things. He ultimately blames Westernized Iranians for the politics of the Pahlavi state. He blames the intellectuals for all that is wrong in Iran:

In my opinion, the main reason (for Iran's crisis) is traceable to leftist materialist thoughts and rightist utilitarian thoughts, both of which are rooted in the West. Both promote cosmopolitan sensibilities among the people.[101]

---

[101] Ehsan Naraghi, *Freedom, Right, and Justice*, pp. 260–261.

Naraghi depicts these Westoxificated intellectuals as soulless beings, without any appreciation of Iranian tradition, obsessed by materialism, and dreaming only of escaping to the West:

I don't know why our intellectuals are indifferent to everything. Why is everybody escaping from Iran? Why is everybody trying to make some money and emigrate to foreign countries? Why does everything belonging to Iran become valueless? Why are Western material and moral goods, just because they are Western, so popular among the people?[102]

However, in contradictory manner, he then goes on to argue:

Today, we need a general mobilization of intellectuals ... Based on our national culture, we can build an Iran in which there is both personal freedom and social justice. In doing so, intellectuals have a significant responsibility.[103]

For Naraghi, the intellectuals are both a source of national aspiration and the agents of Western domination and the corruption of Iranian culture.

2. In discussing contemporary Iranian politics, he almost exclusively reprimands the opposition groups, either liberal or, even more often, leftist intellectuals, for creating the unfriendly and intolerant space for having cultural debate and dialogue.

Naraghi dismisses liberal democracy as Western and alien to Iranian culture. Instead, he speaks of a tradition of debate and argumentation in Islamic Iran. The absence of a vibrant culture of a free exchange of ideas, he contends, is due to modernist intellectuals' indifference to the Iranian tradition of debate. He also argues that the capitulation to "Western" scientific methodology, and "scientism" in general, has made it hard for Iranians to enjoy a vibrant cultural life.

This is all very well as a purely abstract projection of utopia. In the reality of social power struggles, Naraghi used his notion of the ideal community to malicious political and even personal ends. A revealing example of Naraghi's self-serving use of "tradition" to justify the suppression of free expression is an incident that involved a review of two of his books. An Iranian writer, Mohammad Gha'ed, reviewed

---

[102] Ibid.   [103] Ibid., pp. 264–265.

Naraghi's books and harshly criticized him for recycling "old" and "tired" ideas, and dismissed his writings as shallow: "Mr. Naraghi does not have much to say, and what he writes is not that fresh. Nevertheless, he writes a good deal and (it is said that) he also talks a lot. All of the chapters in this book, *The Alienation of the West*, are transcripts of his talks."[104]

The review was published in a national newspaper, *Ayandeghan*. It made Naraghi very upset, so he contacted several high government officials and the editor of *Aynadeghan*, and complained about the publication of the book review and its author.

More interestingly, Naraghi, in a series of conversations with an Iranian philosopher and poet, Ismail Khoi, discussed at length the hazards of the book review. Naraghi's response to the reviewer is almost strange. He seems to blame Gha'ed for being inspired by the West and alien culture in his review of the books.

Naraghi argues that Gha'ed's review is politically motivated. He seems to see himself and his ideas as the embodiment of past Iranian traditions: "The authenticity of a thought and its philosophical value are no longer important. Rather, their political functions are considered the most significant."[105] He also criticized Gha'ed for following the dominant Western-inspired intellectual discourse in Iran: "In present-day Iran, the imported Western ideas are predominant in the intellectual space."

Naraghi avoids any specific response to the criticism of his books. Instead, he engages in personal attacks upon his reviewer: "The inferiority complex I am talking about is not a personal one. It is an inferiority complex that most Eastern intellectuals feel when they encounter the West." Naraghi portrays himself as both the victim of Westoxification and the champion of national pride:

A person [like me] writes something and expresses an idea, and it is normal that his thought has resonance in his country and sometimes on a global scale. What's the problem? Isn't it a symptom of Westoxification that we just value Western thinkers and don't give any credit to ourselves?[106]

---

[104] www.mghaed.com/essays/farewell/Death_of_a_compulsive_preacher.htm
[105] Ehsan Naraghi, *Freedom, Right, and Justice*, p. 53.   [106] Ibid., pp. 54–55.

Naraghi entirely overlooks the substance of Gha'ed's critical comments. Instead, he portrays himself as a victim for having propagated authentically Iranian ideas that are disliked by his Westoxificated critics. He writes: "They don't let any locally rooted thought grow up in this society. There is no doubt that this a big success for foreigners [*baingan*]. If you translate any ridiculous and absurd writing from Western culture, 'the guardians of silence' will say nothing."[107]

Naraghi's harsh reaction against a young writer who is critical of his book takes on a megalomaniacal dimension. He call's Gha'ed, and others who are critical of him, "the guardians of silence." This is a curious notion. Naraghi, after all, had vast access to the media and an intimate relationship with the state, as well as many academic and cultural institutions. It is unclear how he was silenced by these critics. Naraghi describes himself as "the poor guy" who "decides to provide a national and authentic thought" and who becomes the target of the "the guardians of silence." He is "severely attacked." Naraghi even goes so far as to accuse his critics of a crisis at the national level, saying: "They are the main reason for the cultural destruction, cultural exploitation, and cultural silence in today's Iran. Let me be clear, that 'the Tudeh Party' laid the foundations for such a state of affairs."

Ehsan Naraghi presents the story of a man who was born into a family of high social status, who joined the Tudeh Party when secular radicalism was the dominant Iranian intellectual trend, and who, later, from the 1950s on, became the public face of nativism and the Westoxification discourse. He belonged to a particularly paradoxical Iranian political and intellectual elite. His religiously prominent family established the first secular school for girls in Kashan. He was raised by a nationalist reformer and religious scholar with modernist tendencies. Having come of age during the interval of looming interwar unrest and social crisis in Europe, Naraghi entered the University of Tehran's Faculty of Law and Political Science in 1946, during the Iranian oil nationalization movement. Naraghi, like many other students, was drawn to the Tudeh Party of Iran, the pro-Soviet Communist party. He left for Switzerland in May 1947, in the aftermath of World War II, to continue his academic education. He attended the Communist Youth Festivals in Budapest in 1949 and

[107] Ibid., p. 26.

Berlin in 1951, representing "Iranian youth." Naraghi returned to
Iran in August 1952 following the uprising of July 21, 1952 (30 Tir
1331). Hired by Iran's Statistical Center a few days after the 1953
coup d'état, he subsequently lost his government job owing to allegations of having leftist thoughts and of involvement in anti-government
activity. In 1954, Naraghi left Tehran for Paris to pursue a PhD
program at the Sorbonne, where he encountered "spiritual" thinkers,
such as Louis Massignon, who criticized Western "materialist" culture. Upon returning to Iran, he established the Institute for Social
Studies and Research (Mo'asseseh-e Motale'at va Tahghighat-e
Ejtema'i) at the University of Tehran in 1958.

  This entire train of educational and social experience shaped
Naraghi as a "sociologist," one lacking in sociological imagination,
but, ironically, the product of certain social realities of Iranian life.[108]
In the 1960s and 1970s, as a rising political figure, he had close connections to Queen Farah, Amir-Abbas Hoveyda (the prime minister),
and Hussein Pakravan (the head of SAVAK). He was also intellectually
close to Ahmad Fardid and regularly attended the Fardidyyeh meetings. He was therefore involved in an intellectual and cultural project of
cultural nativism based on the ideology of anti-Westoxification.
Simultaneously, in the West, a broad 1960s New Age counterculture
critiqued Western materialism and science in a call for a renewal of
spiritual values. Naraghi, quite cognizant of these New Age tendencies,
wrote his own series of books with anti-Western and anti-modern
content.

  From 1969 to 1975 Naraghi worked for UNESCO. While conducting research for UNESCO and developing his international network

---

[108] A recent memoir by Manoucher Ashtiyani illustrates the intellectual
wonderland of Iran in the 1970s. The author, a Marxist activist-turned-
sociology professor/Heidegger philosopher, spent more than two decades in
Germany apparently studying philosophy with such luminaries as Hans-Georg
Gadamer and Karl Löwith, and attended Heidegger's classes (it is not clear
whether he completed his degree). He returned to Iran – with the
encouragement of Naraghi – got a university position, and was even recruited
to help develop the philosophy of "dialectics" for the Resurgence Party. Two
years later, during the revolution, according to his own account, he was
climbing up a statue of the Shah to bring it down. He ends his memoirs as
a staunch supporter of Khomeini, denouncing "liberals" and "leftists" for not
being true believers in Khomeini (Reza Nassaji, *Questioning and Fighting:
A Conversation with Manoucher Ashtiyani on Contemporary History and the
Human Sciences in Iran* [Tehran: Nashr-e Nei, 2017]).

of connections, Naraghi planned and created the Institute for Social Studies and Research at the University of Tehran. The Institute published more than sixty books in the first decade of its existence. The research policy of the Institute was to support fieldwork. Naraghi preferred to call these "the Eastern insight" against positivism.

Naraghi and the Institute encouraged ethnographical fieldwork in rural areas in Iran. Under Jalal Al-e Ahmad's supervision, the author of *Westoxification: A Plague from the West,* the Institute published a number of highly publicized and well-known "rural monographs." These were largely influenced by the Romantic and "pastoral" anti-modern sentiments promoted in certain intellectual circles, as well as among many elites within the Pahlavi state. The "return" to the "village" represented a political and cultural theme proclaiming an authentic identity for the Iranian nation, in contrast to modernity and the West. German intellectuals, in the early twentieth century, had been involved in a similar cultural movement of "returning" to the country.

Naraghi was only one among many Iranian intellectual figures constituting the contemporary anti-Westoxification campaign. Henry Corbin and Ahmad Fardid were the two principal philosophers of this current, and Naraghi was close to both of them. The anti-Westoxification campaign was taking place in the media, in national and intellectual newspapers and journals.

For a sociologist, within this international New Age intellectual ambit, Naraghi's own narrative of his intellectual path is strikingly non-sociological. He all but disregards events taking place in Iran, and even in the wider world. His intellectual transformation is depicted in a deeply personal way. Naraghi was inspired to help in the creation in Iran of a "nativist," or authentically Iranian, approach to the social sciences, hostile to Western-inspired social sciences. Upon the political front, he was critical of so-called Westoxificated Iranians, charging them with believing in the use of scientific methodology and statistics.

In the last three years of the second Pahlavi reign, 1975–8, Naraghi achieved his lifelong "dream" of a public presence in state political life and influence over its institutions. He regularly appeared in the national media, and wrote for various newspapers and magazines. He routinely advocated an authentically Iranian and "traditional" way of life, decrying the Westoxification of Iranian cultural and political life.

Naraghi projected himself as a man of "wisdom," good sense, and judgment. He was part of a larger group of intellectuals, scholars, and political figures, including Henry Corbin, Ahmad Fardid, Seyed Hossein Nasr, and Daryush Shaygan, who helped to fuel the fire that culminated in the Islamic Revolution. Paradoxically, Naraghi was a man who had always outspokenly feared revolutionary change.

4 | Iranian Cinema's "Quiet Revolution" (1960s–1970s)*

This chapter examines the political and social importance of Iranian cinema in the 1960s and 1970s, as part of the socially wider discursive shift in the Iranian political culture of the period. It analyzes the "New Wave" movies produced in the two decades preceding the 1978–9 Revolution. These cinematic images and narratives, we argue, contributed to shaping the Iranian public's perceptions of the modernization process that was taking place in their country at the time. New Wave cinema helped to influence the broader cultural transformation that we call the "quiet revolution." The Quiet Revolution, in this chapter, refers to a "national imagination" that was fashioned in Iranian cultural institutions, as well as in intellectual circles, during the late 1960s and 1970s. It crossed political lines through the unifying notion of *gharbzadegi* (Westoxification), a term coined by Iranian intellectual, novelist, and social critic Jalal Al-e Ahmad (1923–69) to describe the widespread practice among the upper and middle classes of adopting European culture and fashions.[1]

The theoretical framing of our analysis is based on our reading of Raymond Williams' book *The Country and the City* and Marshall Berman's work *All That Is Solid Melts into Air*.[2] We particularly focus on Williams' ideas of "pastoral modernity" and the "country–city" binary, and Berman's vision of modernity as a unifying experience that embodies the material and spiritual lifeworld. With

---

* This chapter is a revised version of an article, 'Iranian Cinema's "Quiet Revolution," 1960–1978," by Ali Mirsepassi and Mehdi Faraji, in *Middle East Critique*, Vol. 26, No. 4 (December 2017): 397–415.

[1] Jalal Al-e Ahmad, *Occidentosis: A Plague from the West*, trans. Robert Campbell, ed. H. Algar (Berkeley, CA: Mizan, [1962] 1984); for more details on Westoxification, see Ali Mirsepassi, *Political Islam and the Enlightenment: Philosophies of Hope and Despair* (Cambridge University Press, 2010).

[2] Williams, *The Country and the City*; and Marshall Berman, *All That Is Solid Melts into Air: The Experience of Modernity* (London: Verso, 1982).

respect to Williams, in his discussion of Early Modern English literature, he argues that English poets and novelists produced images of the rural–urban divide by creating "a myth functioning as a memory."[3] The countryside is imagined as a Garden of Eden, a place of harmony and community, whereas the city is identified with loss of connections and meaning, and a place of inhumanity. For Williams, these images of the city and the country are merely fictional, functioning as an imaginative surrogate for honestly facing the harsh political and cultural realities afflicting societies undergoing major social change:

Clearly the contrast of country and city is one of the major forms in which we become conscious of a central part of our experience and of the crises of our society. But when this is so, the temptation is to reduce the historical variety of the forms of interpretation to what are loosely called symbols or archetypes: to abstract even these most evidently social forms and to give them a primarily psychological or metaphysical status.[4]

Williams challenges the literary construction of the rural–urban divide, and he argues that they are far more connected than is imagined.

In this chapter, making a related argument, we study the Iranian films produced in the period 1960–78. We point to the construction of the rural–urban divide, and particularly these films' "fictional" construction of Iranian rural life in terms of spiritual identity and authenticity. We also discuss how Tehran, by contrast, is constructed as the space of alienation, corruption, and the fall of humanity. We also use Marshall Berman's discussion of modernity as a unifying experience. This will point to another aspect of how modernization evolved in Iran and then was represented in films. Berman's discussion of Charles Baudelaire in *All That Is Solid Melts into Air* is particularly relevant to our discussion of Iran's New Wave cinema.[5]

Berman argues that a certain vision of modern life tends to split modernity into material and spiritual planes. The first great wave of thinkers of modernity, he contends, "had an instinctive feeling for this unity; it gave their visions a richness and depth that contemporary

[3] Williams, *The Country and the City*, p. 43.   [4] Ibid., p. 289.
[5] Berman, *All That Is Solid Melts into Air*.

writing about modernity sadly lacks."[6] Baudelaire, he contends, was a seminal representative among these Early Modern thinkers. Berman uses the richness of Baudelaire's notion of modernity as a counterpoint to and critique of other, distorted visions of modernity, that is, "pastoral modernism," and what he calls "counter-pastoral" and "cultural despair."[7]

Baudelaire evoked modern life as a continuous struggle between "spleen" and "ideal," the visceral material environment and the high hopes for a better world. Ultimately, he perceived the material world of the "spleen" as invariably undermining our highest hopes, but without erasing the enduring traces of our moral struggles in everyday life through time. But because the "ideal," as an absolute, could never conquer and entirely transform the material world of the everyday, Baudelaire rejected nostalgic and imaginary bids for total moral transcendence. He saw the duty of the artist in exploring the labyrinths of the material world as that of squarely facing the real complexity and uniqueness of the moral web of contemporary modern reality.[8]

Berman, in evoking Baudelaire, is reminding us that the pastoral approach to modern life flattens and fails to see the richness of the spiritual or artistic quality of modernity. For this reason, it sees it reductively in terms of the image of the fall of humanity. This is also the argument that Heidegger makes, and some Iranian intellectuals and filmmakers embraced a similar view under the influence of Fardid and others.[9] The imagined intellectual caricature replaced the complex social reality as a phenomenon requiring sociological analysis.

New Wave cinema's most famous film was Daryush Mehrju'i's *Gav* (*The Cow*), released in 1969. Perhaps more than any other New Wave film, *Gav* introduced an intellectually dynamic, experimental, and open cultural tendency into Iranian cinema. Within three years, over fifty New Wave films had appeared. These films were at once philosophical, political, and poetic, helping to engender a powerful, if ambiguous, new political imaginary in modernizing Iranian society. A leading scholar of Iranian cinema, Hamid Naficy, describes New Wave cinema as "the collaborative synergy of intellectual directors and dissident writers and actors," which forged a substantial social network that contributed to the emergence of New Wave films in the 1970s. He calls

---

[6] Ibid., p. 132. [7] Ibid., p. 134. [8] Ibid., p. 139.
[9] Mirsepassi, *Transnationalism in Iranian Political Thought*.

this emerging style of filmmaking "the dissident cinema": "The collaboration of modernist oppositional writers and dissident filmmakers
enhanced the quality of resulting new-wave movies. [In the political
context of the 1970s,] the act of collaboration itself had psychological,
political, and professional value for both writers and filmmakers, since
it drew them closer as an oppositional and professional community."[10]

Naficy correctly points out the important impact of this new "dissident cinema" in the Iranian cultural politics of the time. He argues
that, in turn, New Wave cinema itself was influenced by contemporary
political and cultural changes occurring at multiple points in Iranian
society:

[The movement] constituted acts of resistance both against the dominant
commercial filmfarsi cinema and against the authoritarian political system.
Undoubtedly, this cinema and its influence on the intelligentsia and the
student population was one of the sparks that ignited the revolution. This
influence did not occur in a vacuum. Rather, it was part of the emerging
formations, dispositions, contingencies, discourses, and microphysics of
power and protest that amplified each other rhizomatically.[11]

Naficy argues that the New Wave movement's original cinematic
style and its high aesthetic quality were a major change in the conventions of Iranian cinema. These films were qualitatively different from
the dominant commercial films typically made in Iran. He correctly
points out that New Wave cinema was also politically informed, and
that it embodied an aura of oppositional resistance.

However, the New Wave and commercial films of this period also
shared a certain common narrative about the emerging modernization
process in Iranian society, as well as distinctive cultural sensibilities.
Both of these different cinematic genres produced imaginaries and
stories of discontent with the modern realities of Iranian life. They
also expressed a longing for the past, or declining forms of life. This
is what Williams describes as "pastoral modernity." Yet, there is something deeply paradoxical about the impact and influence of New Wave
cinema. The very international fame it enjoyed and the specific modernism of its unique vision contributed to its appeal among middle-

---

[10] Hamid Naficy, *A Social History of Iranian Cinema* (Durham, NC, and London:
Duke University Press, 2011), Vol. II, pp. 401–403. For more details on this
subject, see the section on the New Wave Films, pp. 325–431.
[11] Ibid., p. 404.

class Iranians who embraced its denunciation of Iran's authoritarian modernization. The ultimate effect of this paradoxical public embrace was to pave the way for a traditional religious revolution in the late 1970s.

Counter-Modernity and New Wave Cinema

Williams argues that pastoral counter-modernity involves the construction of mythical memory: "And it would then be possible to set up a contrast between the fiction of the city and the fiction of the country. In the city kind, experience and community would be essentially opaque; in the country kind, essentially transparent. As a first way of thinking, there is some use in this contrast."[12]

This memory consists of images of an unspoiled or "natural" rural life. It is contrasted with the corruption of urban development, which is "man-made." The discourse very often is embraced by the first generation of rural migrants to new urban centers, i.e. those who have been forced to seek work. They find themselves in a world without social security, guilds, unions, or any meaningful or protective group organization. They are tempted to embrace an ideology that promises deliverance through the restoration of traditional roots. The discourse of pastoral counter-modernity dichotomizes urban–industrial life with the peaceful life in the countryside now receding into the past. It is a myth functioning as a memory, or a literary representation.

In the late twentieth century, both Williams and Berman have presented two important theorizations of the pastoral. In *The Country and the City*, Williams considers "the pastoral mode" as an ideological construction. These artistic creations, he argues, do not represent the reality of rural or urban ways of living. The world they construct does not exist; nor can it. Yet, in the imaginations of "modern" urban artists and the intellectual elite, who enjoy privileged lives, there is a desire for a more "simple" and "authentic" mode of being in the world. They imagine an organic community with a continuity linking it to an ancient past, estranged from them by a tragic rupture. A gradual and deeply complex historical change is replaced by the projection of a simple, fundamental transformation. This dream of a magical transformation reflects a personal nostalgia for an imagined golden age.

---

[12] Williams, *The Country and the City*, p. 165.

Berman's *All That Is Solid Melts into Air* discusses Baudelaire as a critical voice in the contemporary modernist tendency to split the material and spiritual realms. Berman argues that Baudelaire presents both the "modern pastoral" (uncritical idealizations of modern energies and the bourgeoisie) and "counter-modern pastoral" visions (blanket condemnations of modern people as shallow, coupled with claims for spiritual autonomy in modern art). However, Berman argues that Baudelaire also has a third "voice." This voice captures a deeper and more realistic understanding of modernity. It is his artistic representation of the lives of everyday modern people – prostitutes, petty criminals, and alcoholics – in the ordinary tableau of modern existence. They take on a heroic quality as struggling human beings. This vision in Baudelaire's writings foresees much of twentieth-century literature in the ironic heroism of ordinary people, in their limitations and imperfections.[13] It is a profoundly anti-pastoral vision. In Berman's account, the "pastoral" is any fixed vision of an ideal world that has no real existence, but that omits real human beings through its sheer idealization. It is thereby at once a violent and delusional world, but one that can inspire misguided action.[14]

We can identify five major elements in Iran's New Wave cinema that together can explain the role of the cinema in fostering the Quiet Revolution. The five elements are as follows:

(1) the city and country divide
(2) nature, myth, and Sufism
(3) the pastoral hero as archetypal victim and resistor
(4) the virtuous poor
(5) cultural anxieties and modernization.

Each of these will be discussed with reference to important twentieth-century works of Iranian cinema.

The City and Country Divide

Most movies made between 1960 and 1978 depicted village life and village people as authentic and spiritually good. With few exceptions, the filmmakers and artists of this period were from Tehran or other large cities. Many had been educated in Europe and the United States. It is highly likely

[13] Berman, *All That Is Solid Melts into Air*, p. 134.   [14] Ibid., p. 31.

that their view of the city–country divide was inspired by the *gharbzadegi* discourse, popularized by Al-e Ahmad and others. During this time, many Iranian writers, almost all of them based in Tehran, traveled to rural villages and wrote ethnographical works about them. The general theme of the "village films," as Naficy states, shows "the purity and honesty of villagers favorably with the sophistication and corruption of city dwellers."[15] Majid Mohseni's movies, *Bolbol-e Mazra'eh* (*Nightingale of the Farm*) (1957), *Ahang-e Dehkadeh* (*Village Song*) (1961), and *Parastuha beh Laneh Barmigardand* (*Swallows Return to Their Nests*) (1963), exemplify the village genre. The financial and critical success of Majid Mohseni's *Bolbol-e Mazra'eh* helped to consolidate the village genre. The opening scene is in Tehran, which is depicted as a city of rampant poverty and criminality: robbers, seeing a rural man in the city, decide to steal his money, but the villager proves to be clever and thwarts the villains in their scheme. Then the film switches to a village to depict Shirzad and his sister Golnaz, who live there and work their own land, as well as that of the village's largest property-owner, the landlord. Because of their inner purity and decency, the landlord's son and daughter are in love with Golnaz and Shirzad. The landlord initially disagrees with his children's decisions, but eventually accepts his son's argument that "Being a villager is not a disgrace. She is decent, kind, and beautiful. I want someone like her who is a housewife and is not prodigal."[16] However, the landlord wants his daughter to marry his nephew, who has just returned from Europe and is a boastful, impolite, and incapable young man. In contrast, Shirzad is polite and capable, and is in harmony with nature and his animals. He sings for and talks to his donkey, and in one scene he asks his donkey to knock down a dandy from the city. Shirzad asks his donkey to be calm and gentle when his beloved is riding upon it.

Parastuha beh Laneh Barmigardand further represents this genre. It features an authentic villager, 'Ali, who is determined and honest. Two of his children die from the lack of basic medical care in the village. Seeking a college education for his son, Jalal, 'Ali sacrifices his home and land, and he moves to Tehran so that his son can go to high school,

---

[15] Naficy, *A Social History of Iranian Cinema*, Vol. II, p. 234.
[16] Landlord's Son, in Majid Mohseni, *Bolbol-e Mazra'eh* (Tehran: Studio Diyana Film, 1957).

and then sends him to France to attend medical school. His wish is that his son return to the village to serve its people. He works as a construction laborer during the day and a street performer at night. His wife is a domestic worker. When the father realizes that his son has changed his mind and wants to stay in France, he writes an emotional and patriotic letter:

Because I have nothing in this world to give you as a gift, I send you a bit of your original homeland's earth. This is the soil for which your ancestors sacrificed their lives. Keep it in front of your eyes. Don't forget it. I hope you realize the value of this sacred gift.[17]

Upon reading the letter, Jalal immediately declares: "I shall return to my homeland."[18]

New Wave cinema directors such as Mehrju'i also developed the village genre into a broader aesthetic vision. In fact, his 1970 movie *Agha-ye Halu* (*Mr. Gullible*) presents the city and the country as a binary opposition.[19] The main character, Agha-ye Halu, travels to Tehran to find a wife. The trip starts with the excitement and naïveté of an unworldly man. Upon arriving in Tehran, his baggage is stolen. He wanders about the city and tries to find his address. An unscrupulous real estate agent, recognizing his naïveté, swindles him. When he recognizes the ruse and resists, he is beaten and left alone in the city. While lying in pain upon the pavement, his nose bleeding, the protagonist poetically and proudly repeats, "A man must always tell the truth."[20] We see the honesty of a man of traditional origins confronted with urban disorder and corruption resulting from the modern invasion of materialism and imperial power. He presently falls in love with a beautiful woman called Mehri, and, showering her with gifts, asks her to marry him. When it turns out she is a prostitute, his heart is broken. Yet he chivalrously asks her to give up her job and marry him. He decides this based on a religious or traditional pattern of behavior, rejecting the modern lifestyle around him. The prostitute, suspecting

---

[17] Ali (Majid Mohseni), in Majid Mohseni, *Parastuha beh laneh Barmigardand* (Tehran: Tehran Film, 1963).
[18] Jalal (Javad Gha'em Maghami), in Mohseni, *Parastuha beh laneh Barmigardand*.
[19] Naficy, *A Social History of Iranian Cinema*, Vol. II, p. 234.
[20] Agha-ye Halu (Ali Nasirian), in Daryush Mehrju'i, *Agha-ye Halu* (Tehran: Studio Caspian, 1970).

that he is a poor man, rejects his proposal for a modest but pure-hearted salvation, but then is ensnared in her world as the mistress of a corrupt but wealthy urbanite. Out of material interests, Mehri remains metaphorically wedded to the night, where only a criminal existence is possible. The protagonist seeks to confront the forces of darkness in physical combat. After a fight with Mehri's lover, who beats him, he returns to the country.

The opening sequences, set in Tehran, convey a chaotic vision: people fight for worthless things and steal other people's property in a frightening world of strangers. Images of corruption, anonymity, commotion, immoral behavior, dishonesty, and bullying portray Tehran's modern life as an inferno. The pace of the rural protagonist's speech, meanwhile, suggests the rhythm of a slower and more dignified life. The protagonist's honesty, courage, and purity contrast with the immoral and false behavior of urban crowds. The same tangle of sin, urban chaos, and prostitution is featured in many movies and novels during this era.

The bleak images of Tehran streets, with cars and their blaring horns, express human loneliness. The protagonist is terrified and confused as he wanders in search of his address. Technology and erotic images dazzle him. Craning his neck to look up at an impressive skyscraper, he says: "Amazing, industry has indeed progressed a lot."[21] There is a great irony in this, as progress is also horror. The myriad spectacles of modernity transfix the protagonist: he stops to stare at a women's underwear store, at pictures of superstars, and at an erotic cabaret where a show is about to start. In Tehran, new and unfamiliar sexualities are ubiquitous. Agha-ye Halu stops in front of a store to ask the price of a piece of equipment. The seller's voice, body language, and gestures show that he is homosexual.

Mehrju'i's *Agha-ye Halu* expresses the emotional priority of an authentic, honest, and altruistic pastoral culture, contrasted with a corrupt, inauthentic, and egotistic urban culture. In the moment of seeking to save the fallen woman, and sacrificing everything for her in a great but doomed struggle, he attains a kind of *safa-ye baten* (inner purity). His entire journey could be considered a mystic odyssey. When Agha-ye Halu arrives in Tehran and is getting off the bus, he starts his mystical journey. In an excited voice, he says: "Traveling is a great

[21] Ibid.

thing." At the journey's end, when the bus is approaching his small village, he repeats that sentence in a broken-hearted and thoughtful manner: "Traveling is a great thing. It gives so much experience."[22] He is initially *kham* (naïve) and eagerly excited about Tehran. During the journey, he encounters difficulties and incidents (*azmayesh-e elahi*), and finally he matures (*pokhteh*). In doing so, he finds his "authentic self."

Bolbol-e Mazra'eh and *Parastuha beh Laneh Barmigardand* paint the countryside positively as an unspoiled and pure environment with an organic relationship with its vivid, productive, and simple members. On the other hand, *Agha-ye Halu* shows the city and its denizens as representatives of vice against virtue. In fact, they are delivering a united message. As Sadr characterizes the message of *Agha-ye Halu*: "the only solution offered is to escape the quagmire of urbanism."[23]

Nature, Myth, and Sufism

A telling aspect of New Wave cinema from this period is the perception that modernity is "impure" and "unnatural." Modernization embodies all that is alien and inhumane, and it destroys the beauty of nature, the excitement and mystery of being, and human spirituality. This pastoral vision for the world, as described by Raymond Williams, was a pervasive theme and dominated Iranian films and, ultimately, intellectual discourses leading up to the 1978–9 Revolution.

As mentioned earlier, the New Wave film *Gav* was a pioneering example of man's struggle for dignity and identity in a hard and harsh time. Hamid Dabashi argues that Mehrju'i's *Gav* transformed "the very definition of Iranian cinema."[24] The film broke many Iranian cinematic conventions. Its focus on villagers sought to return to an authentic bedrock of Iranian society and psychology. Its rural locations countered the commercial cinema's fixation on urban life and ersatz modernity. The film represented a thematic turn toward the masses of poor people, the majority invoked in radical leftist discourse. With this film, we see a modernist "village genre" dramatizing the self and the

[22] Ibid.
[23] Hamid Reza Sadr, *Iranian Cinema: A Political Story* (London: I. B. Tauris & Co., 2006), p. 134.
[24] Hamidi Dabashi, *Close Up: Iranian Cinema, Past, Present, and Future* (London: Verso, 2001), pp. 27–28.

other, Iran and the West, in a novel reconstruction of Iranian authenticity.[25]

A critic called it "a historical moment in our cinema," "an authentic cinema," and "an extraordinary leap."[26] Another critic argued that "Mehrju'i is an intellectual," and "the story of *Gav* is mystical and narrates the emotional relationships between human and human, human and animal, and human and nature."[27] Mehrju'i argued, "it's not a film Farsi any more, it's an international movie."[28] One Italian critic wrote, "*The Cow* is a movie with brilliant style" and is "rediscovering Iran … It's a mystical event and … Mash Hasan's cow is mythical."[29] Another critic compared Mehrju'i to Pier Paolo Pasolini, Akira Kurosawa, and Satyajit Ray.[30] Great critical and public enthusiasm greeted the film's release in Iran, generating high box-office revenues.

Gav is about Mash Hasan, who lives in a small village and owns a cow to which he is deeply attached. After Mash Hasan goes to another village for work, the cow mysteriously dies, and the villagers bury it. When Mash Hasan returns to the village and discovers his cow gone, he is mentally and emotionally broken. He starts to believe that he is his cow, and takes to living in the cowshed and feeding on hay. Some villagers decide to take him to a hospital in the city. They tie him up and take him toward the city. Mash Hasan, however, runs up a hill and ultimately falls off a cliff to his death.

Mehrju'i wrote the screenplay for *Gav* with the leading dissident writer Sa'edi. The film adapted *Gav* from Sa'edi's book of eight stories, *Azadaran-e Bayal* (*Bayal's Mourners*). An exhibition permit for *Gav* was made conditional upon a caption stating that the story took place forty years earlier, before the inauguration of Reza Shah's main reforms (in the years 1926–41). However, the film remained banned for a year, as the government brooded over fears that it contradicted "the official image of Iran as a modern nation of promise and plenty."[31] Denied an export permit, the film was smuggled out of Iran in a French visitor's suitcase and entered without subtitles in the Venice International Film Festival in 1971. There, it garnered the

[25] Naficy, *A Social History of Iranian Cinema*, Vol. II, p. 339.
[26] Quoted in Jamal Omid, *History of Iranian Cinema, 1279–1375* (Tehran: Entesharat-e Rowzaneh, 1995), p. 543.
[27] Ibid.   [28] Ibid., p. 544.   [29] Ibid., p. 547.   [30] Ibid., p. 548.
[31] Quoted in Naficy, *A Social History of Iranian Cinema*, Vol. II, p. 346.

International Film Critics' Award. The film's widespread domestic and foreign successes, ironically, opened the way for government support of the Iranian New Wave cinema movement.[32]

Gav presents the village as a contrast to the corruption of the modern city. It idealizes an unbroken and unspoiled unity with nature. In a dialogue between the village chief and another old man, the chief says: "Mash Safar's son has only been trouble, ever since he's come back from the city. It's all he learned out there."[33] Rural harmony between human and nature, and human and human, is represented in Mash Hasan's relationship with his cow.[34] As Naficy states, "Mash Hasan's attachment to the cow extends to a deep psychological bond of love with a sentient being, touchingly demonstrated when he tenderly washes her in the river and talks with her playfully."[35]

The film also features strangers who threaten the village:

These thieves [the strangers], always in a three-man formation, silhouetted against a darkening sky or lurking and scurrying in the shadows of village walls and alleys, form a recurrent visual and psychological motif of fear and anxiety. Ironically, the villagers call these dark, shadowy figures Boluris.[36]

The Boluris are represented as lacking in the belief that unifies any society: "We can't do anything. These Boluris don't believe in anything. We have to leave it to God."[37] These phantom invaders were variously read as Iran's threatening Arab neighbors and as a Western imperialist incursion. The cow itself, as the unique center of economic life in the village, was read as an allegory for Iran's dependent relation on oil. Through these lenses, *Gav* was understood as a deeply political film.[38] Mash Hasan and his wife are repeatedly represented as looking beyond the horizon. Naficy interprets this as a religious symbol of waiting and

---

[32] Ibid., pp. 346–347.

[33] Mashhadi Abbas (Jamshid Mashayekhi) in Daryush Mehrju'i, *Gav (The Cow)* (Tehran: Vezarat-e Farhang va Honar, 1969).

[34] According to Dabashi, "There is scarcely a more loving scene in the history of Iranian cinema than the one in which Mash Hasan feeds his cow": Hamid Dabashi, *Masters and Masterpieces of Iranian Cinema* (Washington, DC: Mage Publishers, 2007), p. 125.

[35] Naficy, *A Social History of Iranian Cinema*, Vol. II, pp. 336–337.

[36] Ibid., p. 337.   [37] Mashayekhi, in Mehrju'i, *Gav (The Cow)*.

[38] Sadr, *Iranian Cinema*, p. 133.

longing for a beloved, a savior, a Mahdi that "constitutes another one of the primal themes of Iranian mysticism, literature, and cinema."[39]

Another film in this category is *Bagh-e Sangi* (*The Stone Garden*, 1976) by Parviz Kimiavi. This film employs "ironic jokes" to "poke fun at authority" and "the contradictions of modernity." A young shepherd drives an old man's sheep using a motorcycle, in rejection of the traditional method of herding on foot. A cleric steals a stone from a tree as though stealing a piece of fruit. The protagonist, Darvish Khan, cuts down telephone lines as soon as company technicians have put them up.[40] Darvish Khan, a deaf-mute, lives with his family in a remote desert. One day, he falls asleep and dreams of an imam. Inspired by this spiritual dream, he makes a stone garden. He hangs rocks and stones like leaves from tree branches. Local people see his garden as a religious shrine and visit it like pilgrims.

A second film in this genre is *Gharibeh va Meh* (*Stranger and the Fog*, 1975), by Bahram Beyza'i. The film contains religious rituals and concepts. The theme of *Stranger and the Fog*, like that of some other New Wave movies, is "the intrusion of a stranger, or a group of strangers, into often small, closed communities which they terrorize and destabilize."[41] An isolated village community by the sea finds a boat containing a wounded and unconscious man, Ayat. The villagers ask the stranger to either leave the village or marry one of the village girls in order to become *mahram* (lit. "confident") with the villagers (in Islamic tradition, men and women should not interact at all unless they are *mahram*). Ayat decides to marry a widow. With the stranger's presence, the harmonious life of the village turns into chaos. Various groups of strangers sporadically attack the villagers and ask Ayat to go with them. In the end, the distressed and desperate Ayat decides to leave his new life and wife. In a small boat, he goes to sea in order to figure out who is looking for him, vowing to "discover what is happening on the other side"[42] (i.e. suggesting the beyond). The whole village starts mourning for him. It seems that death is looking for Ayat. Questioning the identity of the one looking for him, the strangers tell Ayat: "Don't play with us. His songs are everywhere. He has so many things. The earth belongs to Him, the trees, the seashores, the hills, and the four

[39] Naficy, *A Social History of Iranian Cinema*, Vol. II, p. 339.   [40] Ibid.
[41] Ibid., p. 344.
[42] Ayat (Khosro Shojazadeh), in Bahram Beyza'i, *Gharibeh va Meh* (*Stranger and the Fog*) (Tehran: Cinema Theater-e Rex, 1975).

seasons. Our dreams all belong to Him. Think about it, find out for yourself who He is."[43]

Critically, this film introduced "something altogether different from the factual realism of Sohrab Shahid Sales" into Iranian cinema.[44] It presented a "mythologization of Iranian culture," tracing its contemporary ailments to mythical origins.[45] The roots of these ailments are identified in the layers of the collective consciousness. Their subversive derailments are sought in mythological counterattacks. Iranian critics have maintained that the film, and others like it, has "resulted in the most effective challenge to messianism and patriarchy ever mounted in Iranian contemporary art."[46]

The Pastoral Hero as Archetypal Victim and Resistor

We analyze the pastoral hero theme through an examination of four films. The first is *Gheysar* (1968), by Mas'ud Kimia'i. *Gheysar* has been critically read as "an elegy for lost values."[47] Its narrative presents a rebellion against rapid modernization, or the hero's actions as "a substitute for absent social justice."[48] This had a strong resonance in the sociopolitical context of the late Pahlavi era. A young woman named Fati commits suicide by taking poison, and she leaves a letter explaining that she had been raped by Mansour Agh Mangol. Her brother, Farman, seeks to avenge her murder, but is also killed by Mansour and his brothers. Gheysar, the youngest brother, returns from the southern city of Abadan, and decides to kill the three brothers who dishonored his sister and murdered his brother. He murders each brother. However, before the final murder, Gheysar meets Mansour's fiancée, Sohaila. He spends the night with her to complete his revenge.

Using this simple narrative device, the dialogue underlines the failure of the modernizing state to secure justice for ordinary Iranian citizens. This is made explicit in a dialogue between the protagonist and his mother:

GHEYSAR: I have nothing to do in this world but three things. I myself will kill each of them [*the three brothers*].

---

[43] Beyza'i, *Gharibeh va Meh (Stranger and the Fog)*.
[44] Dabashi, *Close Up*, p. 29.   [45] Ibid.   [46] Ibid., p. 30.
[47] Naficy, *A Social History of Iranian Cinema*, Vol. II, pp. 299–300.
[48] Ibid., p. 373.

MOTHER: Don't be naïve. Let the government find them and punish them.

GHEYSAR: The government will find them? You are right. Will punish them? You are right. But you know what will happen? What do you know, mother?[49]

In this scene, a changed reality undermines the traditional wisdom of the elders.

Traditional frameworks of justice have disintegrated and yielded to violence. Ordinary Iranians have no choice but to reproduce comparable violence to survive. This notion is reinforced in a later scene where Gheysar speaks with his uncle:

This world is full of deception. Look what happened to Farman, who was a real man. If you don't kill, you will be killed. Where is Farman now? Where is poor Fati? ... I'm going to kill all of them.[50]

These characters are not from the countryside but from the more traditional section of the city. They represent the older way of life. In many of these movies, where we have an encounter between the city and the country, or modernity and tradition (pastoral and urban), the cinematic representations are more complex, somehow dialectical, with elements of the pastoral being present in the city and used in a symbolic fashion.

The second film, *Tangsir* (1973), by Amir Naderi, is based on Sadegh Chubak's novel. The protagonist gives his twenty years' worth of savings to four city leaders. These include a lawyer, two merchants, and a mollah. He expects them to invest the savings for him, but they later tell him that the money has been lost. When the protagonist attempts to negotiate with them to retrieve the money, they humiliate him and deny that there was ever a deal between them. He becomes quite certain that they are not going to return his money and resolves to kill them. Wielding a gun and an axe, he undertakes revenge. Bystanders, witnessing this personal revenge, are inspired and take his side. They chant slogans and call him Mohammad the Lion. Critical reviews of this film interpreted the narrative as a social allegory: "When street people joined forces

---

[49] Gheysar (Behruz Vosughi), in Mas'ud Kimia'i, *Gheysar* (Tehran: Aryana Film, 1968).

[50] Ibid.

with him, Mohammad's personal revenge became a popular rebellion against oppressors."[51]

The dialogue of *Tangsir* explicitly identifies the modernizing regime with exploitation and injustice. Following an ineffective dispute with city leaders, the disappointed and angry protagonist shouts: "What kind of city is this? The governor is a thief, the lawyer a crook, and the mollah a swindler! All are in it together! Why is it like that?"[52] Other members of the public concede the injustice, implying that it is collectively endured. Yet they urge the protagonist to let the Divine inflict retribution in due time. One man seeks to calm Mohammad by telling him: "Those four are in it together. They've robbed everyone. Let God and *hazrat-e* 'Abbas [holy 'Abbas] punish them. God is witness."[53]

In another scene, following the dispute, Mohammad is watching two blacksmiths who are forging a sword-like piece of iron. Ironically, one of them urges him to await "the Day of Judgment." The transmission of divine justice in a secular context further is implied in a scene where the protagonist is drinking water while an icon of Imam Hossein is dangling behind him. As he drinks, the camera changes its angle to show the image of Imam Hossein. Water and Imam Hossein symbolize the beginning of an uprising in traditional Iranian culture.

Za'er Mohammad openly claims the right to retribution when he states: "Everyone says to wait for God, the prophet, and *hazrat-e* 'Abbas' sword to punish them. What's wrong with me?"[54] He subsequently undertakes revenge and is lauded as a hero for his bravery. The crowds praise him, claiming "God punishes evil" through "men like Za'er." Upon completing his vengeance, the protagonist urges the crowds to follow his example: "I finished God's order. I'm done here. It's up to you not to let such people ruin your lives, steal from you, and exploit you. You must be strong and stand up for your rights."[55] In Ali Shari'ati's language, it seems that Za'er Mohammad rebels against *zar* (wealth), *zur* (power), and *tazvir* (hypocrisy).

The third film is Mas'ud Kimia'i's *Gavaznha* (*The Deer*, 1974). In *Gavaznha*: violent personal revenge was read as an attempt to gain social justice through armed struggle against a government whose

---

[51] Naficy, *A Social History of Iranian Cinema*, Vol. II, p. 375.
[52] Za'er Mohammad (Behruz Vosughi), in Amir Naderi, *Tangsir* (Tehran: Sazman-e Cinema-ye Payam, 1973).
[53] Ibid.   [54] Ibid.   [55] Ibid.

security forces not only failed to protect people but harassed them. This violent and individualized take-charge attitude was both a vestige of the fading improvisational system and a symptom of emerging modernity and capitalism, both of which rewarded individuality and personal initiatives.[56]

The protagonist, Ghodrat, is running because he has committed an armed robbery. He looks for his childhood friend, Seyyed Rasul, to shelter him. Seyyed, residing in a poor multifamily house, helps him. Seyyed, who has now become a heroin addict, had earlier been a brave teenager who had helped other students. Ghodrat attempts to remind Seyyed of his strength in the past and encourages him to stand on his own two feet once more. Seyyed is influenced by his friend and begins a new life journey. He initially strikes the friend and colleague of an actress, Fati, who is harassing her. He then hits the greedy landlord who annoys the tenants, and subsequently kills a drug dealer.

In an interview, Kimia'i said that the purity of the characters (Ghodrat and Seyyed) was lost in a moment. One is addicted to heroin because of his passivity, and the other committed a robbery because of his unbalanced soul. In the end, what keeps them from corruption is their purity.[57] The authorities confiscated the movie for a year, concerned that it could be interpreted politically in terms of Ghodrat being a guerilla. Armed, and concerned about the neighbors' suffering and severe poverty, the characters represented standing up for the poor in Iran.[58]

The film depicts crime and drug addiction as misspent human energies under regimes of oppression. To break out of such endless cycles, the characters embrace a purposeful, revolutionary violence. In one scene, a robber wakes a junkie from his torpor by evoking his lost human qualities under a soul-destroying regime: "Look at you! Look around! Once you were the best. Let me know who made you addicted to drugs. Don't you want to kill him? You are begging the one who made you miserable to make you more miserable. Where is your beautiful knife?"[59] This heroic and activist vision is echoed elsewhere

---

[56] Naficy, *A Social History of Iranian Cinema*, Vol. II, p. 302.
[57] Omid, *History of Iranian Cinema*, p. 696.
[58] Naficy, *A Social History of Iranian Cinema*, Vol. II, p. 385.
[59] Ghodrat (Faramarz Gharibian), in Mas'ud Kimia'i, *Gavaznha (The Deer)* (Tehran: Studio Misaghiyah, 1974).

when one of the protagonists affirms: "It is better to die by a bullet than to die a natural death in the gutter."[60]

The final film is Fereydun Goleh's *Kandu* (*The Beehive*, 1975). In *Kandu*, the protagonist, Ebi, rebels against the city where he has grown up. He feels that his whole life has been a failure. Upon being released from prison, Ebi and Mr. Hosseini spend their nights in a coffeehouse. One night, Mr. Hosseini and some people are playing cards. Mr. Hosseini wins the game. As a reward, he orders Ebi to go to some cafés and eat and drink without paying. Ebi accepts the deal, starting with a café in Lalehzar and finishing in Pol-e Tajrish, severely beaten by bouncers in each café. In the end, he successfully visits seven cafés, with his face covered in blood and bruises under his eyes. Because seven is an epic number in Iranian myths, such as the Seven Labors of Rostam (Haft Khan-e Rostam), and because it is a religiously signifi-cant number, the film raises Ebi's acts to a transcendent level. Entering cafés and drinking without paying his bills, and being beaten by the bouncers, also raises the protagonist's self-esteem, as he refuses to follow social rules. Symbolically, he begins from a café in downtown and finishes in a luxurious modern café uptown. In the middle of the game, he says:

As a kid, many people hit me: police, drivers, salespersons, bullies. After they beat me, I had a weird feeling, as if I felt itchy all over my body. I liked that pain. It was like a release from prison ... I was always beaten. I hate myself that I didn't stand against them.[61]

Gheysar, Za'er Mohammad, Ghodrat, and Ebi all deeply feel the pressure of modern life. They are exhausted by the corruption, ignor-ance, marginality, and inequality in the city. They suffer under its rapid and repressive modernization. With the exception of Za'er Mohammad, who lives on the margins of Bushehr, a city south of Iran, they all belong to the urban lower-middle class of southern Tehran, coming from marginalized communities. Although they know the authorities likely will capture them, they nevertheless choose to rebel against the *status quo*. With the except of Za'er Mohammad, they are all captured. These films suggest that if any hope remains for

---

[60] Ibid.

[61] Ebi (Behruz Vosughi), in Fereydun Goleh, *Kandu (The Beehive)* (Tehran: Seyera Film, 1975).

breaking out of the iron cage, it will be found in small cities like Bushehr, not in Tehran.

The Virtuous Poor

With the rapid modernization of Iranian cities, and particularly Tehran, their populations became increasingly divided along lines of class and wealth. Iranian movies represented the poor and the marginalized of the southern neighborhoods of the capital city. These films represented the victims of modernization as people of virtue, clinging to disappearing moral ideals, with urban centers of rural migration bearing a marked similarity to villages and village folk. The cinematic narratives forged a vision of those with closer ties to the country and pre- modern times as more authentic human beings. In many cases, the poor person from the south of the city, or the village, formed the opposite of the *Gharbzadih* (Westernized person).

The first film to embody this tendency was a very popular commercial film made by Siamak Yasemi, *Ganj-e Gharun (Gharun's Treasure,* 1965). The message of this film is that material wealth and power are ultimately empty and illusory. The narrative implicitly indicts modernization and its aspirations. The film suggests that only a simple and honest life has meaning and virtue, making the good life possible. The movie depicts a rich man, Gharun, who had abandoned his wife and son twenty-five years earlier. Now, Gharun, diagnosed as terminally ill, becomes desperate. Disenchanted because of his illness and loneliness, he decides to commit suicide. He states: "Everybody says Gharun owns everything, but I'm deprived of the best things. Unfortunately, it's too late to know that money serves life, not the contrary."[62] Throwing himself off a bridge into a river, he is rescued by a carefree passer-by named Ali. Gharun lives with him and his family for several days and realizes how happy they are in their simple life. Ali tells him: "When a man leads a happy and simple life, he never gets sick, no matter what."[63] Gharun's diabetes and heart disease are connected to a shallow and materialistic lifestyle, focused on accumulation and forgetting the basics of human decency (family, community, and

---

[62] Gharun (Arman Huspian), in Siamak Yasemi, *Ganj-e Gharun (Gharun's Treasure)* (Tehran: Puria Film, 1965).
[63] Ali Bigham (Mohammad 'Ali Fardin), ibid.

friendship). Gharun concedes that his life has been unreal: "I'm not on a diet any more. Their simple life has changed everything. Now I know what real life is. Their simple life is better than ours. Now I enjoy my life."[64] It turns out that Ali is Gharun's real son, whom he had abandoned in infancy. Finally, family reconciliation, in this narrative, is predicated on a renunciation of modern materialistic obsessions and an embrace of simple traditional values.

Films similar to *Ganj-e Gharun* are known as *abgusht* (meat and vegetable soup), and they often have the story end in favor of the lower classes, even when they are filled with provocative and sexualized presentations of women. For example, a trailer for 'Abbas Shabaviz's *Mu Tala'i-ye Shahr-e Ma* (*The Golden Hair of Our City*, 1965) shows a dancer in a modern cabaret and some sexually provocative scenes. Yet the narrator's voice says: "Such parties and dances in the city are traps to deceive and corrupt youth. This movie is a story of self-sacrifice and friendship among the working class, and of their simple lives and happiness."[65] This theme, like the village genre, was first created in pop-culture cinema and then was professionally developed in New Wave cinema. Although the films in New Wave director Shahid Sales' cinema belongs to an entirely different genre in terms of cinematic techniques compared with movies like *Ganj-e Gharun*, they have many similar ideological and social encodings concerning the lower class and poor people. In *Ganj-e Gharun*, the life of poor people is represented through direct narration, depicting real life as an unproblematic flow of simple experience. In Shahid Sales' cinema, by contrast, this type of life is represented with dignity and respect, along with its challenges and pains.

For example, Shahid Sales' *Yek Ettefagh-e Sadeh* (*A Simple Event*) concerns the daily life of a schoolboy living in a small town, Bandar-e Shah, with his alcoholic fisherman father and his critically ill mother. He is forced to help with his father's fish-smuggling business in order to take care of his mother. Falling behind in his studies, the boy has to do homework and extra work during the recess period while the others play. The film contrasts an existence of joyless drudgery with the 2,500th anniversary celebration of the Iranian monarchy, which

---

[64] Gharun (Arman Huspian), ibid.
[65] Narrator, in 'Abbas Shabaviz, *Trailer for Mu Tala'i-ye Shahr-e Ma (The Golden Hair of Our City)* (Tehran: Iran Film, 1965).

occurred in 1971. The characters portray ordinary people in a modernizing state that withholds dignity from its citizens.[66] Shahid Sales' *Tabiat-e Bijan (Still Life)* was his breakthrough film. It sensitively portrays an elderly railway guard and his family living at an isolated rural junction. Focusing on everyday details and nuances, the bleak but poetic depiction of the guard's approaching retirement powerfully affected Iranian and foreign audiences.[67]

Cultural Anxieties and Modernization

Another major theme in Iranian films of this period, both popular and intellectual, concerns the negative and dehumanizing effects of modernization. This cinematic theme depicts Iranian modernization under the Shah as autocratic and state-driven. However, these movies go beyond merely criticizing the modernization process. They construct modern ideas and institutions as alien and materialistic, destroyers of the human and spiritual qualities of life in Iran. An important example of this genre is Mehrju'i's *Dayereh-e Mina (The Cycle)* (1974), based on Sa'edi's story *Ashghalduni (Garbage Dump)*. Although this film won many awards, upon seeing it with his wife the Shah reportedly left their private cinema in a rage, saying: "Why are these intellectuals always only interested in the dark side of the universe? Why do they only represent the darkness of society?"[68]

Critics interpreted *The Cycle* as the condemnation of a society where everyone is forced to eventually become a dealer, selling themselves and others in an ever-increasing cycle of reified relationships. In documentary style, an innocent boy is transformed into a nauseating bloodsucker. Viewers were forced to reevaluate their own roles in modernizing Iranian society.[69] *The Cycle*, in sum, criticizes the evils of urban life. The film's title was inspired by the medieval Persian mystic Hafez (1315–90): "Because of the cycle of the universe, my heart is bleeding," which transplants the theme to sordid modern conditions. In the film, the city and modernization swarm with poor and corrupted people. Opportunists exploit addicts, whose poverty forces them to sell their (infected) blood. A rural youth, Ali, and his

---

[66] Naficy, *A Social History of Iranian Cinema*, Vol. II, p. 394.   [67] Ibid., p. 395.
[68] Abbas Milani, *The Shah* (Toronto: Persian Circle, 2012), pp. 434–435.
[69] Sadr, *Iranian Cinema*, p. 135.

ailing father become involved in the corrupt and insanitary "free-market" blood industry upon arrival at Tehran's main hospital, seeking a cure for the father. Ali meets a worldly and tolerant nurse, and survives by becoming part of the black market working out of the hospital. By the end of the film, Ali has been drawn into the whirlpool of procuring tainted blood for blood banks, and the exploitation of others. The humor, colorful language, lively characters, and good cast mask a darkly pessimistic vision of the tragic costs of unbridled modernization. The film critically depicts the dark side of the national transition to modernity. In a suggestion of the darkness of this experience, much of the action takes place at night, or around dawn or dusk.[70]

Mehrju'i stated his intention was to show "a human society of vultures, dedicating themselves eagerly to engulfing the lives of others." Mehrju'i's frequent collaborator, Gholamhossein Sa'edi (1936–85), wrote the film's screenplay. Although the government's Ministry of Culture funded the film, its release in Iran was postponed owing to objections from the medical establishment. Finally released in 1977, it was instrumental in the foundation of the Iranian Blood Transfusion Organization.[71]

Mehrju'i's 1972 film, *Postchi* (*The Postman*), was another successful movie, reviewed positively in Iran and abroad, wining prizes at festivals and selling well at the box office. It is based on Georg Büchner's play *Woyzeck*. A French critic wrote: "Mehrju'i, director of *The Postman*, is the discovery of this year's Cannes film festival . . . This discovery made us look at Tehran, not because of Nixon's visit, but because of a brave and intellectual director." Another critic in *Le Figaro* wrote: "This is a symbolic movie, and expresses the human situation against imperialism." Yet another reviewer considered *The Postman* a "socio-political movie" that "well represents life in the Third World."[72]

Taghi, a postman, lives with his beautiful young wife in a small rented home. He works as a postman in a small city and as a servant for a landlord. Taghi is impotent. His doctor is a veterinarian who tries to treat him with herbal medicine. Taghi's daily working life symbolizes ceaseless repetition, and his daily lottery-ticket purchase stands for

---

[70] Naficy, *A Social History of Iranian Cinema*, Vol. II, p. 355.

[71] Asian Film Online, "Summary of the Cycle," accessed August 20, 2015, http://asiapacificfilms.com/films/show/327-the-cycle

[72] Quoted in Omid, *History of Iranian Cinema*, p. 617.

the lack of meaning in his life. His alienation from his nonsensical and low-paid work forces him to seek solutions that incur financial debt. Even though he works two jobs, he can barely make ends meet and always is behind in both his life and work. This "behindness" characterizes his semi-modern life. Trapped by fruitless activities, impotence, low-paid jobs, and installment payments, Taghi unsuccessfully seeks luck through the lottery.

The landlord's young nephew, who is a handsome Western-educated engineer, suddenly returns from the West. Known as Mr. Engineer (*Agha-ye Mohandes*), he represents an archetype of Western-educated Iranians recently arrived from Europe or the United States. These people arrogantly feel confident concerning their knowledge of Iran's problems. They dogmatically advance solutions, as epitomized in the new generation of technocrats in the late Pahlavi period with ambitious modernization plans for Iran. The movie in effect portrays the consequences of the modernizing transformation in Iranian society.

Mr. Engineer decides to destroy his uncle's sheep-raising business and establish a modern business: a pig farm. He also rapes Taghi's beautiful wife. In the scene where Taghi decides upon revenge, pointing a gun at his landlord and Mr. Engineer while angrily shouting, his voice is lost under the noise of a bulldozer's destructive advance. It flattens the house. The arrival of the pigs and the rape of Taghi's wife, both explicitly forbidden in traditional religious theory and practice, have violated personal and national honor. Taghi, who is too weak to fight Mr. Engineer, murders his wife and descends into madness. The Western-educated engineer effectively destroys his uncle's home, his farm, and his life. His plans simultaneously ruin the system of work in the village, and its value-systems. In this film, Mehrju'i seems to be warning society of the infectious virus of modernization, capable of killing all animals and humans.

Another critical film in this genre is Ebrahim Golestan's 1972 *Asrer-e Ganj-e Darreh-ye Jenni* (*Secrets of the Jinni Valley Treasure*). A villager, plowing his field with his single cow, discovers a hidden underground treasure trove of gold. He proceeds to purchase random modern stuff (a refrigerator, a heater, a trumpet, a statue, furniture, and a washing machine) and waste the treasure, without any knowledge of the infrastructure required for his purchases to function. According to Naficy, "This waste parodies what the Shah, the government, and the upper classes did with oil, the national treasure. Like some buildings of the time, the one acquired by the villager is phoney and rickety, but its Styrofoam exterior, however, looks like solid marble."[73]

The villager becomes arrogant and rejects his own family. He tells his wife: "You don't fit with my new life. Stay, if you want to, but you have to serve me, and don't expect much."[74]

A schoolteacher becomes an advisor to the newly rich farmer. He gradually is transformed into a sycophantic architect of the farmer's new vision. The inauguration of the new building and the farmer's wedding parody the Shah's 2,500th anniversary celebration of the Iranian monarchy.[75] The speech at the wedding ceremony satirizes the Shah's empty pretensions and his servile relationship with the United States. The advisor announces:

Today we celebrate not only the joyous wedding of our eminent couple, but also the mind-boggling achievements lavished on us coming from the blessed fount of our beloved bridegroom. If our tongue is short of praise, long is the expression of this proudly erect structure that tells with its golden brilliance of the power and the glory, the wealth and the might, the will and the mind of its dearly beloved founder. This structure comes out from the fertile womb of our ancestral traditions to fuse with the latest technologies and aesthetics of the great American masters.[76]

As the celebrants greedily devour the piled-up delicacies, the advisor grandiloquently claims that the new Iranian architecture requires two domes and one minaret. "A brief cut to the erect minaret between two spherical domes, a phallic symbol, delivers the punch line."[77] Mocking the Shah's nationalist language, the advisor connects the obscene construction to the concept of duality in Iranian philosophy (the battle of light and dark, good and evil, and day and night).[78] In the end, an earthquake destroys the entire building, and the people abandon the villager.

Parviz Kimiavi's 1973 *Mogholha* (*The Mongols*) "deals with the theme of the other – Mongols, modernity, technology, and particularly television."[79] The film warns against the dangerous new powers of

[73] Naficy, *A Social History of Iranian Cinema*, Vol. II, p. 380.
[74] Ali (Parvis Sayyad), in Ebrahim Golestan, *Asrar-e Ganj-e Darreh-ye Jenni (Secrets of the Jinni Valley Treasure)* (Tehran: Kargah-e Film-e Golestan, 1972).
[75] Naficy, *A Social History of Iranian Cinema*, Vol. II, p. 380.
[76] Zeynalpur, in Golestan, *Asrar-e Ganj-e Darreh-ye Jenni (Secrets of the Jinni Valley Treasure)*.
[77] Naficy, *A Social History of Iranian Cinema*, Vol. II, p. 381.   [78] Ibid.
[79] Ibid., p. 390.

information. For example, in one scene, a group of Mongols are asleep in a remote desert as the narrator says: "Because of television, cities are so close together. Distance doesn't matter any more. Not just television, all communication media are making cities close together."[80] The narrative creates a parallel between the historic Mongol invasion of Iran and the twentieth-century cinematic and televisual invasion of the country. This surreal juxtaposition is played out through a depiction of the marital woes of an educated modern couple. The man is employed by a television network to supervise the installation of a new microwave tower for television reception in the remote desert town of Zahedan. While on this trip, the invading Mongols of his wife's thesis appear in the desert, linking the current media invasion and the past Mongolian invasion. In some scenes, the Mongols carry television antennas instead of weapons. The film presents criticism through self-reflexive parody. The Mongols, at one point, complain of their dissatisfaction with their filming conditions to the director.[81]

The films discussed in this chapter are based on dichotomous formulas: purity is contrasted with impurity; spirituality with materialism; authenticity with inauthenticity; and characters and narratives depict these opposites. Nostalgically, the premise indicates countryside, tradition, and human community. This premise portrays an antithesis to the city, modernity, and corrupted human relationships. The films do so by two different methods, depicting both negative and positive features. Movies such as *Bolbol-e Mazra'eh, Parastuha beh Laneh Barmigardand, Gav, Bagh-e Sangi*, and *Gharibeh va Meh*, while from different genres and styles of filmmaking, project pure, simple, authentic, spiritual, and organic characters and spaces. They emphasize the danger of losing them. Movies such as *Agha-ye Halu, Postchi, Dayereh-e Mina, Tangsir, Gavaznha, Kandu, Gheysar, Mogholha, Yek Ettefagh-e Sade*, and *Tabiat-e Bijan* pessimistically present the negative consequences of the transition (marginalized and suppressed, or spoiled and corrupted people, and the unnatural and soulless atmosphere), with the city, particularly Tehran, as a symbol of modernization.

---

[80] Parviz Kimiavi, *Mogholha (The Mongols)* (Tehran: Sazman-e Radio va TV Melli-ye Iran, 1973).
[81] Naficy, *A Social History of Iranian Cinema*, Vol. II, p. 391.

Nostalgia is one of the public products that the combination of these cinematic images created. Among the things that such cinematic nostalgia produces are images and plots analogous to the "pastoral" literary and artistic genre. As Raymond Williams suggests in *The Country and the City*, "the pastoral mode" is an ideological construction.[82] He argues that such artistic creations do not represent the reality of rural or urban ways of living. The world they construct cannot, and does not, exist. Yet in the imaginations of "modern" urban artists and intellectual elites who have it all, there is a desire for a more "simple" and "authentic" way of being in the world.

It is sociologically relevant that almost all of these leading filmmakers came from secular, modern, and middle- or upper-middle-class families. They never lived in villages similar to those poeticized in their movies. Many of them were part of the Iranian elite and had studied in Europe or the United States. They were interested in and influenced by Western ideas and artists, or by Iranian intellectuals who were involved in counter-modernity trends. For example, Daryush Mehrju'i, born into a middle-class Tehran family, moved to the United States to study in 1959. Parviz Kimiavi was born in Tehran, and studied photography and film in France. Sohrab Shahid-Sales was born in 1944 into a middle-class Tehran family and left Iran to study in Vienna, and subsequently Paris. Even Ebrahim Golestan, from Shiraz, came from a culturally and economically upper-middle-class family.

Why would artists, intellectuals, and the political elite be so emotionally and intellectually invested in nostalgia for the pastoral life while participating in a massive social and cultural transformation of the country along lines inspired by Western modernization? What explains this apparent contradiction, if not reckless disregard for reality? The idealization seems to correspond to violently changing property relations and to visions of an ordered and happier past contrasted with the disorder of the present. These utopian fantasies form part of the story of Iranian modernity and can be understood only within the context of Iran's modernization project, with its Western currents and, of course, anti-Western tendencies as well. Moreover, these *imagined* utopias concern the real complexities, ironies, and tensions that modernization brings to a society.

---

[82] Williams, *The Country and the City*, p. 46.

5 A Garden between Two Streets:
"Bearing Witness" to "Iranian Modernities"

The soaring oil revenues produced the conditions, good or bad, and offered the chance for Iranian culture to own one of the most precious museums in the world, with collections of rare twentieth-century art. These collections could seldom be seen even at the most prestigious European museums. In the meantime, in the *Museum of Ancient Iran,* they stocked dead and old Iranian objects that no one ever paid much attention to.[1]

Kamran Diba

Modern Iran: Disjuncture or Continuity?

Reza Daneshvar (1946–2015), a left-leaning Iranian novelist, edited the book *A Garden between Two Streets.* Daneshvar left his homeland after the 1978–9 Revolution and lived in Paris until his death in 2015. The book features his conversations with Kamran Diba (1937–), an Iranian architect and designer, who was the founder of the Tehran Museum of Contemporary Art (TMOCA) in 1977. He too left Iran following the revolution and settled in France. Alireza Sami-Azar (1960–), an architect, art historian, and director of the TMOCA during the presidency of Mohammad Khatami (1999–2005), wrote the preface, which traces the ideas of "modernity" and "modern Iran" through the 1960s and 1970s.

Alireza Sami-Azar's preface to this book is very telling. As he was director of the TMOCA under the Islamic Republic, one might expect some version of the Islamist template, with a critical tone toward modernity and Western cultural influence. Instead, we encounter a surprisingly nuanced and even "heretical" vision for a man in his position. Sami-Azar interprets the museum as a symbol of public desire,

---

[1] Reza Daneshvar, ed., *A Garden between Two Streets: 4001 Days in the Life of Kamran Diba, in Conversation with Reza Daneshvar* (Tehran: Bongah Publishers, 2013), p. 49. (The book was originally published in 2010 in Paris.)

affirming a vista of progressive national existence. He implies that the 1978–9 Revolution sought to transform the "symbolism" of the TMOCA, to express a nostalgic and fearful purview on the place of Iran in the modern world. His perspective on the museum and its place in the Islamic Republic therefore seems positively ambivalent:

Nothing can symbolize better than the Tehran Museum of Contemporary Art the desire among Iranians for progress and show the honor of their presence in the modern world. However, this [the TMOCA] was later used as the mark of the return to the past and fear of the modern world.[2]

This expresses a very sharp statement about the shifting historical visions of Iranian modernity, and its disjunctive relationship between past and present. Sami-Azar, all the while, produces the dominant Pahlavi-era "nationalist" narrative of Iranian modernity as the continuous bridge between the ancient Islamic and the contemporary. In this account, the whole of Iran's history is one smooth flow, perhaps with Zoroastrianism as a great achievement and as a prelude to future civilizational summits of which Iran might be proud:

In my thinking on my historical homeland, there are three essential symbols. Each originates from three periods of Iranian history which always appear: *Persepolis*, as the remembrance of ancient Iran; *Naghsh-e Jahan Square*[3] [*Meydan-e Naghsh-e Jahan*], which embodies the splendors of the Islamic period; and the *Tehran Museum of Contemporary Art,* which stands for the longstanding desire of Iranians for cultural rivalry at the world level.[4]

These remarks, with their thinly veiled antinomies and tensions, should surprise anyone who expects to hear the standard "party line" from the elites of Iran's Islamic Republic. Sami-Azar's seemingly "non-ideological" reflections on the TMOCA show the ambivalence felt by some cultural elites in the Islamic Republic toward pre-revolutionary Iran and its cultural policies:

Most of [the TMOCA's] exhibitions, before the Revolution, such as the Pop Art Exhibition, were comparable to European and American exhibitions. In the two decades of post-revolutionary [Iran], we had ideological and revolutionary exhibitions. These had messages of resistance, sacrifice, and the embrace of Islamic values, as well as a traditionalist outlook on art. During

---

[2] Alireza Sami-Azar, "Preface," in *A Garden between Two Streets*, p. 13.
[3] Translatable as "Images of the World Square."   [4] Sami-Azar, "Preface," p. 13.

the wave of change, and the reformist government [of President Khatami], and the desire to join the global [artistic] movements, [the TMOCA] organized exhibitions in conceptual art and English sculpture. And, in more recent times [Ahmadinejad's presidency], we see a return to the more ideological line, and total indifference to global or domestic trends. These experiences in art represent the visions of the dominant cultural outlook, and their resonance in the Museum's space.[5]

The ambivalence of representatives of the Islamic Republic regarding the Pahlavi past is further displayed in the interaction among these three authors. Sami-Azar, in a rather "generous" manner, expresses his admiration for Kamran Diba, a member of the Pahlavi royal family and the founding director of the TMOCA. He presents himself as a "forgiving" and forbearing person: "All that was, has now passed. Presently, and for various reasons, I have a profound admiration for Kamran Diba and his precious legacy. I have expressed my respect for him upon every occasion when I have had the chance."[6]

Sami-Azar, of course, and perhaps intentionally, presents an apolitical stance. His respect for Diba may not sincerely extend to what, in fact, constitutes the man's genuine cultural legacy. After all, according to Diba in the same book, it was Farah Diba and the Shah himself who endowed and supported the TMOCA's original creation. The following may, perhaps, be a certain political statement on Sami-Azar's genuine commitment to the postrevolutionary Iranian order:

There was a tacit agreement that we [Sami-Azar and Diba] did not wish to trade our positions and manage the Museum at another time. We never considered doing so, either during the period when the Museum enjoyed enormous government support [under the Shah], or in the period when art was riding on a national wave [in the postrevolutionary period].[7]

Further than Sami-Azar's preface, the book contains an interview/conversation between Daneshvar and Diba, whose friendliness of tone only equals the deep ideological cleavages, ambiguities, and half-thought political metamorphoses that it reveals.

---

[5] Ibid., p. 14.   [6] Ibid., p. 25.   [7] Ibid., p. 26.

Pahlavi Imaginings of Western Modernity

The Garden between Two Streets provides a revealing vista into Iranian intellectual, artistic, and policy-making connections, through the Shah dynasty to the autocratic Pahlavi regime, and into how these protagonists envisioned modernity and the West. The perspectives of these influential public intellectuals provide three distinct visions of Iranian modernity. Their voices represent the long struggle of Iranians to negotiate their "national place" within the modern world. This chapter examines the close association between the Shah and his wife, who is widely recognized as a modernist, and the founding director of the TMOCA. The public interactions between these powerful elites show the confused ambivalence of the modernizing Pahlavi dynasty in terms of what constitutes the modern, the West, and, indeed, Iranian culture as the target of their ostensibly modernizing intervention. Two observations follow: firstly, that the book's contents reflect the last two decades of Pahlavi rule; secondly, that the "return to tradition" may also represent a guiding ideological notion within the Pahlavi state. This would explain why intellectuals, artists, and politicos associated with Farah Diba seemed to regularly embrace some version of Persian and Islamic cultural tradition.

The Daneshvar–Diba dialogue on the TMOCA recounts the story of its creation and its later chain of predicaments following the Islamic Revolution. The journey of the TMOCA, told from two differing viewpoints, vividly situates a varied landscape of imaginings on the making of modern Iran. It represents the attempt, by notable Iranian public intellectuals, to retrospectively provide a unifying narrative of essential goodness for Iran's national past and its troubling political present, and a certain "resurgence" of its civilizational wonders in the future. Iran is represented as an eternally splendid Garden, and a source of inspiration to these men of the arts. However, the Garden is flanked on each side by Two Streets, whose alien and unfamiliar quality makes them an unpleasantly polluting distraction. These Iranian public intellectuals see their task as to remove the weeds from the beloved Garden. The purifying endeavor, however, is haunted in advance by a grave risk: will it simply lead us, in the final moment, to a dead end? For the two streets, however difficult and disagreeable the journey they offer, may ultimately be the price we pay to even attain the Garden. Without them, the Garden might very well prove to be unreachable.

Secularism and Nativism: An Interlocking Mosaic?

These three public intellectuals (Daneshvar, Diba, and Sami-Azar) present a puzzling ideological mosaic. Daneshvar, from a secular, leftist background, seemingly appreciates Diba's rather conservative and "traditionalist" perspective. Diba presents himself as having a secular inclination, while also embracing many "nativist" ideas. Though influenced by Le Corbusier (1887–1965), a principal pioneer of modern architecture, Diba declares "tradition" an essential component in his work. Diba portrays himself as belonging to the second generation of Western-educated Iranian students, who returned to Iran with their Western education as a cultural souvenir:

We brought back the souvenir of modernism. I don't mean modernism in its twentieth-century physical aspects, but rather in its spiritual aspects and values as they existed in the West ... However, it was insufficient to import foreign techniques and thoughts to Iran. We had to learn from Iranian traditions, and understand our homeland anew, to integrate our traditional life and culture with Western thought.[8]

The TMOCA, accordingly, was stylized as an underground New York Guggenheim Museum. Nelson Rockefeller, after attending the inauguration of the TMOCA, remarked: "the museum is a synthesis, and complementary restaging of the Guggenheim Museum in New York City."[9] However, tradition also defined the TMOCA, with its various elements of traditional Iranian architecture: *hashti* (a space behind the doorway in Iranian houses), *chaharsu* (a crossroads in an Iranian bazaar), *hayat* (yard), *hauwz* (a traditional pool), a wind catcher, and various floral motifs embedded suggestively within the TMOCA's modern design.

Diba designed and built public buildings and places, Shafagh Park in the Yusef Abad neighborhood of Tehran being his first experience of urban planning, in 1969. It provided buildings for cultural activities involving children and young people. His other well-known achievement was Jondishapur University in Ahvaz, which contained a mosque and a cultural activity center. He built other spectacular mosques, including a prayer room in the Carpet Museum, next to the TMOCA in Tehran. Regarding these creations, Diba states: "building the

[8] www.youtube.com/watch?v=6h5wsIh1h_8
[9] Daneshvar, *A Garden between Two Streets*, p. 154.

mosque was a strange thing in my creative work. Since I come from a Tabatab'i family, my unconscious may be inclined to religious buildings."[10] Although Diba wonders aloud why he may have built mosques and prayer rooms during that time, historical reflection clarifies their relevance to the ensemble of his architectural projects, where Islamic and traditional elements were omnipresent. It was perhaps less the mystery of the ancestral unconscious than the influence of an emerging social movement at the time.

Diba recalls that the president of Jondishapur University once requested he build a prayer room in the corner of the university food court. He turned the prayer room into a social location, and potentially a political space. "They asked me to build a prayer room [in the corner of the food court]. I asked them, why merely a room? Let me make a mosque for you! The university president accepted the idea. Of course, the Islamic movement had not yet started then."[11] Diba placed the university mosque in a location where students were daily required to cross the mosque's yard in order to access other university spaces. He proclaimed: "Jondishapur University mosque is a kind of manifesto. It reads, one is required to pass through the mosque's yard to reach the food court. Now, I'm not a religious person. However, there was a social thought behind this planning." Diba's "social thought" aimed to make the mosque available for all. In designing it, he took inspiration from bazaar mosques, whose construction promotes accessibility to every community member. The mosque thereby became integral to communal daily life and blended into the urban texture.[12] In fact, Diba deserves a nomination for the best candidate among architects sought by the future Islamic Republic during these pre-revolutionary decades. The official clerics of the Islamic Republic, on different occasions, had requested that city officials endeavor to ground mosques within public daily life, to integrate mosques into the growing cities.

Diba's nativist ideas are also exemplified by Shushtar New Town, which the Karun agro-industry commissioned him to build. The project, by his own admission, deliberately avoided imitation of classical

---

[10] www.youtube.com/watch?v=FODYoxDk31c Tabataba'i families are allegedly descendants of the second Imam of Shi'a.
[11] Daneshvar, *A Garden between Two Streets*, p. 137.   [12] Ibid.

Western forms. Neither apartments nor houses would be divided into dining-room, living-room, and bedroom. Diba stated:

We believed in larger rooms, that people might choose their lifestyle. If we place a dining-table in a small room, all that remains to do is to place a few chairs around it. In rural life, however, people use so-called "soft furniture," like mattresses or cushions. They place their bed on the floor and then roll it up, or, place their dining cloth on the same floor and sit around it. So, the large room is multifunctional. Our goal was to think in this multifunctional way, and not to imitate Western models for working-class housing. I really don't like those types of small-room apartments. Our planning concept and chosen model was new at the time. It differed from other existing projects.[13]

Diba seemingly built with a precise ideological concept. He said: "Shushtar New Town was among those rare cities to have been built according to Islamic and regional traditions."[14] "One could feel a pure Iranian atmosphere."[15] Unsurprisingly, his Shushtar New Town project won the Agha Khan Award for Architecture in 1986, owing to its Islamic inspiration.

Interestingly, Diba does not consider himself a religious person. He believes, however, that modern life requires its own spirituality, suited to an accelerated urban lifestyle. His reflections are not far from early twentieth-century art movements such as Futurism or Dadaism, which sought mystery and meaning in the unconscious. According to Diba, urban life has its own spiritual needs: "The more intelligent you are, the more you need spirituality." He explains spirituality in these terms: "There is an inherent human inclination to see the most transcendental phenomenon, to create meaning for one's life, to pursue eternal questions on the meaning of life, to meet spiritual needs, and to achieve a pleasure which differs from material and corporeal ones."[16]

Iran's Ideological Triangle

Sami-Azar belonged to the Islamic Republic's cultural elite, while sharing Diba's modern and nationalist sensibilities. In these individuals, three Iranian modernist cultural tendencies are manifested: the secular-autocratic, the leftist cosmopolitan, and the Islamist-pastoral. These three distinctive Iranian modernist visions require historical

---

[13] www.youtube.com/watch?v=FODYoxDk31c   [14] Ibid.
[15] Daneshvar, *A Garden between Two Streets*, p. 211.   [16] Ibid., p. 70.

location within the pre- and postrevolutionary periods. As represented in *A Garden between Two Streets*, their intellectual commonality is highlighted, while their important practical differences are downplayed. These differences are important, but not watertight, for the three modernist streams have also altered and exchanged elements through porous borders. At root, their distinctive and overlapping trajectories have followed the all-too-human struggle to solve the ever-changing problems of modern experience.

Coming from a distinguished family, Diba was Farah Pahlavi's first cousin. He moved to the United States after graduating from high school in Tehran in 1956. His architecture and urban planning studies at Howard University, Washington, DC, earned him a BA in architecture in 1962, before he obtained an MA in sociology. Prior to leaving the United States for Iran in 1965, Diba visited many galleries and museums in New York City and Washington, DC, drawing deep inspiration. He envisioned building similar artistic venues at home in Iran, and duly established DAZ Consulting Architects, Planners, and Engineers in Tehran in 1967. Diba showed his ideological colors in abstaining from building villas for Tehran's rich population, dismissing them as the "new rich bourgeoisie in Tehran." He instead harbored the populist ideal of creating public places, stating that: "for me, not only was villa building for the new rich bourgeoisie class uninteresting, but I didn't even consider it architecture … I was interested in public works; those buildings that belong to public institutions, not personal life."[17] Diba's artistic view, by his own admission, was influenced by Iranian leftist activities from the Mosaddegh oil nationalization era, and by leftist movements he encountered in the United States. He declared his "Leftist political approach to America … I don't feel any inclination for the American rightists." He proclaimed this left-wing solidarity from his luxury mansion in the Malaga hills in southern Spain.[18]

The Queen's New Iranian Modernism

Kamran Diba had the privilege of close personal contact with Queen Farah. As her advisor on art and cultural affairs, he convinced her of Iran's need for a modern museum. Queen Farah, a keen purchaser of

---

[17] Ibid., p. 75.   [18] www.youtube.com/watch?v=jdR03dd0XhE

classic paintings and photos, requested that he undertake plans for the construction of a modern museum in Tehran. Therefore, although Diba designed and built various projects in the cities of Tehran, Ahwaz, Shiraz, and Shushtar, he is best-known for his construction of the Tehran Museum of Contemporary Art (TMOCA), with the support of Queen Farah.

Kamran Diba was the head advisor in compiling a unique collection within the TMOCA. It includes more than 3,000 items of world-famous nineteenth- and twentieth-century paintings, drawings, photos, and sculptures. The collection includes works by artists of the caliber of Monet, Van Gogh, Pissarro, Renoir, Gauguin, Toulouse-Lautrec, Magritte, Mario, and Braque. It includes one of the most valuable Jackson Pollock paintings to be found outside of the United States, and a Pop Art section by Andy Warhol and Lichtenstein. There is a sculpture park featuring original works by Giacometti, Moore, and artists of similarly high standing. The collection was widely judged as the most valuable and comprehensive Western art collection outside of the United States.

The empress appointed Kamran Diba as the first director of the TMOCA. The museum was inaugurated in 1977, only two years prior to the 1978–9 Revolution. The inauguration and public opening was attended by notable guests from Iran and elsewhere, including the Shah, Queen Farah, the full entourage of Iranian ministers and officials, and Nelson Rockefeller (the former vice president of the United States and governor of New York), among others. After almost twelve years of work, from 1965 to 1978, Kamran Diba left Iran before the 1978–9 Revolution for a brief vacation – which lasted the remainder of his life.

Pahlavi Amnesia and the *Gharbzadegi* Roots Discourse

In the congenial conversations between the two exiled Iranians, Daneshvar, a Pahlavi-era dissident writer, makes brief but sharply critical comments about Diba's self-indulgent life experience and 1960s–1970s Iranian cultural life. In one instance, Diba openly boasts about the TMOCA's prestigious international standing: "The international fame enjoyed by the Tehran Museum of Contemporary Arts is, to a large extent, due to its outstanding collections of noteworthy European and American artists. No other contemporary Museum's collection, anywhere outside of Europe and the United States, can compete with the TMOCA."[19]

This reflection leads to a discussion of the reception of the TMOCA by Western media. A number of international journals and intellectuals were highly critical of the initiative. Diba, clearly annoyed by this reaction, points out that certain Western individuals negatively commented on the creation of the TMOCA and its investment strategy, questioning its useful function for the Iranian public. Diba asserts that these Westerners were simply envious of Iran's progress and had difficulty coping with no longer ruling the "colonies." He strongly suspects their criticism of representing pure arrogance and an unwillingness to see so great an institution created in a former subject of Western imperialism like Iran.

Daneshvar, however, is unconvinced by Diba's argument. He suggests that, perhaps, international criticism of the TMOCA project "could have had a [legitimate] political reason too."[20] Diba, reluctant to acknowledge autocratic Pahlavi rule, proceeds to blame Western leftists for excessive negativity. Daneshvar, in his understated manner, retorts: "it was not only them [Western intellectuals], some dissident Iranian intellectuals were also critical [of the TMOCA]."[21] Diba repeats the identical rationale, arguing that Iranian intellectuals were forever seeking something to criticize. They felt, he states, that the TMOCA had no connection with ordinary people's lives, while some Iranian artists were also upset because the museum did not buy their works. Diba then presents a familiar narrative on the time: "The Leftist thinking dominating radical intellectuals created a provincially limited intellectual environment. The source of their thinking was second- and third-rate translations, old Leftist movement [ideas] from before the fall of the Berlin Wall and the Soviet collapse."[22]

Here, Daneshvar, himself a leftist intellectual at that time, gently asks: "Wasn't censorship responsible for this?" Diba only ignores the comment, and they proceed to another matter. Diba believes that the cultural and artistic projects of the 1970s had nothing to do with state propaganda:

It would be a mistake to consider the burgeoning of 1970s Iranian culture as regime propaganda and its political vehicle. Every period has some needs that

---

[19] Daneshvar, *A Garden between Two Streets*, pp. 16–17.   [20] Ibid., p. 157.
[21] Ibid., p. 158.   [22] Ibid.

its progressive people must meet. The Shah didn't participate in the museum programs simply to draw the attention of Western intellectuals. He didn't have any interest in art, or aesthetic values. For the Shah, they were insignificant, as he completely delegated these kinds of responsibilities to his wife. It is irrelevant to link the museum's activities to the political propaganda of the Shah's regime. Indeed, for the Shah, material development, economic progress, and modernization were his obsessions. He never saw Western modernist culture as a political issue. For example, in urban planning, he thought high-rise buildings were a landmark of progress.[23]

Diba proudly explains an important TMOCA initiative to introduce a modern Iranian artform called the *Saghakhaneh* school of art.[24] Diba seems overly concerned with how the Western world perceives his project, asserting that *Saghakhaneh* was responsible for those Western critics who questioned the TMOCA's lack of involvement in modern Iranian art.[25] Daneshvar, looking most unimpressed, delicately offers his own criticism:

Let me explain my question: as we know, [in the 1970s] the question of identity and self-discovery in the Third World was the critical issue of the day. In Iran, this subject appeared in various guises. For example, Jalal Al-e Ahmad, who was previously a Marxist, went on a pilgrimage to Mecca and embraced Islam. Iranian cinema, meanwhile, began featuring religious elements ... Don't you think that the *Saghakhaneh* movement represented a kind of return to religion, and the quest for identity? Or, as Shari'ati put it, *bazgasht be khish* [the return to self]?[26]

Kamran Diba, with typical Pahlavi-era naïveté, seems unaware of much of the discussion that has taken place concerning this period in Iranian history. He therefore dismisses Daneshvar's argument, telling him that the *Saghakhaneh* school of art involved an abstract art, and that the artists involved were not particularly religious.[27]

---

[23] Ibid., p. 145.

[24] The *Saghakhaneh* school of art was "a contemporary art movement in Iran; the appellation was first used in 1962 by Karim Emami [Emāmi; 1930–2005], the art critic, journalist, and lecturer in English at the Tehran College of Decorative Arts [*Honarkada-ye Honarha-ye Taz'ini*]. It was initially applied to the work of artists, both in painting and sculpture, which used already existing elements from votive Shi'ite art in their own modern work." www.iranicaonline.org/art icles/saqqa-kana-ii-school-of-art

[25] Daneshvar, *A Garden between Two Streets*, p. 163.   [26] Ibid., p. 163.

[27] Ibid., p. 166.

One wonders how Diba can be ignorant of this concept of art. All the symbols, icons, and components comprising this school of art were related to, or were reminders of, the martyrs of Karbala and the Imam Hossein uprising. In the very last months of Diba's directorship of the TMOCA, the museum held an exhibition of *Saghakhaneh* works. The 1978–9 Revolution interrupted it. The exhibition catalogue stated: "there is no doubt that the '*Saghakhaneh*' paintings relate back to Housein Zenderudi. The audience, by witnessing his works, recall *Haram* [shrine], Tekyeh [a place of mourning for Imam Hossein], and Hossenieh [the third Shi'a Imam who is the symbol of resistance]. The whole exhibition revolved around *rouzeh* [the mourning ceremony in memory of the third Shi'a Imam], with crying, the lighting of candles, the sound of *salavat* [praise for Mohammad and his family], and *ya Hossein* [praise for Hossein]."[28]

The Wall Dialectic: Seeing through a Stranger's Eyes as Nativist Inspiration?

Diba was seeking an Iranian identity and aspiring to introduce museum visitors to what was happening on the streets. One could connect the quest for identity of people on the streets and the representations of identity in the artwork. Diba, however, had been unable to connect the dots. Diba saw *Saghakhaneh* as an Iranian form of popular art fully comparable to popular art in the United States. According to Diba, "the only difference was that US popular art used industrial symbols like tin cans, Campbell's soup labels, or photos of Marilyn Monroe, while in Iran *Saghakhaneh* used symbols and icons relating to the people's profound beliefs." According to Diba, "US pop art was 'material,' and *Saghakhaneh* was a kind of spiritual pop art."[29]

Diba describes his Iranian work as avant-garde projects, outcomes of his "dialectical" approach. He states:

I personally was seeking a dialectic: tradition, modernism, and their synthesis. In retrospect, I followed a way to be new, modern, and avant-garde. For this purpose, I had a historical conception, perhaps an unconscious one. [In other words], there was a traditional society that we were aware of; a modernism that we appealed to and felt to be necessary; and my work was a synthesis of these two. Because, I believed, I didn't want to cut away

---

[28] Ibid., pp. 164–165.   [29] Ibid., p. 165.

our roots. What were those roots? Those roots were our authentic fatherland and its culture, as I knew them. And particularly within the architectural field. I saw how this was a substantial wealth, and we could take advantage of it. However, I knew that mere tradition alone was a barrier and prevented creativity. Therefore, I was seeking their synthesis.[30]

Kamran Diba undertook the mission of "creating" modern Iranian architecture, and did so within the discursive limits of the dominant intellectual ideology of the Pahlavi era. As with Ehsan Naraghi, or even Jalal Al-e Ahmad, Diba was obsessed with Orientalist images of Iran and notions of the modern West as representing materialism. This template presented Iran as embodying the spiritual, and Diba envisioned modern Iran's future as further extending this East–West dualism:

We neither had Western technology and nor did their buildings accord with our society. Therefore, we had to invent a kind of building suited to our society. I always looked to our ordinary buildings. I mean, the old architecture ... not landmarks like Persepolis or the Mosque of Shah in Isfahan ... For instance, I was very interested in the "wall." The wall does not have any "ostentatious" style. The wall is a kind of hijab, and hijab has always been a reality in our culture.[31]

Diba seems to look at his own country, and its history and culture, with the gaze of a Western outsider. He argues that his life abroad, and resultant long distance from Iranian culture, produced his deepened interest in traditional Iranian cultural components:

When abroad, and far from culture and home, you become so enthusiastic about your homeland. Therefore, when you return home, you start rediscovering everything. And because of your long-term absence from the country, you observe everything objectively. Those things that look dirty and ugly from a local perspective might look different for a newcomer. For instance, I disagreed with an urban project to demolish an old neighborhood around Imam Reza Shrine, in Mashhad. I believed we should preserve that old neighborhood, just repair and clean it ... A local person might think the neighborhood architecture should adopt the Western style. People like me, fresh from abroad, thought our traditional buildings were much better than modern buildings built of glass and aluminum.[32]

---

[30] Ibid., p. 73.　　[31] Ibid., pp. 138–139.　　[32] Ibid., pp. 89–90.

Diba, however, did not spend a very long time in the West. He perhaps fails to realize that, as a member of one of Iran's elite families, it was his own class and social status that divided him, and his lifestyle, from the everyday world of ordinary Iranians. It was less the time spent abroad that permitted the idealization of Iranian popular culture than the perspective from a tower high above the common social reality of Pahlavi Iran.

Revolt against Modernist Superficiality

Diba clearly represented a unique attitude toward modern Iran, which, at times, produced conflict with other Pahlavi officials. One such notable controversy concerned the neighborhood around the Imam Reza Shrine in Mashhad. This instance, in fact, exemplified the larger controversy between the advocates of modernism and nativism. The modernists, headed by the Shah, aspired to show Iran's glorious greatness through constructing high-rise buildings, highways, and urban monuments. The Shah's ambition to build the fifth-largest army in the world exemplified his approach to modernization. The nativists, Farah Pahlavi and her team, included Diba. These individuals sought an alternative modernity, highlighting Iranian "native" identity and its mystic roots. Diba described the modernists as a "superficial modern generation," bent on destroying old and traditional urban neighborhoods, to replace them with soulless modern buildings. While Diba believed that they should preserve the neighborhood's traditional identity, some officials in the government wanted to destroy this "ugly and dirty neighborhood, to replace it with modern boulevards, apartments, and monuments." Diba charged them with having "the worst thoughts and methods, which were long outdated in the West."[33]

Diba proclaims himself the first to have made statues of ordinary people in his urban projects, and to have placed them in parks or on sidewalks. He says, in an ironic way, that "I was the first person to pull down the statues."[34] Diba was certainly genuine in promoting the public representation of ordinary Iranian people. However, he viewed the endeavor as his exclusive prerogative as an artist. At no point did Diba voice any serious interest in having the ordinary people freely express their own views and ideas. It was his terrain of creative

[33] Ibid., p. 150.   [34] www.youtube.com/watch?v=jdR03dd0XhE

freedom, on their behalf. His populism was therefore elitist, within the tradition of imagining an aesthetic idealization of popular mass culture, but without giving voice or empowerment to those individuals it claims to represent.

Pahlavi Mahabharata: A King Fooled by Glass Water into Getting Wet

In the central yard of the museum Diba created a pool filled with raw oil. At the museum's inaugural ceremony, the Shah, who didn't believe that the black substance was raw oil, tried to touch it. Diba, three decades hence, recalls the scene as a political incident. He says: "In retrospect, I think the contamination of the Shah's fingers with black oil was a historical and political metaphor."[35]

Diba and a group of friends decided, in 1967, to establish an Artists' Club for painters, filmmakers, poets, journalists, writers, and intellectuals. They aimed to create a public space for artists and elites to gather, exchange ideas, have fun, and hold gallery exhibitions for young artists. The club quickly gained popularity among Tehran's elites. A European couple living in Tehran at that time wrote:

There was a time when, to obtain Eastern knowledge, and to escape from the materialism of the West, we Westerners would go to India. Once, on our way there, we stopped in Tehran. One surprising discovery for us was the Artists' Club ... This house, or club, or restaurant, or coffeehouse, was a fantastic place. It was a concoction of East and West. Its atmosphere was authentically Iranian, simple and rural. There was no extravagance. Its furniture was like a coffeehouse, but a coffeehouse with modern architecture and a progressive taste.[36]

Diba states: "Our club was both Western and Iranian. A mixture of rural and Western stuff created a unique atmosphere ... There was a kind of Western freedom, within a totally Iranian or traditional atmosphere."[37]

Diba condemned Iran's modernization process for simply promoting consumerism:

---

[35] Daneshvar, *A Garden between Two Streets*, p. 155.   [36] Ibid., pp. 97–98.
[37] Ibid., p. 99.

Iran, as with many developing countries, adopted the Western consumerist lifestyle, with a rising middle class purchasing refrigerators, cars, televisions, Coca-Cola bottles, and other Western consumerist symbols. Unfortunately, the middle class and newly wealthy classes failed to realize the spiritual or artistic aspects of the modern world. At different social levels, superficial imitation of Western models became dominant, as adequate depth was lacking to reach modernity.[38]

The history of the architecture of [the 1970s] exemplifies how new consumerist values contrasted with our traditional culture. For instance, the two-story houses, suitable for introverted patriarchal families, were replaced by impressive villas. Ostentatious display of wealth was considered immoral behavior in traditional Iranian culture, yet prevailed among the newly rich middle class. The architecture of traditional houses, with their modest façades, had avoided the flashiness of power and wealth. It was replaced by the ugly and pretentious buildings of the newly wealthy people of the middle class.[39]

While criticizing superficial modernization and consumerism, Diba attributed the failure of Pahlavi modernization to resistance from traditional culture:

Although the petrodollar produced a new financial level of independence for our country, Iran lacked Western freedom. The appearance of the new-born middle class resembled the Western middle class, but being modern even as a concept faced barriers. Personal and social freedoms prevalent in modern culture met with implicit difficulties in Iran. Given the problems resulting from traditional cultural resistance, the regime could do nothing.[40]

In this situation, Diba decided to build an arts center, in a modern style, to collect and exhibit international and Iranian artwork:

My dream was to build an arts center in Iran, like I had seen in the West ... [When I returned to Iran], I had enough time to think about my dream, and develop it in my mind ... The only person able to make this ambitious plan feasible, to realize its necessity, was Farah Diba. I knew she would believe in the need for this project. In different meetings, we discussed the plan. She welcomed and supported it.[41]

Farah Pahlavi's funding permitted Diba to undertake the project. He recounts:

---

[38] Ibid., p. 131.   [39] Ibid., p. 141.   [40] Ibid.   [41] Ibid., p. 131.

Inspired by museums I had seen in the United States, I designed the museum. The architecture of the Guggenheim Museum in New York [and such other museum buildings as] Fondation Maeght, in Saint-Paul de Vence, were the sources of my inspiration. Because of the budget deficit, I couldn't visit different countries to see differing museum styles from around the world. Therefore, I drew on my personal observations from our past. It led me to our native style of architecture, particularly the Persian rooftops of Yazd and Kashan. Their round, domed rooftops and their wind catchers gave these cities a distinctiveness unlike that of any other city in the world.[42]

From these varied experiences he devised his conception of an Iranian modernist aesthetic for the Pahlavi era. It was intended to embody the duality of East and West: "I wanted to make the museum a real window on Western and Iranian art. I wanted to make the West available to the public . . . The museum had become a fantastic window on the West."[43]

Due to the oil price increase in the 1970s, a staggering amount of economic activity took place in Iran:

The soaring oil revenue produced the conditions, good or bad, offering Iranian culture the chance to own one of the most precious world museums, with collections of rare twentieth-century art. These collections could seldom be seen even at the most prestigious European museums. In the meantime, in the Museum of Ancient Iran, they stocked old and obsolete Iranian objects that no one ever paid much attention to.[44]

The period we are discussing is well-known as the petrodollar period, which was a very important time. The country underwent much material and physical progress. The problem was, the progress failed to accord with other parts of society. Therefore, a gap divided society. It was exemplified in the corruption and lavishness of the system, without any surveillance. I believe that material progress should correlate to spiritual progress.[45]

Diba openly boasted of the TMOCA's international standing: "The international fame enjoyed by the TMOCA is, to a large extent, due to its outstanding collections of noteworthy European and American artists. No other contemporary museum's collection anywhere outside of Europe and the United States can compete with the TMOCA."[46]

Kamran Diba's vision of modern Iran, upon examination, appears a simple version of Pahlavi elite ideology. We insert a caveat: he was

---

[42] Ibid., p. 132.   [43] Ibid., p. 134.   [44] Ibid., p. 49.   [45] Ibid., p. 160.
[46] Ibid., pp. 16–17.

a far more humble and open-minded person than certain contemporaries, such as Ehsan Naraghi or Seyed Hossein Nasr. Strangely, one can argue that Diba was an apolitical version of Jalal Al-e Ahmad and a less religious version of Ali Shari'ati. He deeply believed in Iran's essential difference from the West, or, in his own terms, in tradition and spirituality versus materialism and technology.

From this, several observations follow:

Diba was a member of the Pahlavi state elite and remained close to Queen Farah. Because he was an architect and was involved in the Iranian artistic and cultural community, he felt an inner mission to accomplish what was asked of him. He was not a simple bureaucrat, and nor was he interested in merely accumulating wealth. Viewed in this light, Diba was a good representative of an "enlightened" autocratic state. He sought to represent the ordinary Iranian people and their hopes. Yet he was neither interested in nor even aware of ordinary people's capacity to think and speak for themselves. There was little evidence, in telling his own story, that Diba ever attempted to request the people's participation in any of his projects.

In the above context, Diba substituted the category "tradition" for a lack of popular voices. The "tradition" category, now become a static and fixed image, replaces the unpoliceable plurality of unpredictable mass opinion. Diba appeared to know neither the social nor cultural realities of mainstream Iranian life in the 1960s and 1970s. He did not have any serious knowledge of Iranian history and culture. Many of Diba's simplistic comments in *A Garden between Two Streets* reveal that he was poorly educated in both Iranian and Islamic history, and his power and prestige derived mainly from his close relation with Queen Farah. However, Diba appears to intentionally downplay the significance of this affiliation.

Diba's basis for knowledge is problematic. His education in the United States seems casual and inadequately serious. He studied only architecture, and only up to undergraduate-degree level – and at a low-ranking university. There is little evidence of his involvement in the artistic or academic community in the States. His connections seem to have been developed later, and mostly because the Pahlavi court asked him to purchase substantial art collections.

In Iran, Diba was known for leading several important projects. These included, notably, the TMOCA. He played a role similar to Ehsan Naraghi's in managing these projects. However, he had no serious scholarly or artistic role as an intellectual or as an art historian. Diba was, in a way, a modern aristocrat: many were aware of his high-powered connections, and he knew the powerful very closely and very well.

In all, Diba's desire for the "spiritual" both served his status as a member of the state's cultural elite and provided him with an escape from the reality of modern life, in Iran and the world. What better way for "a good man" to live "a good life" than in the service of an autocratic twentieth-century monarch? The spiritual, or the category of tradition, offers the luxury of making us blind to the material and social inequalities "out there" in the wider social environment. It is almost certainly a shield against the systemic injustice we are ourselves a part of.

6 | *The Shah as a "Modern Mystic"?*

Mohammad Reza Pahlavi affirmed that the eighth Imam (Reza) had saved him from death in his childhood. In his book, *Toward the Great Civilization*, he declared: "The numerous extraordinary events of my life have convinced me that a heavenly force directs my fate (destiny) on the path he has determined. Everything I accomplish is inspired by this force."[1]

Fereydun Hoveyda

The historian of Pahlavi Iran (1921–78) should identify a transitional conjuncture. It discursively hinges upon the division between post–1921 Phalavi first-era nationalism and the onset of Mohammad Reza Shah's moralizing anti-Western attitude in the 1960s–70s. The two Shahs (Reza Shah, 1921–40 and Mohammad Reza Shah, 1940–78) ruled in two distinct social and political contexts: upon seizing power, firstly, Reza Shah ruled in an ideological climate where the *Mashruteh* discourse remained highly prevalent. Many of his supporters were deeply influenced by the secular and modernist promises of the *Mashruteh*. Secondly, however, the succeeding Pahlavi monarch arose in the post–1953 period, just as nativism and a retreat from the *Mashruteh* tradition swelled ideologically. Political discourse revolved around a return to Islamic and Iranian identities. The unifying feature of the two regimes was that, in both cases, the ruling state lacked absolute agency and was subject to ideologies reflecting the need to hegemonically mobilize consensus within broader social contexts.

The major difference between the two Pahlavi nationalist moments, or state ideologies, meanwhile, comprised two complicating elements: firstly, both were deeply influenced by popular ideas and contemporary cultural media. The first Pahlavi nationalism derived inspiration from *Mashruteh* secular modernism, and the second from the *gharbzadegi* discourse and "Spiritual Islam." The two state ideologies were not

---

[1] Fereydun Hoveyda, *The Shah and the Ayatollah: Iranian Mythology and the Islamic Revolution* (New York: Prager, 2003), p. 75.

generated in a vacuum. Secondly, it is mistaken to exaggerate the discontinuity. The second Pahlavi vision retained many of the earlier elements, such as pre-Islamic Iran. These elements, however, took on new meaning in the 1970s.

Starting in the 1960s, the Pahlavi state faced a choice: either to complement its material modernization polices with a slowly increasing political openness and a form of "guided" democratization; or to rely increasingly on the figure of the Shah as a god-like leader. Pahlavi elites chose the second path, a tragic option for the state. To offer a legitimating ideology for an increasingly autocratic monarchical rule and a rapidly modernizing society, they designed an anti-Western and nativist vision of Iran. The tragedy lay in their imagining the primary challenge to the state as leftist and liberal secular forces, and violently undermining them. The most serious challenge came, in fact, from the Islamists. For the new Pahlavi nationalism, it turned out, the *gharbzadegi*-inspired ideology suited radical Islamist insurgency more than the state.

The first Pahlavi Shah's nationalism, emphasizing pre-Islamic Iranian glory, contained racialist elements in proclaimed superiority over Arabs, and a discursively secular sympathy with the modern European outlook. It was, however, hostile to liberal democracy, arguing for its inappropriateness to Iranian conditions at that time. Considering that merely a decade had elapsed since the constitutional era, its secular and modernist ideas persisted in diluted form, influencing the formation of state nationalist ideology.

A range of discursive spaces pervaded the early Pahlavi state within which dissident intellectuals and scholars articulated varying visions. There was, firstly, extreme Persian nationalism and, secondly, secular and even radical ideas. A Marxist thinker, Taghi Arani, found space to publish a journal, *Donya Monthly*, and discussed mostly secular and progressive ideas. The "new" state ideology of the 1960s, by contrast, was more ostentatious, resembling a prophetic proclamation. Meanwhile, in certain respects, it represented a major retreat from the earlier secular nationalism of the first Pahlavi state.

Toward a Great Civilization

Starting in the early 1960s, the second Pahlavi Shah seemed to initiate two apparently contradictory plans: 1) a massive modernization program, including land reform, women's rights, industrialization, etc.; 2) simultaneously, a shift from orthodox Pahlavi nationalism to an Iranian identity politics inspired by an intellectual combination of Henry Corbin's Orientalist worldview and the *gharbzadegi* ideology (two overlapping visions) popularized during this period.[2] On the eve of Iran's Islamic Revolution, the Shah explained the essence of his national modernization scheme, the White Revolution, in these terms: "Our fundamental aim in building Iran's society of today and tomorrow is to promulgate and fortify as much as possible the true meaning of Islam in our society, so that the society of the era of the 'Great Civilization' will be one truly blessed with faith, purity, virtue, and maximum spirituality."[3]

Is this the modernist voice of sober and responsible national development, coldly efficient but productive and far-sighted, "intelligible" to the West, cut short by the impulsive madness of Khomeini's religious fundamentalism? Its content certainly explodes this category, seeming to subvert the predominant historical narrative of the later Pahlavi era. We are thereby urged to rethink our memories in light of evidence, rather than in too-easy catchphrases.

Mohammad Reza Pahlavi wrote *Toward the Great Civilization: A Dream Revisited* one short year before his fall and the 1978–9 Revolution.[4] The book, from its original publication in Persian, was then translated into French by Fereydun Hoveyda and Soheyla Shahkar, and into English by Fouad Rouhani.[5] The Shah's book aimed to lay out his vision of the future for Iran. It was, to be sure, a globalized vision of Iran's future: "The destiny of our country," he maintained, "is vitally connected with world developments." The globalized world is "seething with experiments in quest of new orientations" and waiting for "a new structure to come into being."[6] This opening passage exposes the Shah's declarations on "true Islam" in a different light. A newly politicized Islam, he suggested, perhaps offered the most hopeful political experiment for the modern globalized world. The Shah openly made this case for Iran in his book.

After ruling Iran for thirty-six years, the Shah wanted to offer his vision of the nation's future and its place in the world. The entire

---

[2] The idea of *gharbzadehgi* was popularized by Jalal Al-e Ahmad. However, for him this was a very political notion, and he used it to undermine the Pahlavi vision of modern Iran. The Shah's critique of the West had similar elements to that of Ahmad Fardid's.

[3] Mohammad Reza Pahlavi, *Toward the Great Civilization: A Dream Revisited* (London: Satrap Publishing, 1994), p. 161.

[4] Ibid.   [5] Ibid.   [6] Ibid., p. 37.

national propaganda apparatus was mobilized at the time to promote the Shah's idea of "the Great Civilization." The media, seminars, and symposiums were organized to interpret this new vision and inform Iranians of the originality of the Shah's vision. Many ideas in the book are familiarly routine, propagated by the Shah in the late 1960s and the 1970s. These concern the need for economic development to join the modern world. The "fundamental and universal difficulties" of the time are "population, nutrition, medical care, housing, education and protection of the environment."[7] In this spirit, the book heralds the emergence of a "brilliant materialist civilization." Yet it inserts a moral protest, faulting modern globalization: "moral and social development have not kept pace with science and industry."[8] In 1968, when the Shah gave a commencement speech at Harvard Law School, we glimpse an early instance of his grandiosity, self-importance, and critical attitude toward the West and modernity.[9]

There is strong evidence to suggest that Shojaoddin Shafa wrote the book. Shafa was the head of the Pahlavi national library, and head of the cultural affairs of the royal house. He was one of the senior speech writers for the Shah. It is said that Amir-Abbas Hoveyda, at his trial, mentioned that Shafa wrote the book on behalf of the Shah:

One journalist took advantage of the brief lull in the proceedings, and asked Hoveyda whether he knew who had been the ghost-writer for the Shah's book, *Toward the Great Civilization*. Fighting for his life in front of the Islamic tribunal, Hoveyda raucously whispered, "Don't quote me, but it was written with the help of Shojaoddin Shafa."[10]

Shafa was a translator of European texts, and his writings were highly critical of the Islamic influence in Iran. He glorified ancient and pre-Islamic Iran. *Toward the Great Civilization* contains elements of this glorification. It evokes "light emanating from the Izads, the divine forces of good," the "path to perfection," as an antidote to the "age of barbarism" and an "atomic hell."[11] However, the text is still more critical of the modern West. The book explains the roots of modern ills: "the basic cause" is the

---

[7] Ibid., p. 43.   [8] Ibid., pp. 38–39.
[9] "The Holy Struggle: The Shah of Iran Proposed a Universal Welfare Legion," *Harvard University Alumni Bulletin* (July 1, 1968): 25.
[10] Abbas Milani, *The Persian Sphinx: Amir Abbas Hoveyda and the Riddle of the Iranian Revolution* (Washington, D.C.: Mage Publisher, 2000), 312–13.
[11] Pahlavi, *Toward the Great Civilization*, p. 49.

"unhealthy social and economic conditions in many of the developed societies of today," resulting from the "excessive welfare and comforts of individuals reluctant to sacrifice their private interests for the good of society."[12] This articulates a corporatist discourse, typical of mid twentieth-century criticisms of the corrosive effect of individual rights. It is put in Islamic terms. There is a moral and spiritual theme, embracing what the Shah calls "the spirit and meaning of the real Islam."[13] These ideas were perhaps closer to someone like Henry Corbin or Seyed Hossein Nasr than Shafa. One can see the tension in the book.

Many high officials, the Shah's subordinates, later expressed strong dismay, and even outrage, at his having written this book. Fereydun Hoveyda, the brother of Amir-Abbas Hoveyda (the long-time Iranian prime minster under the Shah), Iran's ambassador to the United Nations, and the book's French translator had very harsh words for it. He ridiculed the Shah's self-grandiosity:

And he [the Shah] emerged from one of his solitary meditations with the idea of *The Great Civilization*, a book which was published a year before the Islamic revolution. The book developed his dream of transforming Iran into "one of the five great industrial powers of the world" before the end of the twentieth century. He ordered that the book become the "Bible" of the one party he created, at the end of 1976, to replace all other tolerated political groups. "Monarchy," he asserted, "is the powerful underpinning of the Great Civilization, and at the same time the guardian of all its values, and its moral and material achievements."[14]

He also pointed out the Shah's tendency to see himself as a spiritual "saint" in communication with divine power:

In his book, *Toward the Great Civilization*, he declared: "The numerous extraordinary events of my life have convinced me that a Heavenly Force directs my fate (destiny) on the path she has determined. Everything I accomplish is inspired by this Force" ... Notwithstanding all these pretensions and claims about contacts with heaven and the Imams, the illegitimacy of monarchy, as stated in the unwritten constitutional law, remained in force. Even the Safavid kings, who had made Shi'ism the official religion of the state, could not curry favor with the clergy, who considered them usurpers, like any other Shah.[15]

---

[12] Ibid., pp. 45–46.　　[13] Ibid., p. 66.
[14] Fereydun Hoveyda, *The Shah and the Ayatollah: Iranian Mythology and the Islamic Revolution* (Prager, 2003), 25.
[15] Ibid.

The book opens, as we saw, with a plea for global development, but with social justice. This is followed by the claim to unique inspiration in the White Revolution, the "planning" of which "was not a sudden or hasty undertaking." It "developed" in the Shah's "mind in the course of many years."[16] It is "in conformity" with the "cultural values which are part of the special heritage of Iran." The challenge is "the devil of technology," and the "lamentable bewilderment" afflicting "the young generation of so many societies of the world." Only the "virtues and values" of Iranian "national identity" and "cultural heritage" can prevent Iran's "younger generation from going astray."[17] The Shah declares the White Revolution the fulfillment of Iran's anti-imperialist struggle: "One of the most important duties which I considered myself bound to fulfill was to eliminate all of the disparities reminiscent of the age of imperialism."[18] Meanwhile, internally, "military strength" is needed to protect the "Revolution" from "intrigues, agitations, and conspiracies by partisans of the feudal regime," or "'red' and 'black' reactionary movements." The White Revolution is threatened by "terrorists or anarchists who serve the policies of foreigners."[19] The "ambitious aspiration" of the Great Civilization, "justified" by Iran's "several thousand-year-old history" and "creative genius," is a "historical necessity." In a highly imaginative maneuver, the 1921 Pahlavi coup d'état is linked to the unfinished workings of an ancient revolution. It began "twenty-five centuries ago," when the "Iranian monarchy inaugurated a new era in the evolution of human civilization." Another "new era" will now "fulfill the needs of our troubled world."[20] The impending "Great Civilization" is the "principle chapter in Iran's history."[21] It combines the "eternal values" of "Aryan civilization" and the "Islamic period," arising from the "first empire" ever to be based on "justice and humanity."[22] Meanwhile, by contrast, the West is in crisis: "The extraordinary material progress and welfare" resulting from "science and technology" have weakened "ancient moral and social values," and individuals are reluctant to "sacrifice themselves to the interests of society." The result is "one-dimensional democracy." The hands of "authority" are "tied" by "party and union maneuvers." There is a surfeit of "kidnappings, extortion, and the use of drugs."[23] The entire

---

[16] Pahlavi, *Toward the Great Civilization*, p. 67.   [17] Ibid., p. 69.
[18] Ibid., p. 112.   [19] Ibid., pp. 118–119.   [20] Ibid., p. 120.   [21] Ibid., p. 123.
[22] Ibid., pp. 125–127.   [23] Ibid., pp. 136–137.

gamut of social problems in Western societies is reduced to a mysterious spiritual malaise, for which Iran holds the solution. It is a transcendental one. The realization of the Great Civilization will require "divine grace," "solidarity," and "unity."[24]

This chapter focuses on developing the discursive shift toward Islamic spirituality in Pahlavi ideology, and on explaining this new Pahlavi nationalism and it elements: 1) a moral critique of Western modernity; 2) an embrace of Islamic mysticism; and 3) a new cultural identity politics, celebrating the Shah as a modern man of the times, mysteriously linked to Iran's most ancient traditions – as if everything has been destined since ancient times, and the violence of the developing Pahlavi state is an inevitable new Islamic mysticism deriving white revivalist heat from Zoroastrianism. This new form of nationalism is traceable to certain prominent figures in the Pahlavi state, such as Seyed Hossein Nasr and Ehsan Naraghi. It also provided a "nativist" and cultural critique of "Western democracy," and was particularly hostile to "liberalism." In this respect, it served the autocratic rule of the Shah. Ultimately, it was channeled by the Islamists, who claimed the same vision in a more extreme way, and for different ends.

A more conventional political-scientific analysis might prefer to pass over the strangely muddled discourse of the Great Civilization, to emphasize the more "serious" ideological continuity between the modernizing post–1921 coup state-making policies of Reza Shah and those of his son, Mohammad Reza Pahlavi. There are, of course, common elements in early and late Pahlavi nationalism. This is especially so in the emphasis on pre-Islamic Iran. However, in the latter version, we see: 1) an emphasis on the unity and continuity of pre- and post-Islamic Iran (this is an idea that Henry Corbin was very keen on and went to great lengths to spread); and 2) a Persian presentation of Islam. Here there was an attempt to make a finer distinction between non-Iranian Islam and "Persian Islam" as a kind of "spiritual Islam." This, too, was a notion regularly trumpeted by Corbin in his works celebrating Iranian mysticism.[25] The Shah writes that, against the "spiritual vacuum," "no ideology can take the place of religious faith."[26] This refers to "culture," which "restrains" the "emergence of a monstrously

---

[24] Ibid., p. 163.
[25] See Henry Corbin, *The Voyage and the Messenger: Iran and Philosophy* (Berkeley, CA: North Atlantic Books, 1998).
[26] Pahlavi, *Toward the Great Civilization*, p. 160.

material society." It must "exclude unhealthy phenomena" produced by uncontrolled "science and technology," "incompatible with our authentic culture."[27]

A superficially unified ideological modernism of the two Pahlavi monarchs might comprise: 1) the Atatürk legacy of "secularism" from the Turkish experience, an authoritarian ontology inspired by Auguste Comte and the French Revolution; 2) the interwar flowering of 1930s one-state party dictatorships, as an efficient alternative to democratic and capitalist "chaos," and a bid for national order based on ideological "organicism," i.e. the vogue for totalitarianism that enraptured the radical right and left at the time, and was used by Western democracies whenever useful in furthering their clandestine ends; 3) a romanticism that imagines a continuous and unbroken stream of legitimate power embedded in "civilization" (Zoroastrianism contains the germ of the Pahlavi spirit).

These three elements were present in the ideological make-up of the later Pahlavi regime of the late 1960s and 1970s. However, the picture is incomplete without the magic. Western history is equated with "cultural colonialism."[28] Iranian civilization, by contrast, is based on "vitality and creativity," and the "epiphany" of "light," the "source of all beauties and energies."[29] While these ideological belongings fit together neatly like a puzzle, therefore, they omit the inchoate and inaccessible eccentricity demonstrated in the Great Civilization – a mire of confusingly entangled ideas and personal vanities that repels the ordered analytic sensibility. A "Heavenly Force" directs the Shah's every action and Iran's fate. He writes that "no development or change can take root" unless it is "in harmony with the Iranian eternal and creative values."[30] The antinomies between Zoroastrianism and Islam, he implies, are resolved in his divinely guided royal person. It is easier to simply pass over in silence the muddled imaginative texture of the document, to identify its more general contents with known universal categories. Yet precisely to do so is to miss the point, for the rambling confessions and delirious visions of Mohammad Reza Shah – suggestive of private madness, as in the contemporary Iranian classic novel *Blind Owl* – are really the intimate but politically revealing reflections of

---

[27] Ibid., p. 159.   [28] Ibid., pp. 130–131.   [29] Ibid., p. 125.
[30] Ibid. *The Blind Owl* (*Buf-e Kur*), by Sadegh Hedayat, is one of the best-known Iranian modern novels.

a wider cultural and social context.[31] The religious imagination articulated in the Great Civilization, despite its eccentric appearance, was one with Iranian society's Fardidian obsession of the 1960s and 1970s – the quest for a modern Iranian identity embedded in a reconstructed Shi'ism that owed more to European counter-Enlightenment discourses than any specific element in an indigenous Iranian tradition. The eccentric and solitary mind of Mohammad Reza Shah, intoxicated by power and self-importance, simply caught this virus and took it for the invention of his own genius.

Mohammad Reza Shah's plight was apiece with a wider social and political pathology of the Quiet Revolution years. Henry Corbin believed himself to be on an eternal mission from God, each moment destined, within an unfathomable machinery of Providence. He did not arrive in Istanbul – it arrived before him, by divine decree, in a drama in which his role was central (the city's millions were divine extras). Fardid felt chosen by fate across a lifetime, embroiled within a cosmic war, which justified all manner of treachery and cunning against those foolish enough to oppose his righteous crusade. These gentlemen, it appears, were no solitary flickers of eccentricity in the otherwise reasonable era of Pahlavi modernization. Mohammad Reza Shah, too, entertained similar notions of personal responsibility for impending spiritual cataclysms, which must transfigure the world in a preordained destiny: "Twenty-five centuries ago the Iranian monarchy, entering the scene of world history, inaugurated a new era in the evolution of human history."[32] The Shah writes: "History has so decreed that from among innumerable generations the present one should witness the dawn of the most brilliant era that this country has known."[33] It seems the Hour of Judgment for the entire world is at hand, and Iran is at the helm in this divinely ordained unfolding.

Modernity today, the Shah explains, reproducing a contemporary trope, has gone awry. The "highest levels of welfare and progress in human history" face "a disunity which may destroy humanity with all its acquisitions."[34] Mohammad Reza Shah establishes himself within the role of a savior: "first sounded by myself . . . I have frequently given such warnings . . . we must join hands to save the world."[35] The Shah's vision combines a spiritual lamentation with a social critique of

[31] Ibid.   [32] Ibid., p. 132.   [33] Ibid., p. 124.   [34] Ibid., p. 48.
[35] Ibid., p. 47.

existing global conditions. It is manifest in "the unhealthy social and economic conditions in many of the developed societies of today." Yet the critique essentially targets collective moral weakness. Western societies enjoy the "disorder" because "they wish to continue to indulge in the excessive welfare and comforts of their present lifestyle," and "individuals are reluctant to sacrifice private interests to the good of society."[36] He contemplates a dichotomous future horizon between "a path to perfection" and "destruction," linked to the "appalling power of all-destroying armaments" which may "[demolish] the solid foundations of the past."[37] Mohammad Reza Shah then proclaims the ancient Iranian worldview as holding the answers to these mysteries: "the point of view of the philosophy of ancient Iran [is] the most prominent manifestation of this great enigma of destiny."[38] He asks of this "destiny," establishing himself within a millennial role, whether "final victory [will] belong to the light emanating from the Izads, the divine forces of good, or to the darkness of Ahriman, the symbol of evil?"[39] *The Great Civilization* proceeds to explain how "evil" the un-Islamic and morally rootless West is, while Iran harbors the torch for a global spiritual resurrection with all modern benefits intact, free of danger.

Mohammad Reza Shah legitimizes his rule through the national construction of a mythic history. He undertakes the construction of Iran's historic past around his royal person as an inevitability: "the White Revolution was a historic necessity," rooted in the "coup d'état of 1921," also "a historic necessity," a "dawn" destined to "coincide with the resurgence of Iran." A "land in ruins" is restored to "a great civilization," a "nation that will never die," based on "everlasting spiritual and intellectual values."[40]

The Shah borrows from the popular *gharbzadegi* political metaphor of disease. The contrasting era of decline is likened to a disease, "up to the end of the First World War," a time of "lost life energy, like a victim of malaria."[41] Iran's constitutional revolutionary time is thereby dismissed as "weak," "unstable," and "chaotic."[42] The period of democratic opening (1941–53), a rare historical opportunity in which democratic and civil society formations took root, is dismissed as "an agitated period of twelve years," "total disorder," "wasted,"

---

[36] Ibid., p. 46. [37] Ibid. [38] Ibid. [39] Ibid., p. 49. [40] Ibid., p. 60.
[41] Ibid., p. 54. [42] Ibid., p. 55.

"distress," "anarchy," and "foreign influence."[43] Mohammad Reza Shah then reveals that the antidote for this disease lay in Islamic revival. He jubilates over "the role of Iran in spreading Islamic civilization" and the "heritage of Iranian civilization [being] inseparable from Islamic civilization."[44] The Shah therefore calls for a "crusade against negative and destructive factors," the "total mobilization of all national possibilities."[45] It is the road of "faith, purity, virtue and maximum spirituality."[46] In these accounts, the Islamic Republic was not original in citing traditional Iranian Shi'ism as the central mobilizing axis in modern Iranian development and state-making. The Shah ideologically predated the political maneuver, to disastrous effect for his modernizing, authoritarian regime.

The Shah, inspired by this fantastic and baseless ideology of mystical deliverance, collided with disaster, just as the Islamic Republic ran into deepening crisis. Objective reality gets its way, in the real world, except in postmodern fantasies where perception is the only reality. Have we perhaps thereby identified these three religious luminaries as portents of the postmodern academic trend to come? Sadly, each of these great dreamers collided with their real futures, most grimly in the violent fall of Mohammad Reza Shah. It is not that their idiosyncratic minds made Iran's political future other than it might have been. The full range of social and historical conditions for a mass revolution were objectively present. To be sure, though, as with Michel Foucault, they saw what they wanted to see, their personal fantasies projected, while also encouraging others to follow suit through their vivid written works.[47] Foucault, having witnessed the Islamic Revolution, rushed back to the boring, secular vacuum of the jaded European swindle, excitedly proclaiming the fulfillment of his anti-modern postmodern prophecy in a new "politics of spirituality." Corbin, convinced that he had found an alternative to Western modernity in Eastern spirituality, wandered distracted in the valleys of his own mind, while tempting eager European students with mystical Eastern promise. Fardid, who sincerely believed that his mystic illuminations of *occidentosis* heralded a new age, was disappointed to see his ideas wielded crudely in Iran's modern political arena. A strange mystical narrative seduced the French post-structuralist, the French

---

[43] Ibid., p. 61.   [44] Ibid., pp. 128–132.   [45] Ibid., p. 166.   [46] Ibid., p. 161.
[47] Ibid.

Orientalist, the Iranian Heideggerian, and the Shah of Iran at the highest level of state power.

Therefore, *The Great Civilization* belongs within the literary canon of Corbin's weird fantasies, Fardid's labyrinthine narcissism, and Foucault's Orientalist utopia as the dreams of a postmodern left made flesh.[48] Each casting himself as the hero of his own movie, they built their narratives upon a counter-Enlightenment tradition of politics. Mohammad Reza Shah blurs the boundaries of human rights discourse to establish, somewhat later in *The Great Civilization*, the new domain of cultural human rights:

If man is man throughout the world, and human rights are the same for all individuals irrespective of race, sex, and nationality, in accordance with all moral and logical criteria, as well as with the Charter of the United Nations, then it follows that the fundamental provisions and principles governing the destiny of all men should also be the same, even though certain other rules and norms have necessarily to be different as decreed by diverse psychological attitudes and other peculiarities of each nation.[49]

As we presently see in the Great Civilization, this caveat undermines the very principle of universal human rights in favor of the cultural right of Iran, destined to rescue the entire world from nihilism, to suppress dissent and to protect a pure identity. This template is not at all original, but a novel twist on a fashionable discourse. Now we are better prepared to understand the Great Civilization and its place within Iran's Quiet Revolution as a discursive conjuncture. *The Great Civilization* is filled with phobias about the dangers of rampant individualism, and, above all, fears of the Iranian left: "Religious fanatics who did not understand the true nature of Islam allied with the Tudeh Party"; "demands for 'authentic parliamentary democracy' were nothing more than demagogy."[50] To legitimize unchecked state power, while systemically crushing dissent, the Shah attempted a bizarre ideology of national religion, identity, and world revival.

The historical context sheds a mundane political light upon this heady ideological adventure. The 1921 point of ideological departure, before it reached its discursive identity shift and violent terminus some decades hence, was the post–World War I crisis. Fear of Bolshevism spreading to India's millions had inspired the British imperial idea of

---

[48] Ibid.   [49] Ibid., p. 48.   [50] Ibid., pp. 170–171.

ousting the Qajar dynasty, to support a new and loyal – and above all militarily powerful – leadership capable of defeating any potential socialist revolution within Iran. This point is worth pondering: total domination at home, to serve the ends of foreign interests, was inscribed in the regime's very identity. In 1921, Colonel Reza Khan, of Iran's British-advised Cossack Brigade, led 3,000 soldiers in a coup. In 1926, Reza crowned himself *shah-an-shah* (king of kings), adopting the pre-Islamic name Pahlavi. Posters on the walls of Tehran reading "I command" epitomized the ideological crudity, rooted in a military worldview. Political strength was based on the army and police. The regime viewed traditional Shi'a influence as impeding economic modernization and the development of a new Iranian middle class. The 1930s saw the state restriction of seminaries and control over religious endowments. More generally, the parliamentary tradition of the Constitutional Revolution was swept under the carpet and dismissed as "chaos." The new road to national regeneration was from above, based on an Orientalist revival of the pre-Islamic Aryan heritage. The new urban middle class – superficially donning the fashionable pose of "Western" cultural superiority – scarcely understood the religious culture of most Iranians, let alone the anguish and terror of their daily lives under an authoritarian developmental machine bolstered by a massive police state.

The father, Reza Khan, nurtured his own delusions, which shows, at any rate, that he must have dreamed. When Europe's rising political star, Hitler, praised him in the Orientalist terms of archetypal myth as the receptacle of a great Aryan heritage, the future of the world, and the graveyard for moribund democracy, he took the bait. Didn't Hitler, to so many, represent the exciting new wave of the future? In 1941, as Reza Shah drifted closer to Hitler's Germany, based on the totalitarian fantasy of a "land of the Aryans," Britain and the Soviet Union conspired to avert the catastrophe of Iranian oil falling into enemy hands. The shah was forced to abdicate in favor of his 20-year-old son, Mohammad Reza, a move favored by Britain, who hoped to thereby secure imperial stability in Iran and India through an obedient, showpiece, "traditional" monarchy. All of this must have meant a turmoil of confusion for the young man, handicapped by the bubble of outrageous elite privilege and personal doubts. Mohammad Reza lacked his bullying father's military charisma and stature, and, tormented by complexes, hoped to win the approval of both the Iranian masses and the world. At all costs, he would be a great man! History was his, a legend freely to sculpt – if only in his mind. This is the typical Jungian fantasy of transformation, unsullied by inconvenient "materialist" considerations. Of course, reality confronted the young royal heir from behind the dreamy veil. And, surprisingly for a developer, Mohammad Reza hated nothing more than "materialism." Only "Religious beliefs," the "essence of the spiritual life of every society," are "a restraining force in preventing the possible emergence of a monstrously material society."[51] Material development must be combined with "spiritual and moral resurrection" in two "harmonious directions."[52] He was not a nihilistic developer, as in the West, but an Islamic one, undertaking a global spiritual revivalism.

If that was the dream, the reality was more complex. Reza Khan's fall had altered the political landscape: the national parliament had revived from years of gory repression, a wide public coalition intently wresting power back from the weakened monarchy. Mohammad Reza grasped that only unilateral military power could offset this expanding "chaos" (i.e. state-independent, self-political organization among Iran's masses). He found his higher calling and justification in an anti-Communist mission against the self-declared independent republics of Kurdistan and Azerbaijan, sending in the army once the Soviets had withdrawn. Everything was his idea, "developed in my mind during many years."[53] And fantasy rushed to meet reality, as it so often does for the powerful, in those self-deluding rhythms that always portend catastrophe. The former Western colonial powers, aided by the United States, did the rest when the 1951 oil nationalization bid, under the Iranian parliament, culminated in a foreign-sponsored coup d'état that restored dictatorial power to the Pahlavi monarchy. It seemed the United States was all too happy to make the young king's dream come true, just like in a fairy tale.

For a man living entirely inside his dreams it is never easy to share – for does that not compromise the purity of his dream? After the coup Mohammad Reza had a freer hand to live as he dreamed, alone, and his new ideological imagination began to flower accordingly, in phantasmagoric directions undreamed of by his stern, military-minded father. The surrounding sycophants helped to build his short-lived dream palace. This was, indeed, no longer the simple ambit of Hitler's racially

[51] Ibid., p. 159.   [52] Ibid., p. 61.   [53] Ibid., p. 67.

fanciful flattery about the Aryan legacy, but an entirely new Orientalist vista inspired by fresh ideological currents within Iranian society and abroad. Eccentric French Christian exiles dreamed of holy destruction of the secular Third Republic, from deep in the spiritual deserts of the Middle East, and embittered Iranian drop-out scholars on the margins embraced Heideggerian fantasies of a new faith in being. Somewhere, in the lonely summits of power, Mohammad Reza drank of the same ideological waters in his own quest for meaning and identity, within the steel gears of monopolized, modern state power.

The 1949 assassination attempt that Mohammad Reza survived did not awaken the dreamer – it fueled a growing paranoid megalomania about a religious fundamentalist-leftist conspiracy ("Religious fanatics who did not understand the true nature of Islam had allied with the Tudeh Party back in the 40s"), and he envisioned his own role as the captain at the helm of a cosmic force for good in the Great Civilization.[54] He had to seize Islam back from its growing leftist inclinations, put it in the service of the modernizing Pahlavi state. This act would redeem not only Iran, but the entire world! He did not shrink from projecting Pahlavi development as an ideal for modern living everywhere: "Why should it not be our aim to strive toward a Great Civilization of tomorrow ... to fulfill the needs of which our troubled world is deeply conscious" in a "great faith, great will power"?[55] It had its ultimate roots in Zoroastrian light but its highest spiritual pinnacle in the "true Islam," while providing a practical harness for global economic development, one harmonious world, without the "misled, malicious, and insane" qualities of the West, the "bewilderment" and "one-dimensional democracy" that come with the "spiritual health" of the "True Faith."[56] Astonishingly, all of it, Mohammad Reza writes, was "my idea," as if man's fate turned on his every thought.

Mohammad Reza's bizarre personal-cum-political fantasy was fully articulated in his 1978 manifesto, *Toward the Great Civilization*. Ostensibly a declaration of political purpose for the beginning of a world-changing historical renaissance centered on his pre-destined person, it was revealed quickly as the Pahlavi swansong and

---

[54] Mohammad Reza Pahlavi, *Toward the Great Civilization*, p. 170.
[55] Ibid., pp. 120–121.   [56] Ibid., pp. 159, 137, 64–65.

a confession of impotent self-delusion. Mohammad Reza tried to portray himself as the defender of Islam and foe of Communism. If political freedom permits citizens to adhere to Communism as a belief system or organizational belonging, then this is a violation of Iranian cultural purity based on alien, Western prejudices. Iran's culture is "the great faith of Islam, whose monotheistic tenets were very close to the ancient Iranian beliefs."[57] By contrast, "Communism is sheer materialism and rejects religious and spiritual principles" and "is foreign to the fundamental values of our culture and civilization," "as a living cell rejects inappropriate foreign bodies."[58] The same is not the case for the West: "the situation is entirely different insofar as Western democracy is concerned."[59] But, as Mohammad Reza Pahlavi had made clear, Western democracy is rotten with nihilism and a threat to the world's future. Iranian democracy is true democracy, ontologically moored in Islam, and the only salvation for the apocalyptic crisis of modernity. In Iran, "freedom will prevail in an atmosphere of order and discipline, not in anarchy and lawlessness."[60]

If Iran's Ulama had been divided between traditional orthodox Ulama, who generally abstained from politics, and a new fundamentalist wave seeking direct control over government, the new Shah tried to placate both – that is, he posed as champion of the orthodox while adopting the ideological tenets of the new fundamentalism. Mohammad Reza Shah Pahlavi conceived a bizarre mix of the growing *gharbzadegi* ideology and Corbin's eternal Iran, believing this might unite all Iranians behind his development scheme.

The Shah began to advocate this mysterious cocktail in the later 1960s and increasingly grew ideologically intoxicated throughout the 1970s. This recherché, modern nationalist ideology-cum-Islamic spiritual revivalism received full articulation in *The Great Civilization*, published by Mohammad Reza Shah Pahlavi in 1978, just on the eve of the Islamic Revolution that destroyed his regime. Whereas posterity often likes to recall a progressively modernizing regime obliterated by a backward traditional revolution, the Shah's bizarre 1978 ideological proclamation reveals a less clear-cut tale. For *The Great Civilization* reveals the Shah within his cloistered, megalomaniacal, and narcissistic imagination, thoroughly implicated in spreading and believing a bizarrely postmodern reconstruction of Iran's history, in which he,

[57] Ibid., p. 132. [58] Ibid., p. 134. [59] Ibid., p. 135. [60] Ibid., p. 148.

from the earliest Zoroastrian origins, is the savior and spiritual captain bent upon reforming the entire corrupted modern world.

Let us analyze the three elements of the Great Civilization:

The *moral critique* of Western modernity runs throughout the Great Civilization, in references to the "bewilderment of members of developed societies of our age," where "technology rules over man, who is its very creator" and "a vacuum is created which no material welfare can ever fill."[61] National life, without the "firm backing" of religion, "leads to a normless and aimless existence." This clearly reproduces the Heideggerian template of modern secular life as nihilism. Mohammad Reza Pahlavi clearly gleaned this motif from ideological circuits receiving attention in the Iranian intellectual milieu of the time. He takes the next step in the well-rehearsed ideological formula, which equally captivated Fardid and Corbin: only *Islamic mysticism* provides the solution to the modern disaster. Thus: "True faith is the greatest guarantee of spiritual health … No ideology can take the place of religious faith."[62] Ideology is human opinion and optional, while only religion is real and ontological. It is a political program: "Large-scale political consciousness will complete education in its fullest sense. Religious faith as the highest embodiment of spirituality will elevate the soul of all citizens."[63] Yet, while including all citizens, it is not a publicly open or democratic vision. Mohammad Reza Pahlavi's Islam is a secret variant that only he fully knows: "The pride and secret of the complete success of our Revolution lie in this very fact that the principles of this Revolution are throughout inspired by the exalted teachings of the religion of Islam."[64] For much of Iranian society – the politically dissenting voices – have lost the true Islam: "the true meaning of Islam has nothing to do with malicious, demagogic or reactionary abuse of its principles." He admonishes: "our own society has been the victim of such manoeuvres repeatedly both in its history and during the present age," embracing "the opposite of the real spirit and meaning of Islam."[65] We are led to believe that he, personally, has somehow recaptured the lost secret of Islam, and is implementing it as a modernizing and spiritual political order.

This is astonishing indeed. The redistribution of large landholdings among sharecroppers, mechanized farming, urban industrial

---

[61] Ibid., p. 159.   [62] Ibid., p. 160.   [63] Ibid., p. 141.   [64] Ibid., p. 160.
[65] Ibid.

construction, irrigation schemes, forced migrations, the erosion of the handicraft market, and the destruction of traditional villages: are these features of the White Revolution truly derived mysteriously from the esoteric teachings of the Holy Qur'an? Mohammad Reza Pahlavi would have us believe so: "Our nation enjoys the great blessing of living under the most progressive and elevated religious principles, namely those of the sacred faith of Islam." It is the key to civilizational evolution: "the highest guide to individuals and societies at every stage of social evolution."[66]

Lastly, the religious mystery driving the successes of the White Revolution – doubling hospital capacity, increased college enrollment, and rising industrial productivity – corresponds to a public politics of protecting *pure identity*. Mohammad Reza Pahlavi proclaims: "We have absorbed the science and technology of the West ... but we will not admit into our society any unhealthy phenomenon that is incompatible with our authentic culture."[67] In a paranoiac motif, Iran's entire history is characterized as a ceaseless struggle to repel Satan's assaults in multiple guises. The nakedly destructive violence of the Mongols has, lately, been converted into the insidious poison that subverts authentic identity – that is, *gharbzadegi*: "while seeking to benefit from Western achievements, we should remain wary and prudent lest its negative and undesirable elements prove dangerous to our society."[68] He writes: "on this occasion Satan had completely changed his tactics because of his previous failures." The new Satanic assault is "an indirect assault on our identity and values by way of generating a gradual decadence."

The "decadence" is the modern period. This commenced "from the beginning of the 19th century and continued for 120 years," with the "target" in "spiritual and moral identity."[69] The source of the Satanic assault lies in Western secular nihilism. Mohammad Reza Pahlavi writes: "where instinctive passions are not curbed by the constraining forces of religion, morals, and culture," "an appalling catastrophe" can "destroy society." It is manifested "today in many developed societies," exemplified in "murder, acts of terror, kidnappings, use of drugs."[70] These derive culturally from Western nihilism, rather than sociologically from the violent development process as such. Disruptive

---

[66] Ibid.   [67] Ibid., p. 159.   [68] Ibid., p. 133.   [69] Ibid., p. 134.
[70] Ibid., p. 137.

politics within Iran are "Westoxificated": "anarchists, nihilists, and other extremist groups are products of the developed world." We are thereby meant to believe no basis for political discontent exists within Iran. Nihilism is the root of political agitation: the "declared aim of these people to destroy sound social values." Westoxificated dissident activity represents impending doom: "History proves that if the moral and cultural substructure of a civilization becomes its material veneer … it will be unable to prevent the collapse of the whole structure."[71]

In using this bizarre discursive mosaic to legitimize authoritarian rule, the Shah must harshly condemn liberalism and Western culture as, at best, alien to Iranian culture, and, at worst, invasive and corrupting. In the West "there exists only a one-dimensional democracy."[72] It is characterized by an "excess of intelligence and individualism," and "criticism" over the "spirit of patriotism."[73] By contrast, no "foreign ideology has affected the planning of [White Revolutionary] principles," for "the originality of Iranian thought suffices."[74] This is an incredible statement, considering the role of the British in bringing to power the Pahlavi dictatorship in the early 1920s.

Yet the Shah insists that the regime is culturally pure. Through "conformity to cultural values which are part of the special heritage of Iran," the country could "benefit from the material advantages of modern life without selling our soul to the devil of technology" and "falling into that trap of lamentable bewilderment that afflicts many of the young generations of so many societies of the world." It is a matter of loyalty to "our national identity, our spiritual resources, and our cultural heritage."[75] This is how Iranian "democracy" supposedly differs from the Western variant: "In our democracy, complete individual freedom coexists with complete social order and discipline, for it is not a democracy of anarchy." The Shah warns that "acts calculated to obstruct or impede the progress of the country's affairs will not be tolerated or excused." Such individuals are the "misled, malicious, or insane, a type existing in many developed countries." They use "certain incredible ideologies such as Islamic Marxism," an "impossibility," to pursue "retrograde activities."[76] They are ignorant of "the spirit and meaning of the real Islam."[77]

[71] Ibid., pp. 136–138.   [72] Ibid., p. 137.   [73] Ibid., pp. 129–130.
[74] Ibid., p. 63.   [75] Ibid., p. 69.   [76] Ibid., pp. 64–65.   [77] Ibid., p. 66.

Mohammad Reza Pahlavi's use of Corbin is a dualist template. There is Corbin's "eternal Iran," fusing Zoroastrian light and Shi'a Islam into a single Iranian essence: "the Great Civilization of Iran draws its substance ... from the depths of the country's history and culture" over "thousands of years."[78] The White Revolution has been "successful because it has supported Iran's eternal values": "Iranian civilization" is based on the "centrality of light," "vitality and creativity," "historical manifestation of Aryan civilization (what Hegel called the 'real origin of world civilization')." This cultural paradigm "permits individuals to distinguish between beauty and ugliness, between purity and impurity."[79] Moreover, "in the age of antiquity, but also in the Islamic period, is the same human mission."[80] The cultural paradigm settles many existential questions and permits of no dissent or independent thought. It is exactly as jovial Corbin dreamed of for France, that it may be freed from the wicked curse of secular pluralism that guides away from the monolithic truth of spiritual salvation.

We don't know if the Shah knew Fardid or not. Both Shah and Fardid, we do know, were influenced by a similar cultural situation, and they expressed very similar ideological ideas. Mohammad Reza Pahlavi, like Fardid, urges that Iran "avoid the moral depredations that result from adopting Western patterns in their totality."[81] In scholarship on the Pahlavi period, very often the anti-modern and anti-Western tendencies of late Pahlavi nationalism have been overlooked. The anti-Communist hysteria, the grounds for condemning Western democracy as too permissive, are not grasped in their full magnitude as a declaration of Iranian spiritual otherness to Western materialism as post-Enlightenment society as such. Yet the Pahlavi monarch argues that Iran has endured a long period of materialist decline, contaminated by a Western sickness, despite a glorious heritage as the spiritual center of world civilization.

At the general level, there is a blurring of identity politics and a utopian ideology of global renewal. The revival of Iran's heritage depends upon the protection and purification of a mystical Islamic identity which provides answers to the many problems of the modern world, including "population, medical care, housing, education and protection of the environment."[82] The "situation of the world" is

---

[78] Ibid., p. 123.   [79] Ibid., p. 125.   [80] Ibid., p. 126.   [81] Ibid., p. 139.
[82] Ibid., p. 43.

"disorders and disruptions."[83] Freedom is a scourge, for, owing to "public indulgence in a life of material comfort," while "knowledge, thought, art, [and] literature [have] flowered," the "moral substructure which produced all [has] disappeared."[84] Only the Pahlavi regime, we are meant to believe, will "harmonize" the "traditions and environment with the scientific and technical progress of the world," based on an authoritarian development scheme, for "our Sacred Book highly praises work as a sacred occupation of human beings."[85]

---

[83] Ibid., p. 47.   [84] Ibid., p. 138.   [85] Ibid., p. 141.

7 | The Imaginary Invention of a Nation:
Iran in the 1930s and 1970s

Any given society in any given time is produced by the continuously combined, interacting activity of reason and imagination. However, the history of the past is usually presented as a rational or, at least, a rationalized process, which excludes the participation of imagination. Imagination is the privilege of poets, artists and prophets; it creates images, parables, symbols to add an aesthetic dimension to the realities of human existence, or to show a transcendent truth beyond the ordinary explanations of reason.[1]

Mohammed Arkoun

Nation-making is a complex and multilayered process. While a material and institutional process, it is also a creative enterprise. The material and creative process of nation-making has frequently produced conceptual confusion. For some, the nation is a "natural" entity, or permanently existing phenomenon. For others, it is a historically produced creation of collective desires and imaginings. Nation-making, in this account, is a creative enterprise while also being a material and institutional building process.[2] A very intimate connection links the nation as it exists materially and the mode of its representation. Our only access to nations is through our ways of writing about them and producing them in images, which conditions our modes of reflecting upon them. There is also the emotive effect of music. We can only hope that, in thinking about our nation, our basis exceeds mere projected hopes and desires. This is a difficult thing to demonstrate with certainty.[3]

---

[1] Mohammed Arkoun, "Islamic Culture, Modernity, Architecture" in *Architectural Education in the Islamic World*, ed. Ahmet Evin (Singapore: Concept Media/Aga Khan Award for Architecture, 1986), p. 20.

[2] The idea that nations are an exclusively modern construction is also subject to debate.

[3] The debate on the notion of the "social imaginary" centers around works by Cornelius Castoriadis, *The Imaginary Institution of Society* (Cambridge, MA:

This is not to suggest that any citizen of any given nation may arbitrarily produce, from sheer desire, a representation of their nation and national identity. As Mohammed Arkoun puts it: "the 'imaginary' of an individual, a social group, or a nation is the collection of images carried by that culture about itself or another culture – once a product of epic poetry and religious discourse, today a product primarily of the media and secondarily of the schools."[4]

Charles Taylor, the Canadian philosopher, continues Arkoun's line of argument. However, he places more emphasis on the social imaginary as a "popular" category, or a popularly created and publicly accepted mode of knowing one's nation:

A social imaginary is (i) a way ordinary people imagine their social surroundings; it is not a social theory because it is carried in images, stories and legends rather than theoretical formulations. At any point in time, a social imaginary is (ii) complex, involving both how things are and how things ought to be. It is shared by large groups of people, if not the whole society. A social imaginary refers to (iii) a culture's wide-angle and deep background of understanding that makes possible common practices, unarticulated understandings and relevant sense-giving features.[5]

Arkoun and Taylor's related insights are in the social fact of a many-sided struggle to define "social imaginaries." The grave reality of this struggle affects collective power, through the mobilization of populations – with serious political and cultural consequences. The process results in winners and losers, where material and cultural – indeed, even existential – resources may be gained or lost by certain population groups (i.e. ethnic, religious, or status). The public struggle over a defining national imaginary is far more profound than casual reflection might suggest.

The dominant social imaginary, residing at an unconscious but powerful level, shapes the competing discourses to which individuals and communities subscribe consciously. The losers in the struggle over a national imaginary endure great hardship and prolonged suffering in seeking to recover the existential security undergirding intellectual and

MIT University Press, 1987) and Charles Taylor, *Modern Social Imaginaries* (Durham, NC: Duke University Press, 2004).
[4] Mohammed Arkoun, *Rethinking Islam: Common Questions, Uncommon Answers* (Boulder, CO: Westview Press, 1994), p. 6.
[5] Charles Taylor, *A Secular Age* (Cambridge, MA: Belknap Press, 2007), p. 171.

moral confidence. There is, moreover, a great risk of the social imaginary becoming normalized, as if nature and culture were one, in the historical course of societal development. This is the case of the Dalits in India, who have invested tremendous energy in struggling to change a deeply naturalized social imaginary based on caste. It is a mistake to underemphasize the critical role of the elite, both cultural and political, in the production of distinctively shaped social imaginaries.

It is important to differentiate, from the outset, the "social imaginary" from the idea of "intuitive reason" in Ahmed Fardid's thought, or the similar "imaginal" in Henry Corbin's philosophy. Both Fardid and Corbin clearly distinguish between human "reason," associated with historical and empirical realities, and a mysterious transcendental intuition. They privilege the latter (*elm-e baten*, as Corban calls it). This concept of "intuition" has its intellectual roots in Henri Bergson's distinction between quality and quantity, and the demotion of modern science in favor of the lived experience of existential "truth." In the Iranian context, Fardid subsequently invested it with a Heideggerian pathos, charging the modern world with the annihilation of authentic collective meaning (i.e. culture). The "imaginary," here, stands for a cultural revolt against modern instrumentality (science, development, reason, etc.).

The "social imaginary" is, by contrast, precisely a sociological category. Its function is to elucidate social and historical processes rationally, i.e. to demystify the ideological cloaking of power hierarchies.

In the struggle over constructing the modern Iranian social imaginary, this chapter discusses two focal periods in modern Iranian history. It depicts two key intellectual debates, each embodying the broader ruptures in the "social imaginary" of modern Iranian history. These "debates" both concern the relationship between the religious and secular understanding of the world and Iran:

1) a 1930s debate on the legacy of the French philosopher Henri Bergson as a pretext for a radicalized and innovative discussion of Persian *erfan* and Islamic mysticism
2) the "ideological debates" on how to either "reconcile" or reject Marxism with respect to Islamic and Iranian traditions. This took place in the period immediately following the 1978–9 Revolution.

The postrevolutionary discourse about Iran provides a typical illustration of the social "imaginary," as generated over the four decades following the founding of the Islamic Republic. Upon historical reflection, in endeavoring to grasp how Iran has been "imagined" in modern times, we happen upon a broader perspective on the Iranian production of a distinctive "social imaginary." This broader vista reveals how the "imaginative" construction of modern Iran has exceeded merely a space for poetic or literary inspiration. The history of modern Iran is, simultaneously, a historic battle of competing social and cultural visions for imagining Iran's past and determining the nation's future.

Two Debates on *Erfan* and Secularism

This chapter will focus on a specific "imaginary" shift in constructing Iran as a contemporary nation. One can argue that two important debates represent the shift from one complex of ideas about Iran to a different one: 1) a 1930s scholarly debate on Persian *erfan* and the French philosopher Henri Bergson; and 2) the "ideological" public debate on reconciling Islam and Marxism in the late 1970s. This study examines a clear shift, from a modern and cosmopolitan vision of Iran in the post–*Mashruteh* period to a new national social imaginary, defined by religious identity and national tradition. This shift was a more unified and national narrative, re-envisioning the Iranian nation and shared by a substantial Iranian majority. It crossed political and cultural ideologies, and multiple sensibilities, including secular and religious oppositional currents, and the ruling elites themselves. I will also discuss the emerging national imaginary, from the postrevolutionary worldview, grounded in the idea of *bazgasht be khishtan* (return to roots) and *gharbzadegi* (Westoxification). This underwent a shift toward an open-ended pragmatic politics embodied in the ideas of *azadi* (liberty) and *jame'eh-e madani* (civil society).

The Post–*Mashruteh* Period (1930s)

The post–*Mashruteh* period was a critical interval in the evolution of Iranian modernity. Its dominant political and intellectual discourse was modernist. The disagreements centered around adopting various versions of modern ideologies and policy options for Iran. Ultimately, the autocratic vision of modernity prevailed, and the liberals – following a substantial struggle – lost the ideological and political battle, as the founder of the Pahlavi state gained ascendency with his followers.

During Reza Shah's reign, two intellectual groups were marginalized: 1) the anti-constitutionalists, who were defeated in the aftermath of the revolution (1906–11), and 2) the radicals and liberals, who opposed the new monarchy. However, their ideas, and political and cultural sensibilities, continued to ignite upon every possible occasion. The reason for the return to the debate on *erfan* was the sudden fame of the French philosopher Henri Bergson. Here was an educated and celebrated European philosopher who possessed "modern" and Western credentials but who was critical of the modern vision of the world and seemed deeply sympathetic to hitherto disparaged Persian ways of thinking.

The debate on "Bergson," in Iran, symbolically concerned broader issues. More than anything else, it reflected the attempt to articulate the possible role of religion in the nation-making context of modern Iran. Four principle scholars approached the Bergson and *erfan* Nazari problematic: Taghi Arani, Gholamreza Rashid-Yasemi, Mohammad Ali Foroughi, and Ahmad Fardid. Although voicing distinct perspectives, they shared core assumptions and sensibilities. Their interest was in crafting or introducing new ideas, to the end of improving Iranian society. This holds true also of Ahmad Fardid, the only scholar among the four who was highly critical of modern Western thought. He embraced intuitive thought as superior to rational and modern thought. Fardid cared little for orthodox Islam or the Ulama. His interest in "theoretical *erfan*" was a path-breaking innovation, and far from a faithful reproduction of tradition.

1 For Arani, the critical issue was a radical critique of metaphysics, and the viability of materialist and scientific thinking. He was certainly a progressive leftist, and openly advocated a more global and cosmopolitan vision for Iran.

2 Although Rashid-Yasemi's letter on Bergson is poorly presented, it clarifies his vision for the future of Iran. This vision comprises the following elements: 1) the Iranian nation will survive only if it follows the path of *tajaddod* (modernity); 2) a futuristic mode of thought and an embrace of social change; 3) a striving to clarify how, in Europe, the thinkers who praise Iranian mysticism also favor modern and progressive change.

3 Foroughi presents perhaps the most nuanced and, also, conceptually fragile view: 1) he clearly understands that a well-known French philosopher is changing the most important features of modern

thought, and this can be potentially attractive for Iranians; 2) he aspires to distinguish Bergsonian intuitive thinking from that of Islamic mysticism. He departs, meanwhile, both from Arani (over blatant materialism – he calls for the reconciliation of reason and intuition) and Rashid-Yasemi (he is too fair to totally deny the common ideas uniting Bergson and *erfan*).

4. Fardid is the oppositional figure among the four, and, in his militant way, he wholeheartedly embraces Bergson, seeing in him the "fated" continuation of Persian and Islamic mystical tradition.

1 Taghi Arani

Taghi Arani (1903–40), Iran's leading contemporary Marxist intellectual, published the first Iranian account of Bergson's philosophy, as related to Islamic *erfan* (gnosis, mysticism), in 1933.[6] Gholamreza Rashid-Yasemi (1896–1951), a highly regarded and prolific scholar of Iranian and Islamic history and literature, delivered a lecture on Bergson and *erfan* at the Department of Theology, Tehran University, in 1935.[7] Fardid's two articles followed shortly thereafter, in 1938. Mohammad Ali Forughi (1877–1942), an eminent thinker and politician (the prime minister under Reza Shah, and, subsequently, under Mohammad Reza Shah), also published on Bergson's philosophy, in 1938.[8] Fardid was not alone, then, in his preoccupation with the Bergson–*erfan* link as a defining problematic of the modern Iranian nation-making context.

Firstly, let us consider the problematic from a Marxist angle. Arani's critique of Bergson's "spiritualism," in essays published in his Marxist-leaning journal *Donya*,[9] criticized *erfan* from a materialist and

---

[6] Taghi Arani, "Mysticism and Principles of Materialism" in *Writings and Articles of Dr. Arani* (Cologne: Pahl-Rugenstein Verlag, [1933] 1977).

[7] This lecture by Gholamreza Rashid-Yasemi was published as "Falsafe-ye Bergson [Bergson's Philosophy]" in *Ta'lim va Tarbiat Magazine* (Mehr va Aban 1314/September and October 1935).

[8] Fardid notes in his Bergson article that, as far as he knows, only one other article has been published in Iran about Bergson. This is Gholamreza Rashid-Yasemi's "Bergson's Philosophy" (see previous note).

[9] Arani founded *Donya* with the help of other leftist intellectuals (Bozorg Alavi and Iraj Eskandari), and this journal represented the first Marxist publication in Iran. *Donya* was banned by the government after publishing just twelve issues. Later, in 1940, the journal was again published, as the intellectual mouthpiece of the Tudeh Party of Iran.

progressive outlook.[10] Arani's materialism, however, was crude and one-dimensional: "We can only think by using our brain. We know from experience that if the material environment (light, temperature, humidity, etc.) is changed, the constitution and function of living species is transformed accordingly."[11]

Arani relegates ideas and culture to an inferior level, mere by-products, governed by economic relations: "A person in two different settings, in a ghetto or in a palace, thinks differently."[12] His materialist understanding of *erfan* requires a political economy-based inquiry. This establishes the social conditions of its conceptual origin, which permit "mysticism" to survive. Exploring Sufi and mystic poems as valuable in themselves is pointless.[13] Arani's analysis is more nuanced than this reductive premise. He provides a nearly psychological account of "mysticism." Certain habits and attitudes – including laziness, asceticism, infatuation with hallucinatory substances, and superstitious belief – are all aspects of "mystical" rituals, worldviews, and practices. For Arani, these impede a modern and vital Iranian society. Mysticism, a complex ideological system of values and practices, shapes human experience.

Arani is openly critical of *erfan*. For him as a progressive Marxist, committed to modern social change and technological advancement, mysticism is a "backward" worldview. His article "Mysticism and Principles of Materialism" is a comparative materialist analysis of various philosophical and religious traditions: ancient Greek, Chinese, and Indian traditions, as well as Islamic, Christian, and modern European histories. Initially distinguishing between materialism and idealism, he examines the social conditions producing "mystical" and "non-rational" thought, influenced by the Marxist view of religion. *Erfan* is an ideological mask for the ruling class, concealing worldly domination, and a popular consolation, instilling hope for a happy afterlife.

After discussing ancient Greek and medieval mysticism, Arani addresses Bergson's philosophy. Bergson symbolizes twentieth-century "spiritualism" and the modern face of *erfan*. This requires attention in order to understand the new twentieth-century mysticism:

[10] Arani's essays were later published in a collection of his works as a separate book.

[11] Arani, "Mysticism and Principles of Materialism," p. 94.   [12] Ibid.

[13] Ibid., p. 95.

"Bergson's core belief is that mysticism has advanced from the '*khom-reh neshini*' [drinking parties] of Greek philosophy, and the hashish-smoking of Indian Sufis, into Christian mysticism as the highest form of progress."[14] Arani criticizes Bergson's later book, *The Two Sources of Morality and Religion*, disturbed by its "spiritual" beliefs: "Bergson, in his book, *The Two Sources of Morality and Religion*, advocates a kind of 'spiritualism' which he calls *élan* [this is a reference to Bergson's notion of vital impulse], and he considers Plotinus[15] the earliest phase of mysticism."[16] He sees an intimacy between belief in the "unseen," or Bergson's *élan*, and Sufi practice: "Sufis use cannabis, opium, and *dugh-e vahdat* [a yogurt drink mixed with hashish] because they find it permissible and necessary for creating '*jazabeh*' [a mystical stage for seeking the divine truth]."[17] Bergson's philosophy is idealist, the contrary of materialism, which, for Arani, is the proper worldview: "Bergson, as with all other 'mystics,' believes in the pre-determination of morality. However, 'the predestined determinism,' which is the basis of their argument, has a biological cause, meaning that it is ingrained in the soul itself."[18] Arani, therefore, dismisses Bergson's philosophy as an unfounded belief in the "magical" power of the "unseen": "In the second chapter [of *The Two Sources of Morality and Religion*], the author aims to depict logical analysis as false, and he has a fantastic faculty for intuitively sensing the truth."[19] Ultimately, Arani concludes, in Bergson's philosophy, material and social structures are of little consequence: "Bergson's conclusion is clear. His goal is to maintain that spirit transcends the social, and, therefore, we must liberate it from the human social condition."[20]

To be sure, Bergson was a pioneering voice in the broad twentieth-century distinction between consciousness as lived experience and the objective order of scientific investigation. Arani simplified Bergson's intervention, yet rightly recognized the mysticism in Bergson's ground-breaking philosophy. By linking this mystical tendency to comparable traditions in Iranian and Islamic Sufism, he opened the Bergson–*erfan*

---

[14] Ibid., p. 133.

[15] Plotinus (204/5–270 CE) was a major philosopher of the ancient world and is regarded as the founder of Neo-Platonism. He considered himself part of the Platonic tradition, and his philosophy has inspired centuries of Christian, as well as Jewish and Islamic, thought, particularly in the traditions of gnosticism and mysticism.

[16] Arani, "Mysticism and Principles of Materialism," p. 110.   [17] Ibid., p. 101.

[18] Ibid., p. 133.   [19] Ibid.   [20] Ibid.

problematic. This engendered a struggle within the "social imagination" over the meaning of Iranian modernity.

2 Gholamreza Rashid-Yasemi

Gholamreza Rashid-Yasemi (1896–1951) lectured on the same problematic, at the Department of Theology, Tehran University, in 1935.[21] The most likely Iranian candidate for a "modernist" approach to Bergson's philosophy was his subsequent presentation.[22] He highlighted Bergson's philosophy for its policy implications, and, specifically, for the modernization process currently underway under the first Pahlavi Shah:

His majesty the Shah [Reza Shah], the great leader of Iran, in his celebrated address to Parliament, contended that the success of the Iranian nation depends upon diligence and hard work, and that our [development] program should, in name and purpose, be about work. His [Reza Shah's] honored existence has fulfilled this objective. And he is devoting every moment of his life to the advancement of this doctrine, offering the nation a marvelous role model. Therefore, an extraordinary similarity exists between his majesty's actions and executive instructions, and Bergson's ideas.[23]

Rashid-Yasemi's lecture summarizes Bergson's works in detail, discussing *Time and Free Will, Matter and Memory, Two Sources of Morality and Religion,* and *Creative Evolution.* He presents Bergson's philosophy as dynamic and futuristic. The multifaceted relations uniting Bergson's ideas on vitality, free will, consciousness, and religion are presented in their complexity. Yet there is little discussion of Bergson's critical comments on modern rationalism, or on the limits of human intelligence. Nor is there discussion of Bergson's interest in "mystical"

---

[21] Rashid-Yasemi, "Bergson's Philosophy."
[22] Gholamreza Rashid-Yasemi (1895–1951) was a literary scholar, and a translator of Western texts on the history and culture of Iran. He studied at a European high school in Tehran (St. Louis School, which was French-language, and the first Catholic mission school in Tehran). Rashid-Yasemi was an advocate of modernist reform in the Iranian literary tradition. He edited several important classical texts in Persian and was a leading literary figure of the 1930s and 1940s in Iran.
[23] Rashid-Yasemi, "Bergson's Philosophy," 335.

ideas. Rashid-Yasemi ignores possible similarities between Bergson's view on knowledge and the Persian or Islamic "mystical" tradition.[24]

Rashid-Yasemi's discussion of *Time and Free Will* deserves attention.[25] He cites Bergson's dissatisfaction with Hebert Spenser's limited view of time as the basis for his new approach to the subject, which offers a fresh and dynamic interpretation of time and consciousness. Rashid-Yasemi presents Bergson's philosophy of time as consistent with his own modernist beliefs, while understating Bergson's critical view of modern philosophy. He avoids references to Bergson's interest in religion or mysticism. According to Rashid-Yasemi, Bergson argues that "truth" is a fluid and a constantly changing process: "if philosophy is to make headway, it must be based on this [dynamic nature of truth]. An example of the fluidity of the truth is present in our souls, which sparks, and is constantly revitalizing."[26]

Rashid-Yasemi repeatedly uses the Persian word *tajaddod*, meaning "to revitalize" but also (particularly interesting then) "to modernize." He implies that Bergson's new philosophy embodies a higher-level "modernity" than earlier Western philosophies, including those of Kant or Spencer, the targets of criticism in *Time and Free Will*. Rashid-Yasemi, moreover, highlights Bergson's contention that intelligence and logic in man are secondary to freedom. The mere fact of existence provides the absolute basis of human freedom. He emphasizes freedom as inhering in man's inward senses (*hes-e baten*).[27] The lecture subsequently focuses on Bergson's belief in the fundamental importance of change, and constant evolution in all aspects of natural and human existence.

Rashid-Yasemi, following modernization theory, is highly selective in explaining Bergson's ideas. Silent on the critique of modern

[24] The only exception is a reference to Rumi, where Rashid-Yasemi discusses Bergson's view on free will. Here he makes reference to a Rumi poem (even when stating that our will is free, we express the freedom to express our views) on the intrinsic human feeling of freedom of will: ibid., 356.

[25] It also seems that Rashid-Yasemi, in some of his references, confuses Bergson's two books. Some of the ideas that he ascribes to *Time and Free Will* seem to come from his later book on *Creative Evolution*.

[26] Rashid-Yasemi, "Bergson's Philosophy," 356. Rashid-Yasemi uses the idea of progress and the need for *tajaddod* in our ideas and our social condition. He interprets Bergson as championing modernization.

[27] Rashid-Yasemi here refers to a poem by Rumi suggesting that "human" existence as such represents its freedom. This is the only reference he makes to any non-Western philosophers or ideas.

rationalism, and the intuition theory, he lectures the faculty and students of the Islamic theology department on the benefits of modern ideas.

3 Mohammad Ali Forughi

Mohammad Ali Forughi (1877–1942) was an eminent thinker and politician, the prime minister under Reza Shah, and, subsequently, under Mohammad Reza Shah. He published a lengthy chapter on Bergson's philosophy in 1938. He shared with Fardid and others a deep interest in the Bergson–*erfan* link in the context of Iran's modern nation-making.

Mohammad Ali Forughi, in *The History of Philosophy in Europe*, explained Bergson's philosophy in detail.[28] Forughi presents a balanced interpretation, while indicating similarities between Bergson's ideas and Persian mysticism:[29]

Bergson is among the leading philosophers of this time. Some argue that, since Kant, Europe has not seen a philosopher of such high standing. This is because he has marked a new page, and a fresh beginning, in the history of philosophy. His philosophical views resemble those of the early Greek philosopher Heraclitus. His philosophical approach resembles Plotinus, and our [Persian] Illuminationist philosophy, and mystic scholars.[30]

However, Forughi argues, Bergson's philosophy is serious and scholarly: "However, his [Bergson's] ideas are grounded in scholarly research, deliberation, and serious and innate scholarly knowledge."[31] In contrast to Bergson, he suggests, the similarities in the Iranian mystical tradition are less thoughtful and serious.

Forughi writes on Bergson's intuitive knowledge, how "logical analysis" and "intelligence" merely touch the surface or the outer knowledge of objects. Rational understanding – including scientific knowledge – exemplifies practical or instrumental knowledge, useful

---

[28] Forughi's discussion of Bergson is thirty-seven pages long (pp. 254–291): see Mohammad Ali Forughi, *Seyr-e Hekmat dar Orupa* (*The History of Philosophy in Europe*) (Tehran: Zavar Publisher, 1965).

[29] However, Forughi does not give specific references to Bergson's works. It is hard to ascertain whether his summaries of various books by Bergson are based on his own reading or whether they are from secondary sources about Bergson. This is even more the case with Rashid-Yasemi, Fardid, and Arani's writings.

[30] Forughi, *Seyr-e Hekmat dar Orupa*, p. 257.   [31] Ibid., p. 257.

merely for material necessities.[32] For Bergson, "intelligence" and "logic" provide representational knowledge, but not inner truth.

Forughi skirts Bergson's "intuition," arguably his major concept. He explains that, for Bergson, true knowledge embodies the epistemic unity of subject and object.[33] Higher knowledge transcends analysis and intelligence, embodied in "intuition." Forughi identifies intuition with "inward knowing," "knowledge of the soul," or "self-knowledge."[34] Having "objectively" presented Bergson's theory of intuition, Forughi editorializes on the terminological distinctions in Farsi:

For those familiar with the jargon of *orafa* [Sufis, scholars of mysticism], we should note that *darunbini* [inward knowledge] or *janbini* [knowledge of the soul, or self-knowledge], in a practical sense, is comparable to *moraghebeh* [meditation], which, if produced by focused attention, is identical to *moka-shefeh* [revelation]. However, in order to avoid falling into *erfan* [mysticism], and to avoid our arguments becoming *khalt* [spoiled or mixed up with mysticism], or taken as synonymous with mysticism, we will use *moraghebeh* and *mokashefeh*, instead of *darunbini* and *janbini*. Of course, if required, we will not treat *mokashefeh* and *moraghebeh* as illicit words.[35]

Forughi scarcely explained why Bergson's intuition lacked an affinity with Persian or Islamic mysticism, taking for granted that this should be avoided. Bergson's philosophy, a rigorous and serious intellectual system, could not be compared with Persian or Islamic mysticism. For Forughi, a Western philosopher was superior, even if his ideas resembled "typical," "eastern" *orafa*. This was an earlier Orientalism, operating with the Iranian elites' desire to modernize.

Forughi's *The History of Philosophy in Europe* became a classic text. He tempered the reception of Bergson's more controversial ideas. Despite Bergson's enthusiasm for intuitive knowledge and his critique of analytical thinking, Forughi highlighted Bergson's explicit recognition of rationality for practical matters. He refers to Bergson's desire for an integrated knowledge, where combined intelligence and intuition aid in the pursuit of spiritual and material goals. Forughi argues that Bergson's ideas have provoked their own critique. Certain European scholars, he explains, find his philosophy a bewildering return to the "mystical" tradition:

---

[32] Ibid., p. 266.   [33] Ibid., p. 269.   [34] Ibid.   [35] Ibid.

Yet, we should not assume that intuition and intelligence are incompatible, nor that intuitive aptitudes are distinct from the rational faculty. On the contrary, intuition is another form of rational thinking; quite likely, a higher level of intelligence. Its only difference from what we call logical thinking is that intelligence looks at the exterior and does not penetrate the depth.[36]

We see, then, how Bergson was constructed and mobilized as the highest instance of modernist philosophical thinking by Forughi. This was a detailed, if selective, summary of his major works. Yet Forughi's vision of the forward-looking Bergson was merely one reconstruction. Bergson's mystical aspects, marginalized by the modernizing agendas of Forughi, Rashid-Yasemi, and Arani, were centered and celebrated by other Iranian intellectuals. These individuals envisioned a modern spiritual dynamism for grounding modern Iranian nation-making.

4 Ahmad Fardid

Ahmad Fardid (1910–94) used the *erfan* tradition, via Bergson, to produce an Iranian counter-modern social imaginary. In a two-part 1938 article on Bergson,[37] Fardid employed an eminent European thinker to undermine Western secularism. His Bergson is a unique construction. Fardid remained silent on Bergson's Jewish background and his later Catholicism. Opening with a quotation by Jacques Chevalier, Fardid constructs a generic European and radical critic of the Western Enlightenment:

There are a multiplicity of sources constituting present-day Western culture, most embedded in the past, while some [ideas] stem from the modern period. Bergson's philosophical system, concerning [ideas such as] intuition and knowledge, consciousness and action, is among the most influential sources from the contemporary period. Bergson is an original thinker on the verge of building a magnificent palace of truth and spirituality upon the ruins of the two preceding centuries of materialist philosophy. Many contemporary Western scholars consider Bergson's words as signaling the advent of a new civilization, and predict that glimmers of this philosophy will spread everywhere.[38]

---

[36] Ibid., p. 270.
[37] Fardid published two articles on Bergson: "Henri Bergson and Bergsonian Philosophy: I," *Majalle-ye Mehr* (February 1938); and "Henri Bergson and Bergsonian Philosophy: II," *Majalle-ye Mehr* (April 1938).
[38] Fardid, "Henri Bergson and Bergsonian Philosophy: I," 886.

Fardid's Bergson belongs to a group of Western intellectuals who have created the modern West. This explains Fardid's lifetime promotion of certain "Western" ideas, in a self-appointed quest to construct an authentic Islamist–Iranian discourse. The early Bergson and Heidegger were prophets, arising from Western decline. They assisted Fardid in healing the long-suffering "East" from soulless "materialism" and "rationalism." They were the adversaries of "materialism," "positivism," and "rationalism" – three distinct movements conflated into a Western "antireligious" tendency. Within the Iranian context, Bergson's status as a *European* philosopher was of decided importance. Fardid grew interested in Bergson in the 1930s and 1940s, when he was celebrated internationally. Awarded the 1927 Nobel Prize in Literature, Bergson was the leading twentieth-century European philosopher. His contribution critically confronted modern rationalism, through "intuition" and "nonscientific experience." Bergson advanced sophisticated refutations of Cartesian–Leibnizian "rationalism," which drives all mysterious forces from the world. He criticized the positivism prevalent in nineteenth-century European thought.

Rationalism and positivism were the two dominant currents among the Iranian literary and intellectual class, making Bergson acutely relevant. In the post-constitutional period, positivist and scientific rationalism were ubiquitous. Smaller groups of radical intellectuals embraced European socialist and materialist traditions. For a young philosopher from Yazd, transplanted to Tehran, seeking an alternative intellectual path was hardly surprising. Bergson provided an ideal spiritual refuge from positivism and the materialism of the atheist radicals. Fardid's route to rebellion at home grew from alternative Western intellectual movements. All the while, he claimed to emancipate his Iranian heritage from corrupting Western influence.

Discussing Bergson and Spencer, Fardid identified the roots of corruption in excessive philosophical reliance upon scientific epistemic modes for knowing the world. For Fardid, hence, Bergson's philosophy represents the alternative to materialistic and secular philosophical approaches. He writes: "Without any doubt, the major impediment for humanity in its quest for the truth, and the source of evil and uncertainty in life, is the absence of a shared world understanding, leading to an anxious mind."[39] Bergson reaffirms his larger point:

---

[39] Ibid., 892.

"Any fruitful philosophical study calls for peace of mind, stemming from sincere and pure passion."[40] Bergson's philosophy, Fardid argues, shows the mistake in looking for truth in external phenomena, such as in time and "duration." For Bergson, the internal, subjective experience (*batten*, or hidden) and what is concealed in our understanding of time is truth. The "external" and "internal," and the latter as an authentic "self," echoes the central revivalist ideas of Mohammad Iqbal shared by European Romantics.

Bergson and Elm-e Hozuri

For Fardid, Bergson's *Time and Free Will*[41] (1889) was his first serious account of *elm-e hozuri*.[42] "Intuition," central to Bergson, was the principle source of Fardid's attraction. Fardid sought a "Western" scholar to re-affirm an Iranian–Islamic worldview. Bergson's "intuitive knowledge" provided this with a "legitimate" critique of modern rationalism. Fardid used Bergson to revitalize a traditional spiritualist philosophy. "Intuition," or *elm-e hozuri*, intellectually bridged the modern "West" and the "East." It presented an intellectual key for imagining a superior knowledge in the age of science and secularism. It opened a conceptual avenue for legitimizing the transcendent. This intellectual preoccupation was comparable to Henry Corbin's *hurghalya*. Both scholars, through these concepts, theorized a direct, mystical experience of God beyond the post-metaphysical limits of sociological rationality.

Bergson's "intuition" sought to overcome Kantian rationalism, which eliminates the possibility of absolute knowledge. "Intuition" restores it. Bergson upholds two paths to true knowledge: the analytical

---

40 Ibid.

41 Bergson's doctoral dissertation, *Time and Free Will*, presents his theories on the mind's freedom and duration, the latter of which he regarded as a succession of conscious states, intermingling and numerically undifferentiated.

42 The idea that there is one knowledge of the world, representing appearance and coming from knowledge based on reason, and a different knowledge, rooted in deep human insight and "inspiration," has a long history in Islamic theology and Iranian philosophy. In Islamic tradition, *elm-e hozuri* is a knowledge that is learned by heart rather than through education. This is a way of knowing that one arrives at from within, and it is a calling. It is also suggested that it is knowledge that one obtains from reading the Qur'an. Henry Corbin discusses Sohrewardi's philosophy of *eshragh* as *elm-e hozuri*. *Elm-e hozuri* is translated as the "science of the soul" and "intuitive knowledge."

method, and that of intuition. The analytical method provides "relative" knowledge (i.e. quantitative time), while intuition attains "absolute" knowledge (i.e. duration or qualitative multiplicity). For Bergson,
"intuition" connects to the "things themselves," in contrast to an
artificially constructed measurement superimposed on experience.
Time and Free Will explains: "[the] greater part of the time, we live
outside ourselves, hardly perceiving anything of ourselves but our own
ghost, a colorless shadow that pure duration projects into homogeneous space."[43] Living inauthentically, we have an untapped authentic self. Scientific causality is irrelevant within the qualitatively unique
flow of subjective time experience: "we can nevertheless always get
back into pure duration, of which the moments are internal and
heterogeneous to one another, and in which a cause cannot repeat
its effect since it will never repeat itself." In authentic time, the
quantitative is abandoned, with immense romantic appeal for traditional communities, whose spiritual truth claims are threatened by
scientific advancement. So it is also for estranged modern souls,
hungering for a pre-modern belonging. A political space for religious
and mystical experience opens. Bergson relegates political freedom as
a sociological order (democratic institutions) to secondary status:
"we [moderns] live [too often] for the external world rather than
ourselves ... To act freely is to recover possession of oneself."[44] In
a parallel spiritual reality, rational categories and individual identity
cease to exist in favor of pure becoming. Like Corbin's "imaginal" as
the sphere of real and objective truth, Bergson argues that intuitive
knowledge represents the true nature of authentic experience.

For Bergson, modern objectivity is an illusion, permitting control of
the environment: "We have everything to gain by keeping the illusion
through which we make phenomena share in the reciprocal externality
of outer things" because this "permits us to give them fixed names in
spite of their instability" and "enables us to objectify them."[45] This
inspired Proust's meditations on time, where dreams ontologically
superimpose over objective reality in everyday objects (e.g. the made-
leine), conjuring "previous existences," the "thread of the hours, the

---

[43] Henri Bergson, *Time and Free Will: An Essay on the Immediate Data of
      Consciousness* (Mineola, NY: Dover Publications, 2001), p. 231.
[44] Henri Bergson, *Essai sur les données immédiates de la conscience* (Paris: PUF,
      2007), pp. 174–175.
[45] Ibid., p. 173.

order of the years and the worlds."[46] In Proust's masterpiece, the unconscious universe of unique images and past lives conquers drably mechanical modern life, symbolized by the sick insomniac. Corbin adopted the motifs of spiritual time travel and proto-existential choice, as did Fardid. Proust's vision derived from the imagined Oriental essence, embodied in his central image of the Japanese paper flower metamorphosing into innumerable forms.[47] Just as Japanese curios flooded the European art market, inspiring Van Gogh and Monet, so Fardid revolutionized Persian intellectual traditions in the global cultural interzone.[48] He embraced Bergson's "intuition" as the "Western" analogue for *elm-e hozuri* (i.e. intuitive knowledge, or science of the soul). *Elm-e hozuri* is deeply rooted in Islamic philosophy, in Sohrewardi's *eshragh* or "illumination." For Fardid, intuition represented an established knowledge in Iranian tradition. Fardid is utilitarian in his treatment of Bergson, entering detailed discussion of Islamic philosophy – *erfan* specifically. He distinguishes "real" knowledge in contrast to "appearance":

In Islamic scholarly convention, *elm-e hozuri* is the opposite of *elm-e hosuli*. *Elm-e hosuli* is knowledge where the subjective differs from the objective, and the knowledge of objects concerns outward substance. However, *elm-e hozuri* is knowledge with unified subjective and objective elements. It involves knowledge of the soul's essence, or generally, the knowledge of real or ultimate cause.[49]

Fardid not only privileges "mystical knowledge" over modern rationality: "I need to note here, that in the view of our earlier [*ghadim*] scholars, true knowledge comes exclusively from *elm-e hozuri*."[50] "Our forbearance sometimes described *elm-e hozuri* as '*vejdan*' [intuition, conscious] or '*elm-e vejdani*'."[51] He argues that rationality impedes real knowledge: "Bergson in [*Time and Free Will*], and elsewhere, voices the necessity of a return to intuition [*vejdaniyat*] ... One problem, and the major obstacle in recognizing the essence and *elm-e hozuri*, is rational analysis."[52]

[46] Marcel Proust, *Du Côté de Chez Swann* (Paris: Gallimard, 1988), pp. 1–7.
[47] Ibid., p. 47.
[48] Herbert Read, *A Concise History of Modern Painting* (New York: Prager, 1975), pp. 22–25.
[49] Fardid, "Henri Bergson and Bergsonian Philosophy: I," 893.   [50] Ibid.
[51] Ibid.   [52] Ibid., 894.

In the second Bergson article, Fardid discusses *Matter and Memory* and *Creative Evolution*,[53] explaining:[54]

Bergson, in two of his books, *Time and Free Will*, and *Matter and Memory*, discusses intelligence and rational analysis. However, he does not explain what intelligence is, and what its root causes are. In his book, *Creative Evolution*, published in 1907, he covers this, and other questions, including evolution, life, and three kinds of species [plant, animal and human], and evolution.[55]

Fardid devotes four pages to *Creative Evolution*, omitting to discuss the important *Two Sources of Morality and Religion*.[56] Some consider *Creative Evolution* as attacking Darwin's theory of evolution. Fardid perhaps sought an alternative to a perceived materialism in Iran. Fardid opens by discussing Bergson's question, "What is life?":

In the beginning, instinct and intelligence were integrated in animal life. That is why both share common characteristics. There is no intelligence without traces of instinct, and no instinct without intelligence. For Bergson, philosophers have mistakenly thought that the capacity of plants, instinct, and intelligence are three stages of a single evolution. In fact, these three qualities are different aspects of one process. Their relations are horizontal, not vertical.[57]

He then discusses the superficiality of human knowledge based on intelligence: "Intelligence only regards limited aspects of unified truth [*haghighat-e vahed*], areas essential for maintaining bodily life, or beneficial in rejection of harm."[58]

Fardid has two points: firstly, reliance upon human intellect cannot transcend limited practical worldly knowledge. It represents the human situation as equal with all other living species. Secondly, achieving higher understanding requires abandoning the intellect, grounded in

---

53   Henri Bergson, *Creative Evolution*, trans. Arthur Mitchell (New York: Dover, 1998).
54   Many regard Bergson's book *Creative Evolution* as representing an anti-Darwinian theory. Bergson, in this book, criticizes Darwin's "mechanical" view of the origin of human evolution, instead offering his own theory based on a "creative" development filled with exciting moments.
55   Fardid, "Henri Bergson and Bergsonian Philosophy: I," 1112.
56   Charles Robert Darwin, *The Two Sources of Morality and Religion*, trans. R. Ashley Audra and Cloudsley Brereton, with the assistance of W. Horsfall Carter (Notre Dame, IN: University of Notre Dame Press, [1935] 1977).
57   Fardid, "Bergson and Bergsonian Philosophy: II," 1113.   58   Ibid., 1114.

biological principles of self-preservation: "Intelligence is intrinsically practical, creating lifeless and stationary objects. However, its practical accomplishments encourage it to overstep its limits, and pursue the quest for the truth of objects."[59] Yet Fardid offers a hopeful message to his readers: "Fortunately, man is not merely made of intelligence. Parallel to his intellect, a second knowledge exists. A halo all around him, it is testimony [*shohud*]."[60]

Fardid argues that, for Bergson, "Intelligence may seek the truth of matter, but never find it."[61] Yet "Instinct finds the [truth of objects], never pursuing it, unless motivated by intelligence. Instinct will search for the truth of things, and recover it. This is true intuition, in Bergson's view."[62] In conclusion, Fardid urges that genuine knowing is self-knowledge (*shohud*). Intuitive knowledge is the source of all human inspiration, from artistic creativity to the discoveries of "mystics and prophetic revelations, and all those who are seekers of the truth."[63] Subsequently, Fardid enlarged the mystical thesis, encompassing a wider expanse of Western intellectual history. Kant had raised an already existing Western mystical tradition to sublime heights, linked to Iranian Sufi traditions. This awakening was perfected in the currently influential Heidegger. Partaking of this great advancing movement, venerating mysticism and disparaging reason, Fardid envisioned himself heralding an ineluctable Fate.

Marxism and Islam: Ideological Debates

In the postrevolutionary spring of 1980, the Islamic Republic's state-run national TV aired a series called "Ideological Debates." They invited leading political figures from left-wing, liberal, and Islamic parties to debate notable pro-Islamic Republic individuals. Undoubtedly, the prevailing social atmosphere, and the popularity of political Islam, made it hard for secular forces (both nationalist and leftist) to engage in genuine debate with supporters of Ayatollah Khomeini. Many, including Bazargan's Freedom Movement and supporters of other religious groups, declined the offer to participate. Even those who did participate faced a very complicated situation. Many Iranian intellectual and political figures of the 1960s and 1970s spurned secular and modern Iranian ideas, and embraced Islam, *erfan*, and "Eastern spirituality." It was hard

[59] Ibid., 1115.   [60] Ibid.   [61] Ibid., 1114   [62] Ibid., 1115.   [63] Ibid.

to debate with the ideologues of political Islam, which was currently in power and enjoying mass support.

The "Ideological Debates" vividly summarize the sharp contrast between and a major shift in Iranian intellectual sensibilities. They clearly demonstrate the decline of secular and modern thinking, and the aggressive rise of religious thinking. In these debates, Mohammad Taghi Mesbah-Yazdi and Abdolkarim Soroush represent the religious or Islamic Republic side, and Ehsan Tabari and Farrokh Negahdar represent the Tudeh Party and Fedayeen (two major Marxist organizations).[64]

The moderator and Mesbah forcefully focus the debate on religion and materialism, and, specifically, attack the idea of contradiction within Marxist dialectic. Tabari and Negahdar only reluctantly engage in this debate, and repeatedly request discussion of policies and the economy, and matters on which both sides are agreed. There is much back-and-forth discussion on this topic of religion and materialism; finally, Tabari and Negahdar very reluctantly agree to discuss the religious–secular ideological issues.

Mesbah initiates the debate by arguing that it is critical to engage the most fundamental philosophical issues for postrevolutionary Iran, that is, the distinction between ideologies based on materialism and religious thinking:

Our war with others is an ideological battle. It is a struggle of different schools of thought. We want to introduce the servants of God to our God. All the wars and bloodshed are for illuminating the truth ... But, what is now so relevant in ideological questions are the foundations – the discourse and roots of the difference dividing materialist and non-materialist schools. It is, therefore, critical that we discuss these issues.[65]

---

[64] It should be noted that advocating atheism was illegal in Iran before and after the revolution. This restricted Marxist participants in the debate from questioning the other side on such fundamental issues as divinity, the supernatural, the prophets, the imams, and similar religious matters. In fact, a few years after these "debates," over 300 political prisoners were hanged as "apostates" simply for denying the existence of life after death, the resurrection, the importance of prayer, and the sanctity of the Qu'ran. In prison, inmates were careful not to be entrapped by wardens into philosophical discussions, knowing well that such topics could end up with charges of apostasy – a capital offense according to Sharia law.

[65] "The Complete Transcription of Ideological Debates, Mesbah Yazdi, Ehsan Tabari, Abdul Karim Soroush, Farrok Negahdar, spring, 1981," available at: Iranian Students' University News, May 15, 2014 (http://iusnews.ir/fa/news-details/129462/).

Mesbah-Yazdi's use of "war" is a reference to Negahdar's repeated emphasis on the importance of unity in a situation where Iran was at war with Iraq and the imperialist powers. Tabari attempts to argue that Marxism and Islam have many shared ideas, but goes a little too far:

I am, here, also explaining the fact that Marx and Engels' theory is based on a production-based conflict, but, from the perspective of the theory of production, there is no difference (to Islam). The Marx–Engels theory of production is a monist materialism. That is, the essence of the universe is composed of matter. This, according to Lenin's definition, accepted by all those who profess Marxism, is an objective reality. Therefore, the material does not have any precise characteristics as such. Philosophy cannot discover the characteristics and properties of matter. Knowledge, experience, and wisdom should determine it. Marxist philosophy and dialectical materialism are a philosophy of Oneness [*towhidi*] and monistic.[66]

In response to Ehsan Tabari, Mesbah-Yazdi challenges him:

Mr. Tabari noted that Marx's dialectic is a "towhidi" dialectic (monotheistic or monist dialectic). To some, this may evoke the idea that he is speaking of Islamic monotheism [*towhidi e Islami*]. I must explain to the respected audience that he proclaims the unity of the material world. And his notion of *towhidi* dialectic only means that one material reality exists, and not two ... He lacks faith in the supernatural, or the transcendental.[67]

Here, the debate's moderator sarcastically asks Ehsan Tabari if he is suggesting that Rumi and Shirizi were Marxist thinkers. Tabari responds to him:

I do not propose to say that Jalal al-Din Molavi or Sard al-Din Shirazi were materialists or Marxists. I merely explained the history and development of the idea of contradiction [*tazad*] from their perspective, as it is recorded in philosophy ... This idea was not the invention of Marx or Engels, and nor did they discover it. This is a longstanding subject in philosophy, and they have also uttered their own views about it. This subject matter is equally present in Islamic philosophy. I named them because we acknowledge inspiration from this idea, which comes from our own culture. It is a way of thinking that has roots in our own culture.[68]

Mesbah returns to the attack, and, consistent with his earlier argument, advances a radical critique of materialism:

[66] Ibid. [67] Ibid. [68] Ibid.

The materialist worldview, and its various branches, is on the one side, and, on the opposite front, there are theological worldviews. The core issue dividing these two belief systems is whether "being" is only a material reality or whether it transcends the material. If so, there is an absolute truth that all realities, including the material or non-material, are connected in the absolute, omnipresent, and self-contained Spirit. That is the essence of the transcendental Spirit, and this is shared by all believers and negated by all materialists. Materialists believe that nothing is real except for the material world.[69]

The turn of the debate places Ehsan Tabari in a difficult position. He seems adamant about avoiding a defense of his materialist worldview. However, by suggesting that Marxist dialectic is a monotheistic theology, he adopts an indefensible position. In his response, he abandons the defense of Marxist materialism, and instead offers a political argument:

We are not interested in creating any opposition between dialectical materialism and Islamic theology ... within our national borders, there are both Muslim revolutionaries and those who believe in Marxism, and they all defend the Islamic Republic ... Marxism, in its authentic and original meaning, does not express any hostility toward theology or religion.[70]

This is a big surprise. The Tudeh Party's best-known intellectual leader is either unwilling, or unable, to present a better argument. He entirely avoids any serious argument about Marxism and its attitude toward the Islamic religion. As we know, there are Christians and other religious individuals sympathetic to Marxism. There are Marxists who have a sympathetic view of religion. Tabari fails to point to any of those. This is particularly odd, given that he is one of the leading members of the Communist Party in Iran (the Tudeh Party). His response to Mesbah-Yazdi is revealing:

First, I should say, belief in dialectical contradiction does not in any way signify hostility to the sacred philosophy. Hegel had faith in divine theology. Despite this, he also believed in dialectic. Dialectic thrives in a variety of forms, and multiple traditional worldviews, including the Sufi teachings and the Persian *erfan* of Mulla Sadra. Dialectic has deep philosophical roots.[71]

In the two debates presented here we witness the ongoing struggle to define the Iranian national imaginary in two distinct periods of Iranian

[69] Ibid.   [70] Ibid.   [71] Ibid.

history. The above televised argument significantly represents the dominant Iranian intellectual view of the 1960s and 1970s. However, when contrasted with the earlier debates on Persian *erfan*, in the 1930s, it presents an eye-opening panorama on major mutations in the Iranian political and national imaginary.

These two cases frame an imaginative struggle concerning the place of "tradition" (Persian *erfan*, political Islam) and modern ideas (rationalism, materialism, the West) in the making of the modern Iranian nation. Ironically, Iran in the 1930s was a far less socioeconomically developed modern nation than it was in the 1980s. However, the idea of the nation seems to be in contradiction with its socioeconomic reality. One may argue that the Iranian experience challenges the views of those for whom nations are merely material or socioeconomic reality.

What does explain this rather radical rupture between these two moments, a topographic change, occurs in the Iranian national imaginary. In the debate on Bergson, "intuition" is primarily two things: either 1) a new endorsement of Pahlavi modernization, where Iran is at the forefront of modernity, reflecting the freshest Western intellectual visions, rendering the West itself obsolete (here, the postmodern means a new and better modernity, a spiritual modernity, and it is embodied in rapidly modernizing Pahlavi Iran) – this is the regime's perspective; or 2) a modern spirituality that is distinctive but prone to the same flaws as traditional mysticism – this is the view of the radical left. Both views take the modernist optic for granted as the dominant Iranian imaginary. Fardid is the marginal voice, a challenge from the periphery, seeking in "intuition" a means to transform the Iranian mystical tradition into a revolutionary nation-making ideology based on anti-Western hostility. In his own time and place, he represents the voice of the outsider, a pioneer, but also a man far from the political and ideological center of power.

By contrast, in the television debate, the entire panorama has been reversed. Political Islam is now the organized center of political and ideological power. It invites the modernist liberal and leftist voices to come and justify themselves on national television. They cannot openly argue, but seek only to ingratiate themselves with the reigning Islamist regime. How can a Marxist present himself as a friend and supporter of the Islamic Republic? To do so, he must twist Marxist discourse to embrace a political Islamic imaginary, having recourse to the Hegelian dialectics of the Absolute. Yet he is disdainfully shot down by his interlocutors as a "materialist," a traitor, an apostate. The central problematic has become the justification of "identity." This is far indeed from the post–Mashruteh political atmosphere, where, charged with memories of mass anti-colonial struggle, Iranians sought – primarily though Marxist, liberal, and authoritarian statist modes – to transfigure Iran into a modern, democratic, and independent nation. In the context of making the Iranian nation a creative enterprise in the last two decades of Pahlavi rule, the road was paved for the dominance of political Islam precisely by undermining the major institutional and imaginative "achievements" of the earlier period of the Pahlavi dynasty.

8 | *An Elective Affinity:*
Variations of Gharbzadegi

Intellectual Migrations: East and West

This book builds on my earlier study of Ahmad Fardid's thought.[1] I have analyzed the *gharbzadegi* philosophy as the complex site of a transnational circulation of ideas, producing a significant discursive formation in the Iranian political imagination. The young Fardid was influenced by the *fin de siècle* French critique of modern Western rationality pioneered by Henri Bergson. Spiritual Islam, particularly in Corbin's vision, inspired Fardid with a platform offering a new interpretation of Islamic and Iranian traditions. At this point Fardid's ideas were close to European counter-Enlightenment ideology. Fardid subsequently spent eight years in post–World War II France and Germany (1947–55), where he derived inspiration from the Heideggerian critique of Western modernity.[2]

At the Sorbonne, Fardid studied under Maurice de Gandillac (1906–2006), a professor of medieval philosophy. Gandillac was a student of Nietzsche and, in his major book, *The Genesis of Modernity*, was strongly influenced by Heidegger. Gandillac taught that modernity is rooted in the religious imagining of the damned, those who are left behind by progress. In modern subjectivity, the category of knowledge has replaced God, for it is infinitely extended and limitless (for Fardid, carnal soul, or *nafs-e ammareh*). Modernity is therefore divided, like in a split personality, between "rationality" and "subjectivity."

---

[1] Mirsepassi, *Transnationalism in Iranian Political Thought.*
[2] Fardid mentioned Heidegger and German phenomenology in some of his writings before he left for Europe. It seems he was introduced to Heidegger through reading French early in his life.

Within this context, Fardid coined the Persian term *gharbzadegi* (Westoxification) as a "localized," Heideggerian, anti-modern idea. He explains his intellectual transformation while living in Germany:

Everyone knows that I coined the concept of "Westoxification." I was inspired while I was in seclusion somewhere in Europe. I am not saying that I am above Jalal Al-e Ahmad, or vice versa. My knowledge, however, is more [than Al-e Ahmad's]. His way of thinking is different. My lifestyle and my studies are different. From that time [that I offered the concept of Westoxification] to now, I have always been on the "path." I don't claim that since I have offered Westoxification I have attained a total revolution in my mind. But a kind of revolution has occurred in my thinking.[3]

Simultaneously, Corbin, also inspired by Heidegger, presented a new interpretation of Islam as a spiritual tradition. This was based on Persian Islam (*erfan*), and Corbin's ideas became influential within the Iranian intellectual scene.

We therefore see a seminal two-way migration of intellectual ideas into national politics involving Islamic tradition and Heideggerian thought (and perhaps even French Orientalism). This motley cocktail spread from war-ravaged Europe to politically volatile Iran, followed by Iranian quasi-Sufi ideas flowing back into Europe and then returning in newly regenerated form to their Iranian homeland. The Orientalist Corbin exemplified this amazing concoction: he is known as a French scholar of Persian and Islamic tradition, but he was also a deeply Heideggerian philosopher who introduced Heidegger's works to French readers. Corbin spent almost half a century surrounding himself with a self-created institution of students and devotees. Editing and translating Iranian and Islamic texts, Corbin established an idiosyncratic interpretation of Iranian Islam that he labelled Spiritual Islam. Corbin also belonged to the larger Christian anti-modern current that grew out of the Cold War era.[4] Who was Corbin precisely: an Orientalist? A Christian anti-modernist? A lover of Islamic mysticism? A Heideggerian? One can pose nearly identical questions about Ahmad Fardid. These were scholars who crossed intellectual borders and who are best described as transnational thinkers. While exhibiting certain

---

[3] Ahmad Fardid, *Gharb va Gharbzadegi* [The West and Westoxification], unpublished (Tehran: Bonyad-e Hekmi va Falsafi-ye Doktor Fardid), Vol. 1, pp. 18–19.

[4] Wasserstrom, *Religion after Religion*.

qualities of the classic Orientalist, they also sharply differed from the Orientalist model documented by Edward Said. Unlike Said's evocation, they were neither exclusively modernist nor sympathetic to colonial or imperialist desires. On the contrary: non-Western religious traditions deeply inspired them, and they were radically hostile to the modern West in its secular, imperial, and democratic dimensions. We need to think through the theoretical implications of these two examples, for they imply something far-reaching about the limits and blind spots of contemporary scholarship.

This book charts these significant theoretical implications, and their ethical and political resonance, for key beliefs underpinning postcolonial theory. It challenges us to re-think certain assumptions that are regularly taken for granted. These ideas include: 1) that Orientalist knowledge is more nuanced than is usually assumed, based on a formulaic reading of Said; 2) that the authenticity of the local is often more influenced by Western ideas than is supposed; 3) that the modernist and liberal hegemony in the West is, by contrast, on the margins in the non-West; and 4) that the positionality of the postcolonial itself, as a voice claiming to be local, is often a voice (or voices) from the West.

Let's explore some of these ideas and try to develop how they are often related:

1) Ideas, including the apparently "local," "authentic," "traditional," and "non-Western," partake of a broader circulation of intellectual traditions, which travel from West to non-West and from non-West to the West. Each time these ideas are reconstituted, they take on new meanings. It is important to critically engage with them, to grasp the complexity of their place and origin. This applies equally to Orientalism and Islam. It is, therefore, necessary to trace these multidirectional migrations as a transnational space of exchange. They do not automatically exist in a margin–center relationship of hegemonic–subjugation to a monolithic modern other. Fardid is often represented as a case study of authentic Iranian and Islamic intellectual militancy, an anti-Orientalist and anti-Western hero of the authentic. Fardid portrayed himself thus, and his many faithful associates have certainly extended this one-dimensional myth. Upon critical examination, Fardid's ideas are more derivative of Bergson and Corbin in their early phase, and Heidegger in his later years. This is not to suggest

that Fardid was merely a passive receptacle for these foreign ideas. Rather, a serious and even revolutionary exchange of ideas occurred, and it is important to locate its re-forged boundaries through patterns of intellectual exchange. What is clear, however, is that Fardid's thought is not purely local or non-Western. This is also the case with Iranian liberal or leftist intellectuals. They are all embedded in a complex circulation of intellectual traditions and ideas, which rather demolishes the entrenched myth of a local and authentic culture opposing an imported political left. This is simply a falsehood, and yet the cliché thrives in contemporary academia in a deeply harmful manner.

2) We require studies of intellectual migrations from the center to the periphery, back and forth. In the case of Fardid, his notion of *gharbzadegi*, i.e. Westoxification, was conceived in Germany rather than Iran. *Gharbzadegi* traveled to Iran, and we now consider it an Iranian intellectual production (as Dipankar Gupta, in his book on Indian modernity, argues).[5] The major elements of *gharbzadegi* – anti-modernism and the return to Iranian–Islamic tradition – were articulated in Europe. The template was largely conceived in Germany's cultural struggle against "Enlightened" Western Europe, and partly within Western Europe's own counter-modern fringe. Corbin's notion of Shi'ism as Spiritual or Iranian Islam and Heidegger's confrontation with Western rational and secular thought were both European intellectual productions. It is therefore mistaken to hold – as is routinely assumed – that the idea of *gharbzadegi* is an Iranian or a non-Western production. In fact, Fardid was annoyed by Jalal Al-e Ahmad's use of *gharbzadegi* precisely because he did not appreciate the Heideggerian critique of Western metaphysics. Al-e Ahmad saw an ideological opportunity to mobilize the Iranian masses along nativist lines, while, for Fardid, a theoretical genealogy extending to ancient Greek rationalism was at stake. For Fardid, this implied the prospect of a total revolution in human consciousness, an unprecedented spiritual rebirth. This cosmic event, which only he understood through occult intuition, could only be trivialized in the vulgar political pamphlet penned by the former Marxist and avant-garde modernist writer.

---

[5] Dipankar Gupta, *Mistaken Modernity: India between Worlds* (London: HarperCollins, 2001).

3) We need to question the dominant academic orthodoxy in post-colonial and anti-Orientalist discourse upon the following point: the Western discourse on the East (in this case, Islam) is imposed mostly from the outside and frames our knowledge of the East. Corbin was certainly an Orientalist, and a French gentleman. However, he was also keenly interested in specific traditions within Islam, which he spent most of his life researching and writing about. Ironically, several generations of influential Iranian intellectuals – Fardid, Nasr, Shaygan, and Shari'ati – all embracing anti-modernism and critical of Western views of the East, were influenced by his idiosyncratic analysis of Islam. They accordingly produced a view of Islam that took intellectual root in Iran. It is now – in a completely unfounded manner – prized as an authentic and local Iranian intellectual contribution the world.

4) What makes scholars such as Fardid, Nasr, Shaygan, or Shari'ati more authentically Iranian than such secular intellectuals as Ahmad Shamlu or Taghi Arani, et al.? Why is it that European thinkers such as Bergson, Corbin, Heidegger, and Foucault are considered special cases, and not Western philosophers like Locke, Smith, Kant, Marx, and Dewey? There is an optic underlying this routine differentiation – and a false and harmful one.

5) Let us consider Fardid's case more specifically. He studied in Europe for eight years, and, even before then, he mostly translated the works of European and American scholars.[6] At Tehran University Fardid only offered classes in European philosophy. He hardly ever wrote or lectured on what was considered traditional Islam (the exceptions were when he presented his ideas in the West).[7] Fardid was certainly not a practicing Muslim. What gives him more Iranian authenticity than liberal or even left-leaning Iranian intellectuals? Fardid was not shy in reminding us that he was interested above all in a Heideggerian interpretation of Islam. What makes Heideggerian Islam more authentic or local than say, liberal Islam, or a Kantian understanding of Islam? Is

---

[6] Fardid's earlier works were almost all on European philosophy – Bergson, Kant, and Heidegger, or the American educational system, including a piece on John Dewey.

[7] The title of Fardid's thesis was "Le Problème de l'inexistence netiquette dans la philosophie de l'Islam." Fardid attended, in May 1968, the Congress of Orientalists in Ann Arbor, Michigan, and presented "L'Idée de l'angoisse dans la pensée mystique de l'Islam."

this a political position, or a statement about the production of knowledge? And, if political, what politics precisely?

6) Regardless of our theoretical preferences, we must conclude that hegemonic–subjugated knowledge is more complex than the works of some postcolonial scholars or Foucault have articulated. This critical issue requires greater elaboration: why do we assume that liberalism and modernism are the dominant and hegemonic mode of understanding the world, and the political order of things is institutionalized within the liberal political and intellectual framework? This is a great simplification. The mosaic of intellectual and political influence is transforming unceasingly.

7) Therefore, Orientalism, in the Islamic context, requires a more complex conceptualization. Said's evocation of a modernist and Western desire to represent the East as an object of domination is, at best, incomplete and, at worst, naïve. Corbin was militantly anti-modern and anti-Western. He was perhaps closer to Said and postcolonial theorists, but he was also an Orientalist. This conundrum requires an explanation that might destroy certain popular dogmas of postcolonialism.[8]

8) One of the shortcomings of proponents of postcolonial theory is their one-sided and almost extreme attention to what they call the "Western" or "modernist" representation of the "non-West." Here, their main argument is that the voice of the non-West is not represented, or is silenced. This is a good point, and an important contribution. However: firstly, in most cases, they seem uninterested in including non-Western voices and ideas in their discussion. The thinkers they are most influenced by are almost exclusively Western, or Western-inspired. Secondly, one can in fact argue persuasively that the postcolonial approach is most popular in the West. It is the voice of non-Western scholars and intellectuals living in the West, and it is mostly a debate about various Western intellectual currents. What makes Saba Mahmoud, who lives in the United States, or so many

---

[8] However, to be fair to Edward Said, I would like to note that he was primarily focused on the politics of representation (of the Orient) in contemporary Western cultural literature. It is not all clear, nor is it suggested in this book, that Edward Said would have shared the views of some of the most extreme postcolonial theorists of today.

other postcolonial scholars who have lived almost all of their lives in the West, more representative of the Muslim, Arab, or Indian people than Fatima Mernissi, who mostly lived and died in Morocco? Mernissi espoused important elements of liberal and leftist thought while remaining a lifelong Muslim. Are we to conclude that, having fallen into inauthenticity, she should have referred to key postcolonial texts to recover the Straight Path? This is a preposterous idea, yet it is regularly insinuated in the popular postcolonial writings that pervade contemporary academia.

9) Ahmad Fardid (and Jalal Al-e Ahmad) embraced ideas we now identify as postcolonial, but they did it earlier, and in a more "authentically" non-Western way.

This book challenges some of the assumptions of postcolonial and anti-Orientalist "orthodoxy" by presenting the case for a "modernizing" and "pro-Western" state's ideological commitment to ideas and arguments normally identified with the "Subaltern" resistance. More specifically, it challenges the idea that anti-Orientalism and anti-Western ideologies, in the case of Iran and *gharbzadegi*, are either the voice of the Iranian masses resisting the modernizing state's tyrannical policies or, more broadly, that of Muslim resistance to Western cultural and moral domination. This book argues that the Shah's state attempted to use the discourse of *gharbzadegi*, and anti-Western rhetoric, to marginalize the secular left and liberal nationalist forces. Meanwhile, the Pahlavi state maintained close political relations with the United States and other Western powers.

This book's various chapters present strong evidence that the Pahlavi state, and its cultural functionaries, were militantly anti-Western. They were particularly critical of modern ideas, values, and liberal norms in Iran. The individuals and institutions that produced these anti-Western cultural sentiments were not "traditional" Iranian or Islamic figures or part of the "traditional" establishment. On the contrary. From the Shah himself, down to various artists, writers, and philosophers, et al., almost all were educated in the West and lived a "secular" and modern lifestyle, and yet they were militantly anti-Western.

This goes against current notions accepted by postcolonial theorists. However, as demonstrated in the earlier study of Fardid, the founder of the term *gharbzadegi*, the anti-modern ideology emerges from the elite as well as from the masses. It can emerge from such radical intellectuals as Al-e Ahmad and Shari'ati, but also from such conservatives as Fardid, Naraghi, Shaygan, et al. Here, my argument is that the anti-modern idea of *gharbzadegi* was used to undermine the state, but it was also used by the Pahlavi state to marginalize resistance.

The striking discovery in this many-levelled story is that anti-modern and anti-Western ideas do not necessarily originate from the non-West. They are rooted in certain philosophical and political currents within the West. They have traveled to the non-West via non-Western intellectuals, such as Fardid, Shari'ati, or Al-e Ahmad. This occurred either though translations of Bergson, Corbin, Heidegger, or Foucault. Elsewhere, anti-Western ideas are the products of non-Western migration to the West and back (i.e. Fardid, Shaygan, and Shari'ati), or, more broadly, non-Western intellectuals and scholars who live in the West but believe they are of the non-West. It may be that the elective affinity applies to Western and non-Western scholars and intellectuals also.

In more recent times, from the start of the twentieth century to the present, Orientalism has not been in a binary situation opposing East and West. Postcolonial theory overlooks the fact that the Western notion of the East cannot be understood identically as it was in earlier periods. It is now about the circulation of ideas. The theoretical fixation on a monolithic modernity, dredged up from a Heideggerian imagination and reproduced in Foucault's power–knowledge template, does not accurately resemble the twentieth-century transnational history of ideas. Since World War I at least, with the experiences of Corbin in Turkey and Iran and his influence on Fardid during his exile in war-torn Europe, both of whom were enraptured by Heideggerian anti-modernism, we see a complex circulatory pattern constituted of many levels of exchange. The notion of a monolithic modernity based in the West and imposing itself upon the East simply does not conform to the evidence. It is therefore necessary to challenge the binary template that undergirds postcolonial theory, in an almost facile posture of mute "otherness," and a monolithic "modernity" whose "central" precepts are universally imposed upon the "margin." A critical examination of modernity sees a plural and mediated process of circular exchanges, where the reality of stark inequalities in political or economic power should not be confused with the myth of a homogeneous Western worldview exemplifying Western culture, like a tyrant who propagates Orientalism while silencing the local and the authentic. Indeed, to promote this view is to double the nefarious and pathological ideology of the American religious right, for whom a nebulously concocted "Western culture" is uniquely at stake in struggles against non-white immigration, "Islam," the "left" (i.e. especially Barack Obama and his supporters – that is, most Americans), and secular, pluralist culture generally.

The Methodological Limits of Reading Contemporary Anti-modernism

The current literature on anti-modernism, although important and insightful, focuses upon a single intellectual current (i.e. Isaiah Berlin and German Romanticism), or a geographical location, or on one historical period (Jeffrey Herf, and the interwar interval), or, lastly, on a specific political position (i.e. conservative anti-modernists). Narrative history provides a descriptive account of anti-modernism; however, sociological theory provides an explanatory theory. Hitherto studies have either presented a historical narrative or a moral judgment upholding the superiority of the democratic and liberal tradition (Richard Wolin, Mark Lilla). It is critical that we provide the *historical contexts* and, simultaneously, clearly explain the *characteristics* of *various* anti-modern ideas and movements. As we will see, even in the same time and country, e.g. Iran in the 1960s and 1970s, very different versions of anti-modern *gharbzadegi* discourses served the interests of deadly political rivals who swore themselves to be on opposite sides of ideological divides. Therefore, analysis should be limited to neither conservative nor radical anti-modern politics: we must be able to explain both, as aspects of one sociological phenomenon.

What is needed to render intelligible the anti-modern incoherence is a new theoretical framework. What are the conditions of possibility for these movements? How can we explain these movements, in their context-specific differences, without reducing them artificially to a homogeneous sameness – and yet in a relational, non-essentialist mode, which does not reject all continuity, causality, and intelligibility? Through this optic, we can help to break down the barriers in contemporary scholarship: the liberal, reminding us that the Western liberal tradition is the best on offer; and the postcolonial, desperately seeking to identify the root of all evil in a nebulous Western modernity and salvation in some imaginary "other" space. Precisely because close analysis of historical context never bears out the universal moral supremacy of any political ideology, the liberal "normative claim" runs into the unhelpful simplicity of the partisan propagandist. Because every historical context is the site of conflicting and random forces, the facile modernity–other template of postcolonialism automatically produces a key explanation that thins to emptiness against the empirical facts it rejects.

Weber's notion of "elective affinities" was a companion idea to his theory of "institutional carriers." It derived from Goethe's novel of the same name, in which compatible social qualities produce mutual attraction.[9] In Weber's phraseology, it had three principle functions: 1) Weber wanted to attribute a relative autonomy to the social workings of religious ideas without excluding conditioning material factors; 2) Weber meant it as an alternative to "determinism" or "free will," in that society neither chooses its religion, nor is determined by the economic system; 3) Weber intended a sociological objectivity to bridge the fact–value dichotomy, in that class interests and cultural worldviews are interactive with and irreducible to one another. In sum, the "elective affinities" concept argued for a mutual attraction between idea and social status. Ideas must be in a position of influence within a social order in order to be propagandized. Weber wanted to explain the process of becoming a world religion. He identified the mass-base production process with an ideological simplicity.

This chapter explains Islamism, a modern ideological movement, within the broader context of the nativist social imaginary of *gharbzadegi* – as a paradoxically universal phenomenon. Weber's "elective affinities" very effectively explains its internal conflicts and contradictions, why it can appeal simultaneously to state elites, capitalists, proletarian revolutionaries, and bohemian artists, and serve conflicting social interests while retaining discursive coherence. It also explains other forms of *gharbzadegi*, and how they either share features with or differ from Islamism.

To make sense of *gharbzadegi*, in this respect, we need a corresponding explanation for modernity. Seen in this light, the history of neither modernization nor liberal democracy ever developed "naturally" or in a "normal" social situation over time (as Habermas has argued concerning France and England). In every case, society was forced, and, even as it modernized, also developed a hostile and painful

---

[9] Johann Wolfgang von Goethe, *Elective Affinities* (London: Penguin, 1978).

relationship with modernity. Even after society's becoming modern, or modernizing, an intense and even violent struggle continued and proceeded to shape the modernization process in a more "rational" or, as postcolonial theorists call it, "local" way. It is within this conjuncture that the "old regime," the masses, and intellectuals may share similar social and political attitudes that we may characterize as an "elective affinity." This is the case being made for *gharbzadegi* as a social imaginary. It is the general sociological source of anti-modern ideologies and social movements. Both those on the left and conservatives, and the religious and the secular partake of a common social imaginary while believing they confront each other from across irreconcilably opposed ideological divides. The ideology is not the primary mover, but complex and many-sided institutional pressures, mediated through a traceable social imaginary, where worldview and social interest have "elective affinities."

It is *gharbzadegi* as a social imaginary that animates diverse and conflicting social interests. There is only an elective affinity between different groups. The masses starve but do not speak (i.e. they have no channel). The intellectuals may be unemployed and hungry, but they are literate, privileged, and partake of a cosmopolitan intellectual culture. Military intellectuals are concerned with performance in war and the treatment of the masses (because now they come from the masses, unlike before). From these differing vantage points, they recognize themselves.

The Many Faces of *Gharbzadegi*: Fardid, Al-e Ahmad, and Shari'ati

Discussion of *gharbzadegi* in postrevolutionary Iran has produced many scholarly, thoughtful, and realistic pieces on the anti-modern discourse in Iran in the 1960s and 1970s. There are also studies that focus on some of the leading intellectuals who coined, popularized, and polarized the concept of *gharbzadegi* in pre- and postrevolutionary Iran. Ahmad Fardid, Jalal Al-e Ahmad, and Ali Shari'ati are considered the intellectual bearers of the anti-modern and anti-Western discourse in Iran. Some have also presented earlier anti-Western ideas in the work of Ahmad Kasravi, Shadman, and others.

Overall, the explanation for the rise and popularity of *gharbzadegi* in Iran is attributed to either religion or tradition, or both (i.e. Islamic reaction to modern ideas, secularism, democracy, etc.), or to leftist and Third Worldist anti-imperialist currents, and to Iranian nativism. These are primarily based on the assumption that intellectuals or movements propagated *gharbzadegi* discourse to undermine the modernizing and pro-Western Pahlavi state. What if, however, the actual roots of *gharbzadegi* discourse were embedded in Pahlavi state ideology itself? That certainly would undermine several generations of consensus on *gharbzadegi* as uniquely oppositional, or even authentically indigenous.

In an article entitled "Heidegger's Ghosts," Alexander S. Duff provides the context for the Iranian anti-modern discourse within the global setting of social and material elements interacting as "elective affinities" with the *gharbzadegi* social imaginary:

A specter haunts the post–Cold War liberal order—the specter of radical spiritual malaise. This discontent with or downright opposition to the Western-originated, universalist claims of the broadly liberal cultural, economic, and political order takes diverse forms. One can detect it among Iranian revolutionary theocrats, Russian imperialist ideologues, white supremacist "Identities," European neo-fascists, identity-politics partisans, and anti-foundationalism intellectuals of many stripes. But standing behind some of the leading intellectual and political figures in this mélange of counter-liberalism is one animating mind, that of Martin Heidegger.[10]

This suggests that a broader sociological and material base exists for anti-modern ideas. The article evokes a "radical spiritual malaise." By means of this loose grounding for analysis, the article asks why alternative ideologies have failed while the Heideggerian social imaginary is still pervasive. Since the end of the Cold War, an open question has persisted over whether any organizing political principle can successfully compete with the liberal consensus on the secular state, constrained by democratic accountability and the rule of law. To date, neither the remnants of Soviet-style Communism, nor authoritarian capitalism, reactionary fascism, or Islamic theocracy have achieved a successful combination of military strength and political legitimacy even among the citizens of these anti-liberal forces. But the Heideggerian legacy threatens liberal democracy because of the breadth of its appeal abroad and at home.

---

[10] Duff, "Heidegger's Ghosts," 1.

Heidegger's vision exemplifies the struggle between liberal cosmopolitanism and local cultural or moral claims to identity. It recommends itself to virtually every variety of particularism while charging universalist claims with being too thin to provide meaningful sources of human identity. Here is a good explanation for why Heidegger's critique of the modern West is attractive to anti-modern intellectuals and movements, and what is wrong with liberalism.

The Heideggerian template can help to clear up the confusion about the origin and the construction of *gharbzadegi* discourse. It helps to explain how, based on "elective affinities," radical, conservative, secular, and religious intellectuals and political figures have all embraced it from varied perspectives. It both corresponded to their perceived interests and seemed aesthetically compelling. This explains how *gharbzadegi* became a vision of political radicalization for revolutionaries seeking a new revolutionary ideology faced with political setback. For example, many Iranian intellectuals, known as the third line (*Khat-e Sevvom*), who mostly left the Tudeh Party to join a new intellectual circle of liberal Islamists (*Nehzatee Azadi*), were instrumental in using and popularizing *gharbzadegi* in the 1960s and 1970s. Both Al-e Ahmad and Shari'ati belong to these currents, and they are mostly responsible for the radical propagation of *gharbzadegi*. Others in this current were keen to use *gharbzadegi* to delegitimize the secular left or the modernization of the Iranian society. These individuals, however, made an abrupt turnabout. After the revolution, and without any self-critique, they became champions of anti-*gharbzadegi* ideology.

It is necessary to clarify the origin and distinctiveness of the various usages and meanings of the term *gharbzadegi*. Fardid, Al-e Ahmad, and Shari'ati shared several important ideas:

1 "Religion," in the Iranian context, involves the tradition of thinking and doing in the local and customary way. Sacred morality, they hold, as something at the center of life, has declined and is being eradicated. They all three realize this and have no illusion about the viability of returning to or maintaining it.

2 Their project is, in a way, a post-Islamic recovery of tradition. To this extent, they rely on a similar intellectual idea in the West, with a similar concern for the twilight of traditional social meaning and organization.

3 They are also either indifferent or even hostile to religious scholars
whom they perceive as "fighting a losing battle" or as unprepared to
participate in their new project of a "futurist" traditionalism.

To the extent that these three thinkers are displeased with the decline of
religion and tradition, they were, each in their own ways, hostile to
modernity and sympathetic to anti-modernism. Yet the three also had
substantial differences of outlook. Fardid was less interested in articulating a project for the future; he yearned to defeat the modern world,
based on a dark view of the future. His project was apocalyptic.
Fardid's attraction to Nazism, his enthusiasm for Khomeini's leadership, and his proximity to the state security forces are the evidence for
this.[11]

As an intellectual, Fardid was a deeply obscure figure. He wrote in
inaccessible jargon. It is possible that without Al-e Ahmad's popularization of the term *gharbzadegi* Fardid would never have been elevated
in Iran's political and intellectual history. Fardid's concept borrowed
the Heideggerian notion that something intrinsic to Greek rationality
had blocked a spiritual core in human experience and promoted an
objectifying tendency. In this account, the modern sickness had contaminated the West and Iran long ago. Certainly, in the Abbasid
Empire, Islam was already contaminated by *gharbzadegi*, and the
"ontological roots" in the Prophetic era were cut away. Hence, like
Heidegger, Fardid condemned what he called "humanism," or the
priority of the human subject and agency, in favor of a transcendental
mode of intervention. None of this far-fetched, almost cultishly
science-fiction cosmic melodrama would have occurred to the more
down-to-earth Al-e Ahmad.

Al-e Ahmad, by contrast, was an Iranian nationalist and a public
intellectual, disillusioned by the *Mashruteh* project and the Tudeh
Party's failures. He sought a native or national project for his country.
From having considered the Soviet Union the "world's most progressive nation," he became bitterly disillusioned.[12] He was open to bor-
rowing from the West and, strikingly, considered the Israeli experience
as a possible model for Iran. Al-e Ahmad kept a diary while visiting
Israel in 1962, writing: "I as an Easterner [prefer] an Israeli model over

---

[11] See Mirsepassi, *Transnationalism in Iranian Political Thought*.
[12] Jalal Al-e Ahmad, "Introduction" to the Persian translation of André Gide,
Return from the Soviet Union (Tehran: Akhtar Shoma Publisher, 1954), p. 4.

all other models of how to deal with the West. How to extract from its industries by the spiritual power of mass martyrdom, how to take restitution from it and spend the capital thus obtained to advance the country."[13] This "spiritual vision," hinting at future Islamist imaginaries, reveals how Al-e Ahmad saw Israel as "the basis for a power," an alternative model to either Soviet socialism or Western capitalism.[14] Israel had mobilized religious culture to produce economic prosperity, political independence, and cultural belonging for the national population. In discussions of the roots of Islamism, this Israeli inspiration – amidst narrow Cold War options – is frequently overlooked. Many scholars like to trace Islamist ideology to roots in the Qur'an or the time of the Prophet, but this was hardly relevant to the thinking of the seminal Islamist pioneer, sometime Marxist, and literary modernist Al-e Ahmad.

Al-e Ahmad's notion of *gharbzadegi* was a radical and populist one, set upon quite material and pragmatic aims. In this sense, Fardid was correct to repeatedly remind us that Al-e Ahmad had never fully understood the idea of *gharbzadegi* as a philosophical critique and rejection of the Western worldview. Al-e Ahmad turned the notion of *gharbzadegi* into a less substantial, but ultimately more inclusive and pragmatic idea: a conceptual optic to analyze and critique "dependent" modernity in Iran.

Al-e Ahmad's effort was sparked by disillusionment with the (Communist) Tudeh Party's capitulation to Soviet demands. Al-e Ahmad articulated a sharp critique of Western hegemonic power centered around the concept of Westoxification (*gharbzadegi*). This critique attacks Iranian secular intellectuals as complicit in Western power and incapable of effectively constructing modernity in Iran. Al-e Ahmad argued that a "return" to an "authentic" Islamic culture was necessary if Iran was to avoid the homogenizing and alienating forces of sociotechnological modernization. Yet the "return" advocated by Al-e Ahmad is not a simple one. His populist Islam would not reject modernization as such, but re-imagine modernity in accordance with Islamic principles, symbolism, and identities.

[13] Jalal Al-e Ahmad, *A Journey to Israel* (Tehran: Nashr-e Araye-Negah, 1978), p. 50.

[14] Ibid., p. 52.

Al-e Ahmad undertook ethnographic researches into the Iranian pea-
santry that inspired his charge that the "onslaught of machine and
machine civilization" would "sweep away" Iran's entire "local and cultural identity." This was a primarily sociological political criticism:
"Why? So that a factory can operate in the West, or that workers in
Iceland or Newfoundland are not jobless."[15] Yet an epistemic–ontological
inversion followed this initially sociological analysis, resulting in Al-e
Ahmad's relegation of objective or universal knowledge to a secondary
status behind cultural identity. He did not want his ethnographic monographs to become "a commodity for European consumption" based on
"European criteria." Instead, Al-e Ahmad aimed to produce a "renewal of
[Iranian] self-awareness" based on "our own criteria."[16] By this, Al-e
Ahmad meant that he hoped to mobilize the Iranian masses using culturally familiar symbols. This is still a secular orientation. Al-e Ahmad took
the step into Heideggerian thought when he started to conceive the Iranian
predicament in terms of "a disease," an "accident from without,"
"spreading in an environment rendered susceptible to it."[17] He thereby
depicted Pahlavi modernization as culturally alien, and implied that an
authentically Shi'a Iranian path must exist. Yet this had less to do with
traditional Shi'ism than with European Romantic critiques of modern
scientific knowledge in favor of an instinctive peasant proximity to the
earth: "the peasant's horse will have bolted to the safety of open land
before the seismograph has recorded [the earthquake]."[18] Upon the
same basis, Al-e Ahmad rejected shallow ideologies ("all of these
'isms'" leading to "mechanization") in favor of ontology – Iran's
"historico-cultural character," in the direct inspiration of "beauty
and poetry."[19]

Ali Shari'ati continued and extended Al-e Ahmad's critique by
articulating a positive theory of Islamic ideology as a modernizing
force. Shari'ati as a young man was a nationalist affiliated to the
National Front. Later he became more radically politicized as
a student in Paris, drawn deeply into the Third Worldist movement,
the politics of the Algerian FLN, French existentialism, and Franz

---

[15] Hamid Dabashi, *Theology of Discontent: The Ideological Foundation of the
Islamic Revolution in Iran* (New Brunswick, NJ: Transaction Publishers, 2005),
p. 59.

[16] Michael Hillmann, ed., *Iranian Society* (Lexington, KY: Mazda Publishers,
1982), p. 17.

[17] Al-e Ahmad, *Occidentosis*, p. 27.   [18] Ibid., pp. 27–28.   [19] Ibid., p. 136.

Fanon. From these experiences, Shari'ati became convinced of the need for a single ideological basis if Iranian national liberation was to succeed. He drew liberally from Marxism to construct a populist and activist Islam. Rather than a binary between East and West, he aspired to a dialogue between the two to articulate a viable modernity. Shari'ati, in his book *Red Shi'ism*, argued that the best of Iranian Islamic tradition and modern Western radical ideology might be combined in a solution to the modern world's problems. He observed the trials of Western capitalism and Soviet socialism, seeing both as riven with failings. Shari'ati was interested in Iranian identity politics, but less upon an anti-Western than on an anti-capitalist basis.

Through these readings, the discourse of authenticity emerges as a dialogic mode of reconciling local cultures with modernity rather than as a stubborn determination to avoid modernity at all costs. Their calls for a revitalized and politicized Islam represent attempts to negotiate with the universalizing tendencies of modernity, rather than the gathering storm clouds of a clash of civilizations.

Shari'ati was more complicated, and perhaps intellectually more naïve, than either Fardid or Al-e Ahmad. In an ironic way, he was both more secular, and more religious, than the other two. He was more influenced by Marxism and radical revolutionary ideas, especially the secular Third World discourses of the 1960s. Simultaneously, Shari'ati was far more concerned with offering a positive, or alternative, interpretation of Islam: as anti-capitalist, anti-liberal, and very revolutionary. It is harder to make a case that Shari'ati was genuinely a consistent anti-modernist. However, Corbin and Heidegger were his important influences.

One can suggest that the Shari'ati approach to Islam can potentially lead to a liberal Islamic discourse – a kind of liberalism that is less secular, and more communitarian and sensitive to social justice. Some may take this as unrealistic for two reasons: Shari'ati was influenced by Corbin and by Heideggerian notions of authenticity, and, particularly, Marxism. Also, "religious liberalism" contains an inherent tension: while liberalism embedded in religion might seem an attractive idea, it shatters upon the rocks of rival authenticity claims upon being institutionalized.

Addressing the young and the middle classes, Shari'ati reconstructed Shi'a Islam to entail a religious obligation to revolt against regimes based on injustice, i.e. all existing state power worldwide. The only successful revolution, moreover, must spring from authentic religious roots, and not alien Western ideologies. The "backwards-looking" Iranian Shi'a clergy were useless for this purpose. Only a dynamic, modern intellectual vanguard could assume leadership. Shari'ati envisioned the "modern calamities" in terms of the universal human rootlessness inflicted by the machine: "Humanity is every day more condemned to alienation, more drowned in this mad maelstrom of compulsive speed." He implied that the qualitative, poetic side of human life had been lost: "Not only is there no longer leisure for growth in human values, moral greatness, and spiritual aptitudes," but "traditional moral values decline and disappear as well."[20]

Shari'ati, however, transcends this essentially Romantic view to construct Shi'a Islam as a revolutionary organizational machine based on "the war of religion against religion," i.e. a revived, authentic revolutionary Islam versus the existing but inauthentic conservative orthodoxy. Shari'ati used these ideas in explicitly Heideggerian manner as rival tendencies perennially engaged in battle within the Shi'a tradition, but with only one ontologically legitimated idea. He maintained that "true Islam," the "revolutionary sort," had been "forgotten." Rejecting the superficiality of "one-dimensional facts," Shari'ati based his red Shi'ism on a politics of the "self."[21] The Heideggerian element in Shari'ati is fused with revolutionary Marxism. The true enemy was the "petty bourgeoisie," the "dirty connection" which had spoiled true Islam.[22] The real aim of Islam, Shari'ati held, was the Marxist one of building a "classless society" on earth, to be governed by the modern intelligentsia.[23]

The author of "Heidegger's Ghosts," Alexander S. Duff, therefore makes a good point in arguing that Heidegger's ideas in Iran, in the anti-modern *gharbzadegi* discourse, concerned a "futuristic" project:

Several leading Iranian thinkers prior to and following the 1979 Revolution were formed by their understanding of Heidegger, drawing on his thought in both the diagnosis of the toxicity of Western civilization and their aspiration

---

[20] Ali Shari'ati, *Marxism and Other Western Fallacies: An Islamic Critique*, trans. R. Campbell (Berkeley, CA: Mizan Press 1980), p. 32.
[21] Ervand Abrahamian, *Radical Islam: Iranian Mojahedin* (New Haven: Yale University Press, 1992), p. 116.
[22] Dabashi, *Theology of Discontent*, pp. 122, 141–142.
[23] Abrahamian, *Radical Islam*, pp. 113–114.

for a future-oriented, permanent revolution that would retrieve something of an Islamic past lost beneath the stomping boots of history.[24]

The author of "Heidegger's Ghosts" only makes certain factual errors. It was not Shari'ati but Ahmad Fardid who introduced Heidegger and his philosophy into Iran, and in the 1930s rather than the 1950s. Also, Shari'ati, while in Paris, collaborated with Frantz Fanon and was influenced by Jean-Paul Sartre. Shari'ati was also influenced by another Parisian scholar, Henry Corbin, and his idea of Shi'ism as the core Persian spiritual tradition. Henry Corbin was the first person who introduced Heidegger to France, and first translated the works of Heidegger into French.

We see, in this tangle of examples, a circulatory dynamic. The same type of explanation applies to Corbin. He was a product of the crisis of the Third Republic and the Franco-Prussian War, when the Catholic Royalist movement finally yielded to the secular republican movement – who embraced the Rights of Man while practicing colonialism. Corbin went to the Middle East, looking for his lost utopia for France. Corbin hated France because it had betrayed the Catholic monarchist tradition, to install a secular republic. The Turkish and Iranian intellectuals Corbin encountered were hostile to France because of its imperialist designs on their national sovereignty. Corbin and these intellectuals found common ground in being hostile to France. Yet their reasons were entirely different. Despite this difference, together they helped to spread the *gharbzadegi* social imaginary and expand its popularity. To hear Corbin's criticism of the West, rooted in a deeper tradition, from De Maistre, but above all World War I and Heidegger, was a blessed occasion for many. Not so for the left or liberal streams in the Middle East – but they faced their own tragedy. The new USSR practiced a ruthless geopolitics, and the charge of collaboration with Western power hung over those embracing Western ideologies.

To add to the complexity of this picture, Foucault followed the trail of Corbin. This was another French intellectual with very different concerns. A student of Louis Althusser, who had yet grown disillusioned with the "vulgarity" of French Marxism, he hated the secular republic in France. This hostility arose not from a religious standpoint, but a disillusioned leftist one. The revulsion against "secular humanism" inspired Foucault to seek a "way out" of modernity through

---

[24] Duff, "Heidegger's Ghosts," 2.

revolutionary Shi'a Islam. He associated "secular humanism" with the "disciplinary society" that had destroyed the soul, that had thrived in the relative anarchy of pre-modern societies (the mad as visionaries, public torture of heroic criminals, unrestrained bucolic sexual pleasures in the villages, etc.). Foucault, visiting Iran during the revolution, wrote articles extolling "spiritual Islam" and "mythical" or "spiritual" politics as exciting new political possibilities beyond Western liberal norms. These views derived less from Foucault's Marxist teacher, Althusser, and more from readings of Louis Massignon and Henry Corbin. Foucault derived from these sources a premonition that something new, unprecedented, and perhaps mystical was emerging in the 1978–9 Revolution. Celebrating the revolution's "mythical leaders," Foucault went so far as to castigate Iranian secular and non-religious forces, charging them with reproducing a dull Western model (i.e. constitutional, reformist), rather than entering the new and exciting terrain of spiritual politics. Foucault saw in the 1978–9 Revolution an instantiation of his quasi-mystical thesis of the "death of man," i.e. the epistemic reign of the human sciences. In short, he adopted a Heideggerian optic of ontology triumphing over epistemology. Foucault rejoiced at the 1978–9 Revolution as the escape from an "imposed teleology" – a mystic and irrational outlook, reflecting personal intellectual obsessions more than social reality.[25] It portended, he excitedly urged, "a different way of thinking about social and political organization, one that takes nothing from Western philosophy."[26] The Enlightenment, he maintained, with "objectivity" and "rationality," was the "revolutionary enemy."[27]

Foucault ridiculed Marxism, and the left affirmed his hatred for capitalism and democracy (as "modernity"), and ultimately he embraced an anti-modern ideology very similar to Corbin's. Foucault, a Bataille- and Nietzsche-inspired scholar, had an undertow of religious obsessions. There was also a certain elitism – a preoccupation with the beauty of private rituals and experiences, sheltered from the banality of modern mass society. These elements

[25] Michel Foucault, *The Essential Foucault: Selections from the Essential Works of Foucault, 1954–1984*, ed. Paul Rabinow and Nikolas Rose, revised edition (New York: The New Press, 2003), 332.
[26] Janet Afary and Kevin Anderson, *Foucault and the Iranian Revolution: Gender and the Seductions of Islamism* (University of Chicago Press, 2010), p. 186.
[27] Ibid., p. 185.

fostered in Foucault, a comparatively privileged and celebrated intellectual, an indulgence toward *gharbzadegi* – the attraction to the arcane, the sacred, a fusion of individual and higher abstract principles like divine oneness, and, above all, a rupture with the money nexus of modernity.

The masses in Iran, and other semi-colonized countries, faced a different reality. They could hardly have been attracted to *gharbzadegi* for the same reasons as Foucault. Yet they did become attracted to it, from an entirely different horizon of experience. Their social interests were not Foucault's. But the "elective affinity" existed between Foucault and the Iranian masses. Nothing indigenous compelled the Iranian masses to embrace *gharbzadegi*. Iran's modern history shows another direction. There was genuine multi-class mass enthusiasm for the rule of law and national autonomy in the Constitutional Revolution, starting with the tobacco revolt and culminating in a constitutional monarchy. Then there was World War I, which entailed considerable hardship, and the 1921 British-sponsored coup that set up a dictator in order to protect British India from Russia. Even so, in the National Front interim, there was still mass Iranian support for a "liberal" and "Marxist" politics. After the United States-sponsored 1953 coup against the popularly elected Mossadegh, the second such coup in a century, real disillusionment with the West viscerally set in.

The Permutations of the Twentieth-Century Iranian Left

A striking feature of modern Iranian intellectual history is how Marxism has been situated within a powerful anti-modernist current. This phenomenon reveals the underlying pattern of discursive circularity in local–global flows of ideas. Early Marxism in Iran was clearly modernist and proudly cosmopolitan (1930s–40s). This was evident in Taghi Arani and the early Tudeh Party, whose ideas affirmed an egalitarian and democratically (via education) modernizing Iran, linked to other modern nations in an anti-imperial struggle. This was no closed or elite party, but a broadly inclusive coalition of politically motivated groups and individuals. Many Iranian nationalists and liberal intellectuals maintained informal ties with the Tudeh Party. Moreover, the Tudeh Party boasted a brilliantly creative avant-garde whose literary experiments – Sadegh Hedayat exemplifies this – pushed the frontiers of modern artistic and political self-expression. Moreover, the Tudeh did not follow the authoritarian secularist stream (i.e. the Soviet Union or Kemalist Turkey) that excluded the involvement of religious-minded individuals and groups. The participation of religious people inspired by Marxist and socialist ideas was important to the growing Iranian left. "The Movement of God-Worshipping Socialists" is one example.[28] Ali Shari'ati, who was zaffiliated with this group, generously borrowed from Marxist theory to articulate this modern Islamist ideology.

However, the post–1953 period witnessed a dramatic rise in anti-modern sentiments among many Iranian intellectuals. This allowed Marxists, of which Al-e Ahmad is the prime example, to embrace the anti-modern ideologies already spreading among Europeans disgusted with the Depression and two catastrophic world wars. Simultaneously, a significant attempt was made among Iranian intellectuals to creatively localize Marxism within a new nativist idiom.

In the twentieth century, Marx's ideas were encountered within non-Western contexts in two opposing directions. While the affiliation with Marxism remained fashionable, Marx's ideas were "localized" in Soviet, Chinese, and Indian variants. A striking instance is the Mujahedeen, who, capturing the transnational imagination of several generations, derived inspiration from Marxist ideas. Through this optic, anti-imperialist and anti-capitalist Marxism was privileged over the universalist and cosmopolitan features of Marxist thought. Within this anti-imperialist and anti-capitalist tradition, important individuals pioneered the use of Marx to express anti-modern and anti-liberal sentiment. Ironically, their contribution has been the most enduring feature of Marxian radicalism, even as the Marxist heritage has in other respects faded with the collapse of the Soviet Union and Marxism as a genuinely existing world power.

Recently, with this decline in Marxism, many former Marxists have reconceived Marxism in an anti-modern style – with strong Heideggerian and occult overtones – and selectively extracted elements from Marx's corpus to this reconstructive end. They blindly celebrate

---

[28] The Movement of God-Worshipping Socialists (Nazhat Khoda Parastan-i Socialist) was founded in 1943 in Iran. The group was led by Mohammad Nakhshab. They were initially known as the League of Patriotic Muslims. Its ideology was a fusion of Islamic sentiments, Persian nationalism, and socialist ideas.

anti-liberalism with a moral passion devoid of constructive substance and advocate a pre-modern ideological line of marginalization, identity, and memory. Indeed, the contemporary anti-modern camp has hijacked Marx, something the nineteenth-century founder of radical modern sociology and scientific socialism himself would have certainly deplored.

The "traditionalist" anti-modern current – in Iran and elsewhere – had always viewed Marx with hostility and deemed him the modernist enemy. They deplored Marx as the fountainhead of modern atheism, throwing cherished faith into doubt. Fardid and even Shari'ati viewed Marx as a "humanist" and charged him with being post-transcendental. The power of Marx's vision saturated the rudiments of their worldviews all the same, and all modern revolutions – religious or secular – have an elective affinity with Marx's modern revolution in the human imagination.

Viewing Modern Iran through Elective Affinities

Thus, the "elective affinity" between Western and Iranian intellectuals, and these intellectuals and the Iranian masses, is highly complex, requiring a transnational optic, but it is also historically intelligible. A similar logic of "elective affinities" can explain the relation of Iranian state elites and the Iranian masses, as well as important Iranian public intellectuals. The Pahlavi quest for self-stability lured it into the web of self-destruction, because its self-interests seemed erroneously to conform to the *gharbzadegi* discourse, even as revolutionary social agents made the same fatal estimation.

The Pahlavi regime faced a critical choice: to open up, or to advance dictatorially, making the Shah a god-like figure – and they chose the second path. Again, in circuitous manner, the regime appropriated ideological components conveniently from everywhere. Intellectuals opposed to the regime did so also, but much more effectively. The masses faced a brutally violent and frightening situation, of economic, political, and cultural violence, plus the national humiliation of arrogant foreign rule, and had been let down previously by other popular ideologies. Now, the public space of images and narratives becomes truly significant. The experience of New Wave cinema fostered a mixture of hope in "tradition" and "Islam," and a rejection of the "modern," "corrupt," etc. How do most people make political decisions? Quite quickly, desperately, without the luxury of a lot of time to reflect, and with a firm conviction about their own interests and those of their family or entourage, and also with a belief in what they have learned from their upbringing. It is often a big gamble, not made alone, and with high risk. There can be an elective affinity between revolutionary masses and intellectuals.

What is the upshot of studying this complex pattern of "elective affinities"? Firstly, it places in doubt one vaguely argued thesis of "Heidegger's Ghosts" and many fashionable postcolonial arguments. It is a major mistake to argue that the Heideggerian project, as "Heidegger's Ghost" seems to suggest, provides more social or cultural space for the local. It is entirely the opposite case. Islamist, or other so-called anti-modern and "local" currents, are far more oppressive of other "local" traditions. They have absolutely no tolerance, either in practice or ideologically, for minorities and local communities.

The "local" is really a merely "imagined" local. It is, in fact, global and transnational, and, ironically, it is invoked by Western scholars and intellectuals rather than those inhabiting the "local space." Even Islamic intellectuals and scholars, those who either live in the West or have studied in the West, use the notion of the local. Traditionalists rarely do so. The Shah and his associates, who, almost all educated in the West, adopted a "cosmopolitan" and Western lifestyle, also celebrated the uniqueness of Iran as a local cultural place. For them, too, this category of the "local" was entirely imaginary. It had little to do with the harsh and troubled transnational spaces which are the only real terrain for struggle and change in our world.

Mistaken Modernities?

In a *New York Times* article entitled "Westoxication & Modern Toxicity," anti-modernist sentiments in contemporary India are explained using *gharbzadegi* as perhaps the most popular word to criticize the pre-revolutionary Iranian experience of modernity. It reads: "Terms used in India to characterize the adoption of the material trappings of Western life, without also embracing Western values of equality." The main difference between the Indian and Iranian version of Westoxification is the generous, and maybe naïve, image of "Western modernity" among Indian writers. Interestingly, the op-ed in *The New York Times* refers to the genealogy of the debate in Iran:

The Iranian intellectual Jalal Al-e Ahmed coined the term "Westoxication," as opposed to Westernized. He was referring to those who embrace Western technology and the high life while negating the equality of opportunity. In the Indian context, a more appropriate term would be "modern toxicity," as opposed to "modernity." Unless we in India embrace modernity in its completeness, the dreams of India as an emerging economy would be impossible to achieve.[29]

This view projects an almost utopian image of modernity as a socially liberating project, and it rejects the Indian version as the modern trappings without the egalitarian substance. One can assume that, at least in the case of India, there is still hope for the "real" modernity. *The New York Times* op-ed, meanwhile, seems to present a more balanced and sociologically grounded view of Westoxification. It is a Habermasian critique of modernity in the Indian context. For example, it refers to a piece by Sitaram, published in *The Hindustan Times*:

This is the modern Indian paradox. Those considered "modern," in terms of flaunting the latest gadgets and fashion, simultaneously perpetuate age-old prejudices based on caste and gender.

Any curious observer might wonder why this situation is defined and explained in terms of Westoxification discourse (*gharbzadegi*). Why not an unfulfilled modernity or, in Habermas' words, an incomplete modernity? What are the social roots of the toxicity? Why is modernity geographically organic to the West, and not India?

Al-e Ahmad, too, was critical of modern statesmen and intellectuals who, using modern and Western material resources to perpetuate high status, flaunted the rhetoric of democracy and equality, but were indifferent to the poor. However, the piece on India is focused more on the problem of modern development in India, and not the entire Enlightenment project. This piece also refers to the Indian sociologist Danker Gupta and his book *Mistaken Modernity*, in which he defines: "a modern society as one that has the following characteristics: 'Dignity of the individual; adherence to universalistic norms; elevation of individual achievements over privilege or dis-privilege of birth and accountability in public life'."[30]

---

[29] Ben Schott, "Westoxification & Modern Toxicity," *The New York Times*, op-ed (April 12, 2011).

[30] Gupta, *Mistaken Modernity*, p. 2.

This holistic and almost utopian view of modernity is now used to undermine it. This is particularly interesting in the case of India. One may argue that, in the non-Western context, the development of modern India is a relatively successful story. Both Gandhi and Nehru had a balanced view of the local traditions and conditions in India, and recognized the complicated and diverse situation post-independence. Their vision of modern and democratic India has led to the development and survival of a stable and democratic India for over seventy years.

However, Indian intellectuals and scholars, both inside and, particularly, outside of India, are the leading proponents of postcolonial discourse and militant anti-modernists. How do we explain this? Is it the case that a high expectation of modernity's possible achievements is the source of the anti-modern current in India? As it stands, the very categories of the "nation," "democracy," "development," "history," and other sociologically related terms, are charged by Subaltern and postcolonial scholars with being a poison that has undermined the indigenous agency of the multiple Indian populations. These influential scholars thus uphold a variant of *gharbzadegi*, in the language of Foucault and sometimes Heidegger, but also citing Marx, in which an indigenous cultural revival shall usher in the utopia of social justice that "modernity" has promised but never achieved.

If we take these various examples – from Fardid to Corbin via Heidegger, the Islamist ideologues Al-e Ahmad and Shari'ati, the complex Iranian left, and the postcolonial vogue from India to America – into account, there is no such thing as the "authentic anti-modern." Anti-modern ideas and discourses, like modernists of liberal or secular persuasion, are circulatory, the pieces are flying everywhere, traveling back and forth, being recycled, modified, and presented perhaps as local or authentic. Liberalism and even the West are often attacked in monolithic terms in the contemporary "orthodoxy" of academic writing. Any defense instantly brings down the charge of "liberal" or "imperialist" upon the head of the sceptic. Yet even what we call liberalism or modernism is subject to the circularity of ideas and discourses. French liberalism differs from Indian liberalism, as Marxism in Italy differs from its Chinese counterpart. These are both global and local, the products of the exchange of ideas and ideologies, practiced and reconfigured in each specific time and place. The recognition of this deprives many "radical" scholars of a polemical straw man cherished for its harmless convenience in contemporary academic writing. If we cannot bash the "liberal" and "modernity," then how shall we save the world, in the fantasy realm of our fashionable academic publications? Yet to relinquish the straw man in any form is to view social history through a more nuanced and complex optic.

It is hard to imagine how an issue in the French Third Republic (Corbin's torment) might have inspired Iran's Islamist conjuncture, as only one principle element among dozens more (some from Russia, or India, etc.), and how Iran's conjuncture, in turn, inspired movements elsewhere. Yet this is precisely what happened. We can take this argument a step further. The image of the 1978–9 Revolution as the authentic anti-secular project has now become the unspoken paradigm of the culturalist left. One may wonder whether, had Iran taken a different course in the late 1970s, today's academic left might have been very different.

Bibliography

Abrahamian, Ervand, *Radical Islam: Iranian Mojahedin* (New Haven: Yale University Press, 1992).

Adeli, Mohammad Hossein, "Consumerism and Narcissism," *Bonyad Monthly*, Special Issue, (April 1978): 42–46.

Afary, Janet and Kevin Anderson, *Foucault and the Iranian Revolution: Gender and the Seductions of Islamism* (University of Chicago Press, 2010).

Al-e Ahmad, Jalal, "Introduction" to the Persian translation of André Gide, *Return from the Soviet Union* (Tehran: Akhtar Shoma Publisher, 1954).

  Occidentosis: A Plague from the West, trans. Robert Campbell, ed. H. Algar (Berkeley, CA: Mizan, [1962] 1984).

  A Journey to Israel (Tehran: Nashr-e Araye-Negah, 1978).

Arani, Taghi, "Mysticism and Principals of Materialism" in *Writings and Articles of Dr. Arani* (Cologne: Pahl-Rugenstein Verlag, [1933] 1977).

Arkoun, Mohammed, "Islamic Culture, Modernity, Architecture" in *Architectural Education in the Islamic World*, ed. Ahmet Evin (Singapore: Concept Media/Aga Khan Award for Architecture, 1986).

  Rethinking Islam: Common Questions, Uncommon Answers (Boulder, CO: Westview Press, 1994).

Asian Film Online, "Summary of the Cycle." Accessed August 20, 2015. https://search.alexanderstreet.com/preview/work/bibliographic_entity%7Cvideo_work%7C2063586

Avesta, Mehrdad, "An Interview with Avesta about Literature and Erfan," *Bonyad Monthly*, No. 17 (August 1978): 82–87.

Banuazizi, Ali, "*Olum-e Ejtema'i*, a Quarterly Journal of Social Sciences, ed. Ehsan Naraghi and Daryush Ashuri, Tehran: Institute for Social Studies and Research, University of Tehran, 1968–," *Iranian Studies* 2, No. 1 (winter 1969): 45.

Bergson, Henri, *Creative Evolution*, trans. Arthur Mitchell (New York: Dover, 1998).

  Essai sur les données immédiates de la conscience (Paris: PUF, 2007).

  Time and Free Will: An Essay on the Immediate Data of Consciousness (Mineola, NY: Dover Publications, 2001).

Berman, Marshall, *All That Is Solid Melts into Air: The Experience of Modernity* (London: Verso, 1982).

Beyza'i, Bahram, *Gharibeh va Meh (Stranger and the Fog)* (Tehran: Cinema Theater-e Rex, 1975).

Bill, James A., "Review: *From Palace to Prison: Inside the Iranian Revolution* by Ehsan Naraghi, trans. Nilu Mobasser, Chicago: Ivan R. Dee, 1994," *The Middle East Journal* Vol. 49, No. 1 (winter 1995).

Bonyad Monthly, "A Western Tribe among the Ethnic Iranians," *Bonyad Monthly*, Special Issue (April 1978): 34–35.

Bonyad Monthly Research Group, "Racism and Apartheid," *Bonyad Monthly*, No. 15 (June 1978): 3–13.

Castoriadis, Cornelius, *The Imaginary Institution of Society* (Cambridge, MA: MIT University Press, 1987).

Centre Iranien pour L'Etude des Civilizations, *L'Impact de la pensée occidentale rend-il possible un dialogue réel entre les civilisations?* (Paris: Berg International, 1979).

Corbin, Henry. "An Interview with Henry Corbin: The Inner East," *Bonyad Monthly*, No. 1 (March 1977): 6.

The Voyage and the Messenger: Iran and Philosophy (Berkeley, CA: North Atlantic Books, 1998).

Dabashi, Hamidi, *Close Up: Iranian Cinema, Past, Present, and Future* (London: Verso, 2001).

Masters and Masterpieces of Iranian Cinema (Washington, DC: Mage Publishers, 2007).

Theology of Discontent: The Ideological Foundation of the Islamic Revolution in Iran (New Brunswick, NJ: Transaction Publishers, 2005).

Daneshvar, Reza, ed. *A Garden between Two Streets: 4001 Days in the Life of Kamran Diba, in Conversation with Reza Daneshvar* (Tehran: Bongah Publishers, 2013).

Darwin, Charles, *The Two Sources of Morality and Religion*, trans. R. Ashley Audra and Cloudsley Brereton, with the assistance of W. Horsfall Carter (Notre Dame, IN: University of Notre Dame Press, [1935] 1977).

Davari, Reza, "An Interview with Reza Davari," *Bonyad Monthly*, No. 5 (August 1977): 32.

Dubos, René, "Against Technology," trans. A. Azarang, *Bonyad Monthly*, No. 10 (January 1978): 14–17.

Duff, Alexander S., "Heidegger's Ghosts," *The American Interest*, Vol. 11, No. 5 (February 25, 2016).

Editor, "The End of the Age of Sandwich Images," *Bonyad Monthly*, No. 10 (January 1978): 13.

"Freedom Means Having No Wish," *Bonyad Monthly*, No. 18 (September 1978): 3–4.

"The Pars News Agency: A Way against the News Imperialism," *Bonyad Monthly*, No. 14 (May 1978): 47 and 174.

"Persons of the Year 1977," *Bonyad Monthly*, Special Issue (April 1978): 12–17.

Ellerin, Milton, "A Report of the Revival of Nazism in Europe," trans. Farah Barari, *Bonyad Monthly*, No. 19 (October 1978): 20–22.

Faghiri, Abolghasem, "Village Culture: Kaka Siyah," *Bonyad Monthly*, Special Issue (April 1978): 166–167.

"Village Culture: Kharkan Daughter," *Bonyad Monthly*, No. 20 (November 1978): 53.

"Village Culture: New Year's Game in Shiraz," *Bonyad Monthly*, No. 14 (May 1978): 92–93.

Fardid, Ahmad, *Gharb va Gharbzadegi* [The West and Westoxification], Vol. I, unpublished (Tehran: Bonyad-e Hekmi va Falsafi-ye Doktor Fardid).

"Henri Bergson and Bergsonian Philosophy: I," *Majalle-ye Mehr* (February 1938).

"Henri Bergson and Bergsonian Philosophy: II," *Majalle-ye Mehr* (April 1938).

"Presentism of Persian Academy," *Bonyad Monthly*, No. 4 (July 1977): 5.

Fatemi, Said, "Historical Cryptology of a Religion," *Bonyad Monthly*, No. 8 (November 1977): 43.

"I Was Crude, Attained Experience, and Burned," *Bonyad Monthly*, No. 14 (May 1978): 8–11.

"An Interview with Said Fatemi: Myths," *Bonyad Monthly*, No. 2 (May 1977): 63–64.

"The Presence of Old Myths in Modern Thoughts," *Bonyad Monthly*, No. 5 (August 1977): 18–23.

"Social Symbols of Ancient Gods of Iran," *Bonyad Monthly*, No. 7 (October 1977): 14.

"Thirty Centuries of Human Anthem," *Bonyad Monthly*, No. 4 (July 1977): 17 and 66.

"The Universalism of a School," *Bonyad Monthly*, No. 9 (December 1977): 24–25.

Forughi, Mohammad Ali, *Seyr-e Hekmat dar Orupa* (*The History of Philosophy in Europe*) (Tehran: Zavar Publisher, 1965).

Foucault, Michel, *The Essential Foucault: Selections from the Essential Works of Foucault, 1954–1984*, ed. Paul Rabinow and Nikolas Rose, revised edition (New York: The New Press, 2003).

Goethe, Johann Wolfgang von, *Elective Affinities* (London: Penguin, 1978).

Goleh, Fereydun, *Kandu (The Beehive)* (Tehran: Seyera Film, 1975).

Golestan, Ebrahim, *Asrar-e Ganj-e Darreh-ye Jenni (Secrets of the Jinni Valley Treasure)* (Tehran: Kargah-e Film-e Golestan, 1972).

Gupta, Dipankar, *Mistaken Modernity: India between Worlds* (London: HarperCollins, 2000).

Hercules, Frank, "To Live in Harlem," trans. Hadi Dastbaz, *Bonyad Monthly*, No. 19 (October 1978): 14–15 and 27.

Herf, Jeffrey, *Reactionary Modernism* (Cambridge University Press, 1984).

Hillmann, Michael, ed., *Iranian Society* (Lexington, KY: Mazda Publishers, 1982).

Homayunfar, Ezzatollah, "Messenger of Peace," *Bonyad Monthly*, No. 1 (March 1977): 4.

Hoveyda, Fereydun, *The Shah and the Ayatollah: Iranian Mythology and the Islamic Revolution* (New York: Prager, 2003).

Jacobson, Dan, "Memories and Dangers of Travel to South Africa," trans. Farah Barari, *Bonyad Monthly*, No. 18 (September 1978): 23–28.

"Memories and Dangers of Travel to South Africa, Part 2," trans. Farah Barari, *Bonyad Monthly*, No. 19 (October 1978): 16–19.

Jazayeri, Ezzatollah, "A Letter from Sweden: Let Nobel Heroes Know That We Are Heroes As Well," *Bonyad Monthly*, No. 3 (June 1977): 21.

Jozi, Mohammad Reza, *"Review of Position of Philosophy in the History of the Islamic Iran," Bonyad Monthly*, No. 9 (December 1977): 56–57.

Kadivar, Mohsen, *Government of the Guardian* (Tehran: Nashr-e Nei, 1998).

Khodadadian, Ardeshir, "Avesta Literature," *Bonyad Monthly*, No. 18 (September 1978): 32–33.

"An Introduction to the History of Culture and Civilization of the Ancient Iran," *Bonyad Monthly*, No. 14 (May 1978): 19–32.

"A Review of Pre-Islam Literature and Languages," *Bonyad Monthly*, No. 17 (August 1978): 18–19.

Khosravi, Khosro, *Khark Island during Oil Domination* (Tehran: Mo'asseseh-e Motale'at va Tahghighat-e Ejtema'i, 1963).

Kimia'i, Mas'ud, *Gavaznha (The Deer)* (Tehran: Studio Misaghiyah, 1974). *Gheysar* (Tehran: Aryana Film, 1968).

Kimiavi, Parviz, *Mogholha (The Mongols)* (Tehran: Sazman-e Radio va TV Melli-ye Iran, 1973).

Lawrence, Bruce B., *Defenders of God: The Fundamentalist Revolt against the Modern Age* (Columbia: University of South Carolina Press, 1989).

Lilla, Mark, *The Reckless Mind: Intellectuals in Politics* (The New York Review of Books, 2001).

The Stillborn God: Religion, Politics, and the Modern West (New York: Vintage Books, 2008).

Mazluman, Reza, "Imitation and Social Frustration," *Bonyad Monthly*, No. 17 (August 1978): 4–7 and 86–97.

Mehrju'i, Daryush, *Agha-ye Halu (Mr. Gullible)* (Tehran: Studio Caspian, 1970).

Gav (The Cow) (Tehran: Vezarat-e Farhang va Honar, 1969).

Meybodi, Alireza, "The Beggar of Freedom," *Bonyad Monthly*, No. 20 (November 1978): 4.

"Consummation of History," *Bonyad Monthly*, No. 1 (March 1977): 32.

"The Crisis of Self," *Bonyad Monthly*, No. 3 (June 1977): 4–5.

"Linguistic Doctrine for Language," *Bonyad Monthly*, No. 4 (July 1977): 5.

"New Years and Yesterdays," *Bonyad Monthly*, Special Issue (April 1978): 8–11.

Milani, Abbas, *Eminent Persians: The Men and Women Who Made Modern Iran, 1941–1979*. Vol. I (Syracuse, NY: Syracuse University Press, 2008).

The Shah (Toronto: Persian Circle, 2012).

Miller, Arthur, "Literature and the the Consumer Society," trans. Mehdi Khamush, *Bonyad Monthly*, No. 16 (July 1978): 14–17.

Mirsepassi, Ali, *Intellectual Discourse and the Politics of Modernization: Negotiating Modernity in Iran* (Cambridge University Press, 2001)

Interview with Alireza Meybodi, Los Angeles, CA, April 26, 2015.

Political Islam and the Enlightenment: Philosophies of Hope and Despair (Cambridge University Press, 2010).

Transnationalism in Iranian Political Thought: The Life and Times of Ahmad Fardid (Cambridge University Press, 2017).

Mirsepassi, Ali and Mehdi Faraji, "De-politicizing Westoxification: The Case of *Bonyad Monthly*," *The British Journal of Middle Eastern Studies* (December 2016): 2–21.

"Iranian Cinema's 'Quiet Revolution,' 1960–1978," *Middle East Critique*, Vol. 26, No. 4 (December 2017): 397–415.

Mohseni, Majid, *Bolbol-e Mazra'eh (Nightingale of the Farm)* (Tehran: Studio Diyana Film, 1957).

Parastuha beh Laneh Barmigardand (Tehran: Tehran Film, 1963).

Nabavi, Ebrahim, *Through an Unbaked Brick: Interview with Ehsan Naraghi* (Tehran: Jame'eh Iranian, 1999).

Naderi, Amir, *Tangsir* (Tehran: Sazman-e Cinema-ye Payam, 1973).

Naficy, Hamid, *A Social History of Iranian Cinema*. Vol. II (Durham, NC, and London: Duke University Press, 2011).

Naraghi, Ehsan, *The Alienation of the West* (Tehran: Amir Kabir, 1974).

The Development of the Social Sciences in Iran (Tehran: Nikan, 1965).

Freedom (Tehran: Afkar, 2004).

Freedom, Right, and Justice: A Talk between Esma'il Khu'i and Ehsan (Tehran: Javidan, 1976).

Hormoz Ki's Talk with Ehsan Naraghi (Tehran: Jame'eh-e Iranian, 2002).

Impossible Fate (Tehran: Elm, 2003).

From Palace to Prison: Inside the Iranian Revolution, trans. Nilu Mobasser (Chicago, IL: Ivan R. Dee, 1994).

What Oneself Had (Tehran: Amir Kabir, 1974).

Naraghi, Ehsan and Ata Ayati, *A Glance at Social Research in Iran* (Tehran: Sokhan, 2000).

Naraghi, Hasan, *A Brief History of Iran: From the Aryans to the End of the Pahlavi Dynasty* (Tehran: Atiyah, 1999).

"Historical Building of Kashan's Telegraph Center," *Tasvir*, No. 29 (March 1964): 21–25.

Kashan in Mashruteh (Tehran: Mash'al-e Azadi, 1976).

"Shah 'Abbas's Tomb in Kashan and Its Historical Documents," *Honar va Mardom*, No. 24 (October 1964): 46–49.

Social History of Kashan (Tehran: Moasese-ye Motaleat va Tahghighat-e Ejtema'i, 1966).

"Tayer-e Qodsi or Mohaghegh and Fazel Naraghi's Poetry," *Tasvir*, No. 187 (May 1978): 47–50.

Nassaji, Reza, *Questioning and Fighting: A Conversation with Manoucher Ashtiyani on Contemporary History and the Human Sciences in Iran* (Tehran: Nashr-e Nei, 2017).

Nur, Zia', "*Vahdat-e Vojud* and Its Display in Masnavi," *Bonyad Monthly*, No. 2 (May 1977): 20–25.

Omid, Jamal, *History of Iranian Cinema, 1279–1375* (Tehran: Entesharat-e Rowzaneh, 1995).

Pahlavi, Ashraf, "Human, the Third World, Rights, and Justice," *Bonyad Monthly*, Special Issue (April 1978): 3.

"A Space to Think," *Bonyad Monthly*, No. 1 (March 1977): 3.

Pahlavi, Mohammad Reza, *Toward a Great Civilization: A Dream Revisited* (London: Satrap Publishing, 1994).

Pajuhesh, "The Horrendous Domination: How the West Made Eastern 'Brains' Homeless," *Bonyad Monthly*, Special Issue (April 1978): 47 and 174.

"Racism," *Bonyad Monthly*, Special Issue (April 1978): 68–72.

Pierce, Paul Sh., "The Dreams of Black America," trans. Hadi Dastbaz, *Bonyad Monthly*, No. 18 (September 1978): 20–22.

Proust, Marcel, *Du Côté de chez Swann* (Paris: Gallimard, 1988).

Raja'i Zafrei, Mohammad Hassan, "Village Culture: Ta'ziyeh in Rural Areas," *Bonyad Monthly*, No. 16 (September 1978): 84–85.

Ranjbin, Naser, "The West and the East from the Eastern Man's Point of View," *Bonyad Monthly*, No. 10 (January 1978): 32–36.

Rashid-Yasemi, Gholamreza, "Falsafe-ye Bergson [Bergson's Philosophy]," *Ta'lim va Tarbiat Magazine* (Mehr va Aban 1314/September and October 1935).

Read, Herbert, *A Concise History of Modern Painting* (New York: Prager, 1975).

Sadr, Hamid Reza, *Iranian Cinema: A Political Story* (London: I. B. Tauris & Co., 2006).

Sa'edi, Gholamhossein, *Ahl-e Hava* (Tehran: Mo'asseseh-e Motale'at va Tahghighat-e Ejtema'i, 1966).

   Ilkhchi, An Azeri Village with Sufi Dwellers (Tehran: Mo'asseseh-e Motale'at va Tahghighat-e Ejtema'i, 1963).

   Khiyav and Meshkin Shahr (Tehran: Mo'asseseh-e Motale'at va Tahghighat-e Ejtema'i, 1965).

Sa'edi, Gholamhossein and Sirus Tahbaz, *Yush* (Tehran: Mo'asseseh-e Motale'at va Tahghighat-e Ejtema'i, 1963).

Safa'i, Ebrahim, "Khayyam and Meterling," *Bonyad Monthly*, No. 20 (November 1978): 37–40.

Sahand, S., "The Age of Technology," *Bonyad Monthly*, No. 18 (September 1978): 85–86.

Sami-Azar, Alireza, "Preface," in *A Garden between Two Streets: 4001 Days in the Life of Kamran Diba, in Conversation with Reza Daneshvar*, ed. Reza Daneshvar (Tehran: Bongah Publishers, 2013).

Schott, Ben, "Westoxication & Modern Toxicity," *The New York Times*, op-ed (April 12, 2011).

Sedgwick, Mark, *Against the Modern World: Traditionalism and the Secret Intellectual History of the Twentieth Century* (Oxford University Press, 2004).

Seifpur-Fatemi, Nasrollah, "Review of *Sufism*," *Bonyad Monthly*, No. 6 (September 1977): 74.

Shabaviz, 'Abbas, *Trailer for Mu Tala'i-ye Shahr-e Ma (The Golden Hair of Our City* (Tehran: Iran Film, 1965).

Shams, Shahkar, "*Gharbzadegi* in Production System," *Bonyad Monthly*, No.9 (December 1977): 3.

Shari'ati, Ali, *Marxism and Other Western Fallacies: An Islamic Critique*, trans. R. Campbell (Berkeley, CA: Mizan Press, 1980).

Tabarra'ian, Safa al-Din, *Soft Like a Sponge: Evaluating Ehsan Naraghi's Role in the Second Pahlavi*. Vol. I (Tehran: Moasseseh-ye Motale'at-e Tarikh-e Mo'aser-e Iran, 2013).

Tajoddini, Mohammad Reza, "The East and the West," *Bonyad Monthly*, No. 10 (January 1978): 37.

Tamimi, Farrokh, "The East or the West," *Bonyad Monthly*, No. 10 (January 1978): 30.

   "A Letter to His Excellency," *Bonyad Monthly*, No. 16 (July 1978): 12–13.

Taylor, Charles, *A Secular Age* (Cambridge, MA: Belknap Press, 2007).

   Modern Social Imaginaries (Durham, NC: Duke University Press, 2004).

Traore, Mahama Jansoon, "The Ugly Reflection of Colonialism," trans. Parviz Shafa, *Bonyad Monthly*, No. 19 (October 1978): 23–37.

Vahidi, Iraj, "Revival of Iran's Global Stake," *Bonyad Monthly*, No. 7 (October 1977): 3.

Wasserstrom, Steven, *Religion after Religion: Gershom Scholem, Mircea Eliade, and Henry Corbin at Eranos* (Princeton University Press, 1999).

Williams, Raymond, *The Country and the City* (New York: Oxford University Press, 1973).

Wolin, Richard, *Heidegger's Children: Hannah Arendt, Karl Löwith, Hans Jonas, and Herbert Marcuse* (Princeton University Press, 2001).

www.iranicaonline.org/articles/saqqa-kana-ii-school-of-art

www.mghaed.com/essays/farewell/Death_of_a_compulsive_preacher.htm

www.roozonline.com/persian/news/newsitem/article/-9e497d6f02.html

www.youtube.com/watch?v=6h5wsIh1h_8

www.youtube.com/watch?v=FODYoxDk31c

www.youtube.com/watch?v=jdR03dd0XhE

Yasemi, Siamak, *Ganj-e Gharun (Gharun's Treasure)* (Tehran: Puria Film, 1965).

Zarrinkub, Abdolhossein, *Continuation of a Search for Sufism in Iran* (Tehran: Amir Kabir, 1983).

Trail of the Search for Sufism (Tehran: Amir Kabir, 1978).

The Worth and Legacy of Sufism, 5th edition (Tehran: Amir Kabir, 1983).

Index